The Cannibal's Wife

The Cannibal's Wife

A Memoir

Yvonne Maes

with

Bonita Slunder

HERODIAS

NEW YORK LONDON

Published by HERODIAS, INC.
346 First Avenue, New York, NY 10009
HERODIAS, LTD. 24 Lacy Road, London, SW 15 1NL
www.herodias.com

Manufactured in the United States of America
Design by Charles B. Hames
Jacket Photograph by Musya S. Sheeler

LIBRARY OF CONGRESS CATALOGING-IN-PUBLICATION DATA

Maes, Y. M. (Yvonne M.)
The cannibal's wife : a memoir / Yvonne Maes ; with Bonita Slunder.
p. cm.
ISBN 1–928746–03–9
1. Ex-nuns Biography   2. Sexual abuse victims Biography.
3. Sexual misconduct by clergy.   [1. Maes, Y. M. (Yvonne M.)]
I. Slunder, Bonita.   II. Title.
BX4668.3.M34A3   1999
271'.9002—dc21
[B]   99–32952
CIP

BRITISH LIBRARY CATALOGUING IN PUBLICATION DATA

A catalogue record of this book is available
from the British Library.

ISBN 1–928746–03–9

1 3 5 7 9 8 6 4 2

First Edition 1999

Acknowledgments

The Cannibal's Wife owes its existence to a number of people who dared to stand by me when it would have been easier to turn away. In particular I wish to thank my younger sister, Isabelle Maes Bossuyt, for her unshakable belief in my integrity and my older sister, Clarisse Maes Radvak, for bending her ear to the keyhole at Wimbledon. Rose Gregoire kept me sane by her sharing through Labrador boil-ups, berry picking and hikes on the ice. I could not have survived the grueling meetings without the support of Phyllis Clarke. Sister Marjorie Moffatt clarified issues and courageously admitted her own inability to support me.

Marguerite McDonald provided me with a shoulder to cry on. Margaret Kennedy and Jenny Fasal, both in the UK, fired off challenging letters my superiors would not. Dermot Monaghan's scribbled comments proved to be insightful feedback. For teaching me to write less "on the nose" I thank Bonita Slunder. Margaret and Andrew McCooey and Barry Bond, all in the UK, were unstinting with competent legal advice. Over her evening meal Evelyn Keener listened to the large and little catastrophes I faced in bringing this abuse to light. Ed, Mary and Daniel Hayden revived me with Saturday night picnics in their living room followed by a game of scrabble.

All through this process the Labrador community gave me a reason to live. From Linda Anderson, Gillian Decker, Shirley Flowers, Anita McNeil, Hilda Lyall, Joyce Corbin, Nancy Hamel, Harold Fewer, Linda Boland, Susan Sparks, and Joy and Nelson Schaefele to Nancy and David Nuna, Maxine Snow, Rose Montague, Judy Norman, Manish and John Luke Nuna, Paul Jack, Sylvester and Christine Nuna, Apenum and Lynn Pone, Bart Jack, Father Fred Magee, Judy and Harvey Hill, Janet and Theresa Gregoire, Edward Nuna, Janet O'Donnell, Lori Morina, Jackie Monamie, Pirson Williams, Barbara Coffey, Manikatnin Nuna, Elizabeth Penashue, Philomena and Dominic Pokue, Anyette Nuna, Mary May Osmond, Emily Flowers, Jackie McCarthy—these allowed me into their lives where I found warmth and understanding.

Others further afield in Canada helped see me through: Aunt Martha Ketsman, Katherine and Janise Maes, Annie Mohr, Sisters Claire Jobin, Alice Konefall, Lorraine St. Hilaire, Leonne Valois, Vera Hoelscher, as well as Roz Silversides and Louise Smendzick all in Manitoba; Kathleen Kufeldt in Newfoundland; Annie and Leo Matthyssen and their four children in Quebec, Dr. Tony Eccles and Sharon Hodkinson in Ontario. Those from the US who stood by me include Srs Arnadene Bean and Virginia Ginet of Oregon, Ray and Ann Higgins and Sr. Mary Berchmans in California; Barbara Hardy in Maine; Jan Kahnback in Florida; Tom Economus in Illinois, Sharon Palma in New Mexico.

Several individuals from across the seas merit a vote of gratitude: Gerard Mathot, Srs. Julienne Lefebvre, Eulalia Leoatla, Filipina Tebalo and Br. Henry Aubin in Lesotho, Sol Durbach in South Africa, Fr. Rene Paul in Kenya, Srs. Elaine Kelly, Mary Moylan, and Daphne Norden in the UK, Fr. Tom Quadras in India, Fr. John Pearce in Australia, Lieve Van den Bosch and Denise Delvaux in Belguim and Sr. Maureen Connors in the Solomon Islands.

Each of you
A lighted candle
Together a flame
Thank you

Madiepetsane

In northern Canada the dark night sky is often painted with the spectacular iridescent colours of the *aurora borealis*. Inuit legend says these magnificent lights are torches carried by spirits to guide the way for the living. Rays of bright green and waves of ice blue dance like magic across nature's pitch-black canvas. I have spent many sleepless nights staring at the flickering sky from my home in Labrador. In a whimsical way I have often wondered, is one of those spirits looking for me?

Tonight, I'm sleepless once again. I reach for my journal of Africa #1. It's a light green Hilroy exercise book No. 990, narrow ruled. I leaf through the tattered yellowing pages. The neatness of my entries surprises me as I flip to 1969 and begin to read. Far from this northern night I relive my time in Lesotho, Africa.

FEBRUARY 21, 1969
Two hours of sleep—drove a woman named Pulane and Chief Tsiu to the Maseru police station to report an attack on the woman's life—ritual murder attempt it seems!

I can recall that night like it was last week—not thirty years ago. I was a new missionary tutor at Mazenod Teacher's Training

College in Lesotho, Africa. I had been in the country just eight months and already experienced some remarkable extremes: four-blanket nights in July, dusty winds off the Kalahari in August, giant aloe blossoms in December, and the scorching drought of February. Like the people, this land never ceased to amaze me.

Mazenod College was an attractive red limestone building constructed around a quadrangle of much-trampled grass. Dormitories occupied two sides of the quadrangle, classrooms lined the third, while the kitchen and dining area completed the square. Across a dusty passage and beyond a huge clump of pampas grass stood the red limestone convent. All the buildings had corrugated metal roofs that creaked in the wind and thundered in the rain.

There were ten small bedrooms and one dormitory for the sixteen nuns who lived at Mazenod. My age of twenty-eight entitled me to a bedroom. It was a tiny room with a cot, a wash stand, a mini-desk with chair, and a slender clothes closet. Since our custom at that time limited us to just two outfits, the clothes closet was adequate for everything except our blankets. Nightly temperatures in June and July often dipped to thirty degrees Fahrenheit. Our small paraffin heaters took the chill off at bed time, but paraffin was in short supply. Each night around nine-thirty when the electric generator shut down, we extinguished the heaters. This made having four or more blankets a necessity. We stored the blankets and heaters in a common cupboard when warmer weather came along.

At Mazenod, moving from one activity to another usually meant stepping outside. I loved that. I drank in the exotic smell of mimosa blooming in August and the queen-of-the-night in December. It excited me to have constant contact with the elements. It reminded me of the prairie farm in Manitoba where

I grew up. City life at university and then in the convent had deprived me of wind and rain. But in Africa, where donkeys brayed outside my classroom window and the sun took a mere twenty minutes to disappear each evening, I basked in the splendors of nature. Sometimes, when I thought about where I was—finally in Africa—I felt blessed to be fulfilling a dream I'd kept since adolescence. Only then I had imagined I would follow in the footsteps of Doctor Tom Dooley in the book *The Night They Burned the Mountain Down.* The idea of serving others and bringing healing attracted me. Back then religious servitude was definitely not part of that dream—a husband was. But then, dreams shift, life changes. *Africa.*

It was the people—the nuns, the students, the villagers—that exhilarated me most. Their customs both thrilled and baffled me. Greeting with both hands was not difficult to master. But the new rules for greeting were far from tangible and brought me to tears on several occasions. I thought it rude to walk into the dining room and announce myself regardless of any and all conversations. The Basotho found me rude when I failed to do so. I was embarrassed by my poor pronunciation yet every time I entered a room I had to loudly proclaim *Dumelang Bo'Me—Hello Mothers.* It took some getting used to. Each time I'd brace my shoulders, close my eyes for a second, then barge in with my loud greeting. Eventually I grew to like it so much that when I returned to Canada I kept the custom.

The customs and etiquette I had learned in my first few months in Africa helped little when it came to the night of February 21, 1969. It all began when someone pounded fiercely on my window. I bolted up with a start.

Stunned by the rude awakening, I peered around at my sparsely furnished surroundings. It took me a second to figure out where I was—tucked into a corner of the large senior students' dormitory—the mother's room. This was my first night as acting dorm mother for sixty young Basotho women. As I recall, there were many 'firsts' that night.

"Ivoni, it's Julienne here. We have a woman who needs to go to the police station. Would you drive her?" Sister Julienne's husky French Canadian accent echoed urgently from the window. She was a small, capable woman serving as the principal and my superior. We got along well. Both of us liked playing archaeologist by scavenging local *dongas* in search of Bushmen arrowheads, skin scrapers, and termite hill-smashers.

"I'll be right out," I responded. Quickly I pulled on my gray skirt, white blouse, and that tight, itchy, white veil that I resented because it kept the wind from my hair and my ears. In fact, I hated dressing differently. The nun's garb made me stick out like a pigeon in a flock of canaries.

The night air of the Lesotho summer had a refreshing coolness about it—something I appreciated. As I tip-toed through the dorm and out onto the *kikuyu* grass that matted the quadrangle court yard, I couldn't help but notice the velvet African sky. There was no moon, so the Milky Way fanned out with unusual clarity like a million sparkles just beyond my grasp. I smiled at the five stars of the Southern Cross as it twinkled down on me. My heart raced with excitement and anticipation.

"Ivoni, you have to take the chief of Ha Paki with you; that is the custom. The woman's name is Pulane. She barely escaped being murdered for ritual medicine. I'll send some sisters with you."

I happened to be the only available licensed driver at the training college. I grabbed the keys to the *kombi* and opened the sliding door so the three sisters and the panting Pulane could climb in. Pulane sat directly behind me. The entire nerve-wracking ride she panted down my already hot neck.

The sisters directed me through the rocky track and around enormous aloes to Chief Tsiu's neatly thatched *rondavel*. My headlights bounced off the porch and onto the low cross-shaped mud wall that served as a windbreak for open air cooking.

Chief Tsiu emerged through the doorway looking like a burly bear roused from a winter sleep. He grunted and climbed onto the front seat beside me.

I offered to take the three sisters back to the convent. Celinia was a primary school teacher and not particularly strong. The other two were student teachers in training. They nodded.

After dropping them off, Pulane, Chief Tsiu, and I wended our way along the hilly terrain to the capital city, Maseru, sixteen miles away. Without warning, Pulane began shouting and shook the frame of the seat in front of her, which happened to be my seat. Her hot breath made me shiver with anxiety. I spoke virtually no Sesotho and Pulane spoke no English. To make matters worse, I had to drive on the left side of a pitch-black unmarked tar road on a moonless night.

Terrified her disruptive behavior would force me off the road, I looked over at the Chief with quick, pleading glances. Chief Tsiu was bilingual but he was also taciturn.

The half hour drive felt like the road to hell—long and hopeless. I dared not ask Pulane to move over, mainly because I didn't know how, but also because I didn't want to cause her any more discomfort. Self-assertion was not my strong point, and I had internalized a big dose of *God loves the cheerful giver.*

The police station was a dilapidated colonial left-over. Flies buzzed against the small filthy windows that hadn't seen a wash rag in decades. Several large, hard-shelled beetles bashed themselves relentlessly into the bare single light bulb that dangled from the ceiling. They fell to the rough plank floor where they spun noisily and collided like bumper cars. Heavy, dark, wooden benches ran along two walls. At the far end, a woman wrapped like a cocoon in a traditional Basotho blanket sat slumped into herself. Just the top of her head showed. A uniformed man sat behind the counter that stretched along the third wall. He tapped a pencil impatiently as he questioned a tired looking middle-aged man.

Behind the policeman a door opened onto a dimly-lit corridor. Another heavy wooden bench was pushed against one wall that faced several small doors. I could hear angry voices wafting toward me. The smell of bleach warred with the odour of rotted wood and human grime—in that atmosphere we waited. Chief Tsiu kept mumbling to Pulane in what looked like an attempt to calm her. Several times she stormed outside into the dark with Chief Tsiu following.

Three poorly-clad men came in and shuffled about in soleless shoes without ever crushing a spinning beetle. I strained to grasp even a word of the various clouds of conversation that flitted about the room. *"Eh em Ntate!"* meant *"Yes indeed father."*

From time to time I concentrated on the flies—their buzzing had a more familiar ring to it than did the Sesotho. In a bizarre way it was soothing. My reluctant companions returned to wait once more and the old adage *patience is a virtue* repeated in my brain.

Then, *'crack'* a gunshot pierced the air outside. Nobody stirred. I sat very still, straining my eyes toward the door, waiting for a scream, a thumping of feet, running. Silence. Tsiu must have read my discomfort. He whispered, "Just a night watchman signaling another night watchman in the area."

I forced an appreciative smile then marveled at how well this man spoke English.

Finally Tsiu and Pulane made their statements and then Pulane disappeared into one of the little doors in the corridor.

"They want to keep her in a cell for the night—safety," explained Chief Tsiu.

My jaw dropped. Of all the scenarios I had imagined, this one had never entered my mind. I shook my head in disbelief. All that waiting for justice and the victim gets locked up!

By the time I dropped Tsiu at his *rondavel* the first light of dawn streaked across the Maluti Mountains. Later, at morning break, as I walked into the staff room for a cup of coffee, Sister Celinia greeted me excitedly. "I didn't sleep a wink until I heard you drive in the yard," she exclaimed. "Did you know Chiefs' are usually the instigators of ritual murders? I feared for your safety."

My eyes must have bulged, "No. I wasn't aware of that," I confessed, glad no one had told me sooner.

Celinia giggled nervously. "You remind me of our legend about the cannibal's wife, Madiepetsane. She escaped his cooking pot by playing tricks on him."

From that day on Sister Celinia called me Madiepetsane. I felt accepted into my new country simply because I had done something to help.

When word got out about some of my creative solutions for everyday problems, like scaling the fence that enclosed the school compound so I could attend community development meetings in the neighbouring villages, other sisters picked up on my new nickname. I must admit, it was rather unbecoming of a nun to slip (however modestly) over an 8 ft. wrought iron gate wearing a veil and skirt. But how else was I to get in for supper, prayer, and study supervision? The conventional method was to yell one's lungs out like a love sick wildebeest until someone came to unlock the gate. That meant disturbing others, so I took the route of *why trouble another if you can do it yourself?* I preferred independence and accomplished the transfer from one side of the fence to the other within seconds. My skirt hooked a few times, but it never ripped.

Slowly, Madiepetsane grew on me. At first, I enjoyed the laughter the nick-name evoked; it certainly was a conversation piece. Children and adults alike would sing the song about her. Strangely enough, it was to the tune of John Brown's Body. I never learned how that came about. I did learn that the legendary Madiepetsane played harmless tricks that never hurt anyone. She was amusing. We had a lot in common. I never wanted to hurt anyone either.

Later on, I sensed that her escapades were more than innocent pranks. They had to do with survival itself. Most of them involved magical transformations—things I could never imitate. Yet, Madiepetsane never struck me as a strong character. She didn't take a strong stand for either herself or anyone else. She was just a female figure in a peculiar legend about a husband who tried constantly to cannibalize his wife.

I often wondered why she ended up in the same life-threatening situations over and over again. Much like battered wives who return to their husbands, she kept going back. I thought perhaps the common rumour was true—for some women that's just the way it is. They have no choice. No help. No hope.

All in all, I grew to feel pity for this namesake of mine. The only thing she had going for her was her magical power. When I asked about this I was never given any insight, and I concluded it was either a much protected or much forgotten legend. I left it at that and went on with my busy life.

But now, three decades later, I'm tormented by this pitiful image, yet I refuse to let her go. Instead of asking why Madiepetsane kept going back to her cannibal husband, I now ask why he attempted to cannibalize her in the first place.

The Fourth Commandment

I remember the day I turned ten—August 11, 1949. It was a hot, sunny day in Dugald, Manitoba, and the smell of ripe wheat clung to the air like invisible dust. I was one of six children born to Nathalie (nee Van den Bosch) and Alphonse Maes, Belgian immigrants who settled on the bleak and often harsh Canadian prairies in the late 1920s. Dad was fifteen years Mom's senior and a foot taller. A thick mop of black wavy hair topped his narrow face, broad shoulders and long, lean body. By the time I knew him he was slightly stooped. Whenever he disapproved of something I did, he would glare silently at me with his deep blue eyes and I would obey. Whoever said *silence is golden* obviously never met my Dad. With cattle, Dad was patient; but a tractor that refused to sputter to life with his cranking sent him into a rage. His drug of choice was chewing tobacco. He spit gooey, dark brown blobs of it into the wood box. Every time I encountered one of those blobs on my hand as I picked up a stick of wood to stoke the stove, I swore—under my breath of course.

Mom wore thick glasses which enlarged her green eyes into watery saucers. This disconcerted me because she looked like she was crying and I felt I had to comfort her. Every Saturday morning I pin-curled her silky brown hair and combed it out just in

time for her and Dad to go off to the Belgian Club that evening. I
envied her clear, olive complexion and I imitated her ready smile.
From shoulders to knees she resembled a well-corseted cylinder.
Once, when Queen Elizabeth visited, Mom dressed up in a
Victorian period outfit and barged her way to the front of the
crowd. The Queen spotted her and stopped to chat. I inherited
Mom's hair, complexion, and attractive legs but Dad's height and
frame. I don't know where the extra brown tint in my hazel eyes
came from.

By age ten I was at least six inches taller than my twin
brother, Albert. I was ashamed of my towering height. Girls, I
learned early on, weren't supposed to overshadow boys.
Magazines and advertisements of the era always showed petite
women standing next to tall, powerful men. It felt like a mortal
sin for me to be so gangly—a freak of genetics that made me
stick out like the ugly-duckling. I hated to have my picture taken
with Albert unless I could lean against a building or disguise my
height somehow.

For our birthday that year, as every year, Mom gave us a bar
of Baker's chocolate. The sweet, dark squares, divided in eight
equal pieces, were loosely wrapped in waxed paper. I ate one
square really slowly—to savour every morsel of flavour. Albert
ate only half of one square. What he lacked in height he seemed
to make up in self-control. Perhaps it was a DNA exchange gone
awry. He lacked height, I lacked self-control. I still don't know
how he could limit himself to half a square of chocolate at a time.
It was our one birthday present and we could do with it as we
pleased—share it, eat it all at once, or save it. We could even
munch away greedily while other members of the family looked
on with envy. The pleading eyes of my little sister, Isabelle, made
this impossible for me. I did share with her. I permitted her to
scrape her front teeth over the edge of one square. My generosity

was just enough to leave a small set of teeth marks in the dark chocolate, and a feeling of kindness in my heart.

As I continued to grow, there were many mornings I cried from the aches in my legs. Mom assured me I was just sprouting too fast. By the time I turned twelve I was five foot two and as tall as my mother.

Albert didn't sprout (as Mom always assured he would) until he was sixteen. He then outgrew me. That finally put an end to my height dilemma—he solved it by growing taller.

Although Albert was my twin, our lives were very different. Because he was a boy he could play outside and seemed to have many more adventures than I did. I always had chores to do—everything from caring for the chickens, to baking, cleaning, and shining shoes.

It was this unfairness that possessed me to run away from home that year I turned ten. Clarisse, my older sister, had moved away to attend high school in Transcona. My other sister, Isabelle, was too young to be any help to me. The three boys were outside while I was stuck in the house. My tasks for the morning included cleaning the kitchen floor and baking a cake. Both jobs required strategy as well as strength. My skinny arms were exhausted after scraping off the floor a week's worth of Manitoba gumbo, tracked in by seven pair of farm boots. After washing I had to wax—then defend my fine accomplishment from ruinous feet until it dried. That was the boring part. I was a prisoner waiting for the wax to dry. When it finally dried, I had to stoke the coal stove so the oven would be hot for baking.

I detested making cake batter. Every muscle in my arm would ache as I whipped it with a wooden spoon. If I were lucky, Maurice would be around the yard somewhere. He loved this task. His whipping turned out the fluffiest cakes I'd ever eaten.

But on this particular morning Maurice was nowhere to be found. He had taken Albert and Isabelle and gone with Dad to clean out the granary. If they were lucky they might find a nest of mice, spot a gopher, or sit beside Dad and shift the gears of the tractor. Mom was out in the garden hoeing potatoes in the hot sun.

I felt sorry for myself and pouted. I hated being a girl. It wasn't fair. I felt like Cinderella. As a matter of fact, I began to believe I was just a slave. Uncle Albert had told me once that I was a mistake. He said that because I was the second born of twins and so unlike my brother, that I probably shouldn't have been born. I even imagined I was adopted—an orphan my parents had taken in out of pity. Come to think of it, I *was* different from the rest of the kids. Maybe they made up the story about Albert being my twin just to keep the neighbours from asking questions. After-all, he was a runt and I was a giant—so how could we be twins?

My ten-year-old imagination continued to boil. I tossed the wax rag into the centre of the floor and decided to run away. I'd show them I wasn't a slave. They would miss me when the work wasn't done.

Outside, under the big sky, I felt waves of excitement and fear. Determined to teach them all a lesson, I marched towards the west—towards Winnipeg. After maybe two hundred feet I decided that perhaps the big city wasn't such a good idea. The thought of all those strangers scared me. I turned east on a dirt road and headed toward the Tonoski homestead a half mile away. Before reaching the halfway mark, the blazing sun hurt my eyes and my mouth was parched. I stopped at a ditch but couldn't find any tadpoles to tell my sad story. My feet hurt and the little sparrows that pecked at the gravel didn't chirp or try to cheer me. Soon I forgot why I was trudging eastward.

All I wanted was a cool drink of water. The ditch water was too muddy to drink so I turned around and headed home. At first I walked slowly, then I speeded up as the thought of cool water and the smell of cake baking teased my senses. Soon I was running.

Judging by my thirst I assured myself that I'd been gone for hours. I presumed my entire family would be frantically searching for me. Each one would give me a warm welcome back and a grand apology for having treated me like Cinderella. This thought made me grin with smug satisfaction. I burst through the door. The house was empty—not a soul around. My wet rag lay limp on the floor just where I had thrown it. The gallant image of my welcome home burst like a big balloon. I let out a huge sigh of resignation. I drank a pitcher of water from the borehole bucket then dropped to my knees and continued where I'd left off waxing the floor. This was my fate and I couldn't find a way out.

∴ ⁖ ∴

My period started at age eleven. So did the terror of my father. I remember how he tormented Mom for her big breasts and ridiculed her for falling asleep whenever she read even one page of a book. Soon Clarisse, who returned home on weekends and holidays, was getting the same treatment from the boys in the family as well as Dad. I knew I'd be next. And there was nothing I could do except hunch my shoulders. Mom constantly nagged at me, "Straighten up, Yvonne! Why do you always slouch?" She knew why. Why didn't she leave me alone?

That summer my Aunt Lizzy and Uncle Smitty came over for a Sunday meal with my five cousins. I loved Aunt Lizzy. She was a pear-shaped woman who always gave me a special greeting. She was my wonder aunt—a woman who appeared much too seldom and left much too soon. I liked the five cousins as well and my Uncle Smitty, who quietly smoked his pipe and listened.

Everyone squeezed around the table and admired the piping-hot roast chicken I had slaughtered, plucked, and gutted the day before. I got up to get a basket of fresh biscuits I had baked earlier. Without warning, as I walked past my father, he pulled me down onto his lap. I squirmed but he held fast, clutching my budding breasts. "She'll be a big-breasted wife for someone," he announced with a snicker as if talking about a cow. I felt blinded by rage at having my breasts used as brag bait. Just like Clarisse and Mom, the degradation had started. Dad hadn't noticed me in years and now this. A few cousins glanced at me squirming, grinned with embarrassment, then looked down into their plates. Aunt Lizzy and Mom ignored it all. Uncle Smitty puffed a few rings of gray smoke from his pipe. I felt humiliated.

"Yes, she'll be a big-breasted wife for some lucky man," Dad repeated as if it would make it so. Eventually, he got tired of the groping and loosened his grip. I pulled away and crept into a corner for the rest of the day. I skipped supper—I had no appetite. That was my first brush with nausea.

Not more than a week later Mom solemnly called me to stand beside her as she mended a pair of denim overalls on the old Singer sewing machine.

"Yvonne—um—I want you to watch out for Dad." She paused and wiped her eyes. "He did something to Clarisse." Again she paused and her voice cracked as if the sick reality were a choking clump of sawdust. "I told him never to do that again to any of the girls." She avoided looking at me and I knew this must be a serious matter. Then she added, "If he does something to you, you could have a baby and—well—good girls don't have babies until they're married."

I was totally confused. Living on a farm I had a good idea of the mating process. The chickens always made a big fuss. It struck me as noisy, rough, and rather one-sided. The male seemed to be in charge while the female seemed to resist the activity. I saw how roosters chased hens and how the hens ran away squawking as if for their lives. But the rooster persisted and the hen usually ended up fiercely pinned down, her beak in the dust, her comb bleeding from his violent attack. After the mating he would strut off while she dashed for cover ruffling her feathers. Poor hen, I always thought.

On the other hand, I remember nights when I lay awake listening to a cow bellow until a bull was brought to her. After the mating she was calm and quiet.

I shrugged at my mother's grave warning. There were two things I didn't understand. Firstly, I couldn't imagine why my Dad would want to do that with me, and second, how in the world I would ever protect myself if he did. I would have to be very disobedient—even break one of the Ten Commandments. That was unthinkable. It all seemed so ridiculous and confusing. In humans, mating was something only grown-ups did. It was one of those weird things. I had no desire to *mate* with my father. But now I was afraid. Dad had groped me in front of the others, so there was no telling what he would do next. Would Mom have warned me if it wasn't a serious matter? My sense of danger grew but I had nowhere to place it. I tried to bury it, but I was unsuccessful. I had no one with whom to share my dilemma, and the entire thing made me feel dirty and even more angry for being a girl. Did my twin brother have to worry about Dad sneaking into his bedroom or touching his private parts? I felt sick to my stomach. I assured Mom that I'd be careful, but I didn't know how. Was I to serve him his meals from the back of the stove or the opposite side of the table? Mom hadn't given me any suggestions.

If he grabbed me, how was I supposed to get away? If I disobeyed him would I go to hell? Would God forgive me for breaking Fourth Commandment—Honour Thy Father and Thy Mother? Life became a nightmare of contradictions. The 'bad girl' feeling grew deeper—my body seemed to cause a lot of problems. I was not only a mistake but I was bad as well.

I began having nightmares about snakes chasing me. I'd run and run until finally I'd wake up, terrified. If I went back to sleep, I'd be thrust back into the same dream. So I'd stay awake and by morning I'd be weak from fatigue. As the years passed, this nightmare became a regular occurrence and I became more exhausted.

Mom never again brought up this subject. She never asked how I was doing with Dad or if I needed to talk. There was a thunderous wall of silence between us at all times. It bonded us and it separated us.

.· ·. .·

My days at the one-room country school, with its library of twenty books, ended after grade eight. The nearest high school was at the end of a bad road and had a terrible reputation. This seemed to worry my father, and it was clear he had an idea that would insure we wouldn't have to go there. One summer day, he drove the twenty miles into Winnipeg and came back the owner of a house—a dilapidated three-storey rooming house in the heart of the downtown area. Mom, Albert, Isabelle and I moved there on the first day of September 1953. The stairs and hallways reeked of stale grime regardless of how I scrubbed them. The single bathroom responded even less to my Dutch Cleanser.

Mom had arranged for a friend's daughter to show me the way to St. Mary's Academy. She took one look at me and said,

"Yvonne, you can't go to school in that!" I looked at my farm slacks in dismay. "You'll have to find a skirt for today and then buy a uniform." I'd never worn a skirt to school before.

Boarding a noisy, lurching public bus, dropping coins into a slot and asking for a transfer was all new to me too, and quite terrifying. After leading me to a door marked 9B, in a building that was bigger than our dairy barn, my guide vanished. I knocked on the door. An awesome creature dressed totally in black—except for a strip of white around her face—greeted me. "What's your name?" she asked. Behind her in neat rows sat more girls than I had ever seen in one room. I couldn't remember my name and eventually recognized it on a list she handed me.

I had just met my first nun! She was tall and graceful in her imposing habit. She taught me grade nine. At times she twitched her nose, and I wondered if she had ears hidden under that headgear—if so, could she twitch them like my brother Maurice? Once she asked me if I had enough to eat. I stammered, "Yes, I have eggs, milk and chicken." I felt she really cared about me. I admired the fact that these nuns had pioneered the education of girls in Manitoba. They struck me as independent women who ran their own show. Furthermore, a few of them served as missionaries in Africa. Sadly, they had no children and no husbands.

On weekends and holidays, Mom sent me to the farm to do laundry and other chores. I resented her for that—sending me out there with no way to defend myself. I believed that as long as I was not alone with Dad he wouldn't touch me. I was right. Once I had figured that out, I cajoled, coerced, and enticed Isabelle to stay at my side whenever Dad was around. However, there were times such as feeding the chickens in the early morning that I couldn't drag Isabelle along. Dad would come along and hug me and pant down my neck. This terrified me and caused me endless nightmares.

He often vented anger at me while accusing Mom of spending too much time at the rooming house. I noticed Mom was happier in the city than on the farm.

The summer I turned fifteen, Maurice, Isabelle and I ran the Dugald farm. Dad had taken Albert to another farm for the summer and Mom was supervising the rooming house in Winnipeg. One particularly sunny day I recorded in my diary: *Pickled beets and cucumbers and canned peas and beans. Also stung by 2 bees as I finished nailing the shingles on the north roof of the house.* What I did not record were the forays into the garden to gather the vegetables, the armloads of wood to keep the stove blazing, and the buckets of water I hauled from the pump room in the barn. Nor did I record the meals I prepared, the cows I milked, and the chickens I fed.

Once, after harrowing a field with a cantankerous little tractor, Isabelle came in for lunch motion-sick and crying. Maurice insisted she go back out to finish harrowing the field that very afternoon. She was barely twelve years old. He was nineteen and did an amazing job coaxing the various machines, especially said tractor, into running smoothly.

Maurice loved dancing and didn't mind having me along once I was sixteen. When Saturday night rolled around, we hurried through the chores and sped off to the Fort Rouge Legion Hall where a live band played. Soon I could do all manner of steps from square dances to fox trots. At midnight, the band stopped playing and Maurice and I drove back to the farm to catch some sleep before morning chores and Sunday mass. After then it was back to the rooming house and homework.

I had little time or energy to socialize with my schoolmates. Once, I spent a weekend at a girlfriend's farm. She lived with her older brother and his housekeeper. There was no laundry to do, no baking, no cows, no chickens, and no wood to split. It felt strange and surprisingly boring.

Family functions became a problem for me. Once Dad noticed that I was a good dancer, he would haul me to the dance floor and spin me around to an old-time waltz—clockwise and counter-clockwise—until I was dizzy. If I stepped on his toes he would groan at me as if I had failed him in some terrible way. People cleared the dance floor when they saw Dad coming with me in tow. I was the puppet for his stardom.

One night when I was sixteen, I awoke to a strange pleasurable sensation in my groin. Isabelle, sleeping beside me, had accidentally wedged her heel against my pubic bone. The sensation increased and flooded my body. It was a feeling that made me sweat and shiver. It seemed to ripple right through me—as far as my ears if I moved even slightly; and if I remained very still it died away. About a month later, I engineered for it to happen again. This time the sensation reached such an extreme that I squeezed my eyes closed and then it became painful. I didn't know what to make of it all, but I knew it was sexual. Could this be the rubbing they talked about in religion lessons, I wondered in alarm? The rubbing that was supposed to be mortal sin? Until then, I thought mortal sin was difficult to achieve, requiring serious intention and action. Was this serious intention? No one was hurt by this. For the next few days I was tormented over hell fire, and determined the safest route was never to do this rubbing again. The next time I felt aroused, I rolled up into a tight fetal ball in the farthest corner of the bed and held myself perfectly still with a vivid picture of flames licking at me. Eventually I fell asleep. After two more episodes the sensation vanished as mysteriously as it had come.

My first real date was with a garage mechanic a few years older. After a movie we returned to my cold rooming house.

I boiled water on a gas burner and prepared some instant coffee. Mom liked him and he told funny stories. I was nervous wondering how to say good night, so I did nothing. He simply kissed me on the forehead. I returned to the kitchen and stared at the kettle. It was covered with grime. Any boyfriend who saw how my family lived and still had an interested in me would surely be a gem, I thought. I never heard from the mechanic again.

At eighteen, I suffered a broken heart over a handsome German immigrant. One evening, we hugged so hard that one of my blouse buttons popped. He stuck to necking and never touched me, so I felt safe with him. Out of the blue he stopped calling me. I concluded that he was jealous because I had danced with another man. I refused to call him to find out what had brought about his turn from hot to cold.

A few months later, I met an Canadian Air Force navigator from Nova Scotia. On New Year's Eve, the officers mess served a candle-light steak supper. The music was lively, and by midnight we became a swirling, twirling jive-pair. He behaved very well until one night driving me to the farm he stopped on the side of the road and slid over beside me. Soon his hand was under my skirt. I hugged him more closely thinking that would show sufficient affection for him to remove his hand. I was wrong. I considered jumping out of the car and walking the few miles home in the sub-zero weather, but gave up that idea because it would hurt his feelings. I felt somehow to blame. What message had I given him to make him think this was okay? I did the least offensive thing I could think of—I put my hand over his and pushed. His hand didn't budge. That galvanized my anger. I yanked away from him and turned towards the door. He drove me to the farm and I never heard from him again.

By the time I entered university, our rooming house had been declared unfit for human habitation and torn down. Reluctantly,

Mom went back to the farm. Isabelle and I lived in a tiny apartment, and I took on various summer jobs to pay for rent and food. On weekends, I still returned to the farm to help clean, milk cows, and do laundry. My father's sexual advances continued. Through clever cow blockades and by conveniently having a pitchfork handy while alone in the barn, I was able to ward off most of his unwanted attentions. I tired of his constant attempts, his panting down my neck, his groping hands, yet I was never brave enough to say anything. I just did what I could to avoid him.

∴ ∵ ∴

My even, white teeth, hazel eyes, and well-formed eyebrows led me to believe I was borderline beautiful. But on the other hand, my straight brown hair, round face, and large ears indicated *plain*. I measured five foot-five and weighted 135 pounds. Every summer my olive complexion darkened to bear brown.

Overall I felt weak, stupid, and sniveling; weak for not standing up to Dad, stupid for landing a mere bursary rather than a scholarship for university, and sniveling for needing the approval of others. Other times I felt strong and useful because I knew how to plant and harvest, milk cows, twirl a baton and speak Flemish as well as English.

My dreams of the future oscillated like the prairie temperatures. Within a single hour I imagined myself on a farm, in a courtroom, in a developing country and hanging diapers on a clothes line with a toddler clinging to my skirt and a baby in a bassinet nearby. The image of myself working alongside Tom Dooley, the medical doctor who worked in Laos and wrote, *The Night They Burned The Mountain Down* set my heart into high speed.

Every time I read the comic-strip Blondie, I notice how she stood glued to the kitchen sink while Dagwood roamed the world. Friends laughed as Punch beat Judy, and they swooned over Elvis Presley. I did neither. I figured I must be different. Sometimes I liked being different. I was proud to be a farmer, a daughter of immigrants who made it to university. But more often I felt overwhelmed and far removed as if observing the world from the roof of the dairy barn. There was a hollow place inside me—a yearning to belong and to find a niche other than the kitchen sink.

∴ ❖ ∴

Around that time I met a wonderful young farmer named Lorne Bossuyt. He was a gentle, kind man with expressive eyes and warm laughter. We became good friends and began dating.

On Valentine's Day 1959 he brought me a box of chocolates and took me to see *Inn of the Sixth Happiness* starring Ingrid Bergman. That movie left me in a dreamy daze. Bergman portrayed a woman who saved children from a war zone by traveling on foot across a range of mountains in China. I remember how Lorne looked at me in the cafe afterwards. His eyes were sad but he smiled and said, "That's what you want isn't it Yvonne? To go off to some far away place and help people."

I nodded. "But not China with its complex rice paddies. Perhaps Africa or Laos."

Over the next few months I lay awake not only from the usual snake dreams but also from confusion about my goals in life. Lorne was becoming serious. He possessed so many of the good qualities I wanted in a partner, but I was hesitant.

One cold Sunday afternoon in early April things came to a head. I had not eaten or slept in days. Three exams loomed over me as I stared blankly at my texts. The print refused to stay in place. Some letters danced out at me, growing larger and twisting before they retreated and blurred. They seemed to grow skirts—long white wedding skirts or black nun's garb.

I snapped the book closed, grabbed my jacket plus a gray blanket and strode to a solitary spot on the banks of the Assiniboine River where I knew I'd be alone. The winter ice had just broken up and the flood waters raged onward to the Red River, eventually reaching Hudson's Bay and the Arctic Ocean. Huge ice floes crashed against each other, heaved into the air and careening in wild circles. White and black robed images appeared—swirling daintily on the sheets of ice.

I gazed a long time, shivering, despite the cocoon my blanket made around me. My life felt as cold and rudderless as the ice floes. Eventually, the weak sun sank low into the leafless branches of the majestic elms that lined the streets of Winnipeg. What laws govern the sun's movements? The roiling water? The salvation of human beings? Maybe I could focus on God's laws instead of human laws. Maybe I could be a spiritual mother and not a biological one. I could help developing people with agriculture all the while promoting God's law of love and justice as a spiritual mother. Would I find belonging in the community life of a nun? Could I give up marriage with its promise of intimacy and support? Gone forever would be my chance of bearing children, of farm life. I could see Lorne's face, sad in the dull glow of the setting sun.

I paced the frozen river bank seeking to put my newfound argument into a logical order. I howled at the raging waters. God was my first priority after all.

JOURNAL APRIL 10TH, 1959: ASSINIBOINE RIVER
If I can't cheerfully do what God wills for me, how would I ever cheerfully do what a wife and mother needs to do? Nun it is.

Lorne and I went bowling that evening. The pins seemed to shift and sway, and my stomach started to do the same, so I sat out and watched. Afterwards, at the A & W restaurant Lorne sipped his root beer. I looked on unable to take any food or drink. "You are quiet tonight, Yvonne. Still thinking about far away places?"

I nodded. A lump grew large in my throat as I reached over and tapped his hand. "I think I should be a nun," I blurted. "I'm healthy and educated. I could make a difference—like Ingrid Bergman. I guess I need adventure too."

Lorne was skeptical but never tried to dissuade me. He deserved the best of me and I wasn't able to give that—so in fairness I needed to move on. I felt lonely but knew I had to take that risk or forever resent having chosen a more comfortable path. We prayed together for guidance whenever we dated. On our last evening Lorne held me close for a long time in silence. Just before leaving he kissed me tenderly and whispered, "Yvonne, just be a good nun or this isn't worth it." I turned away and fled to the porch.

My next hurtle was breaking the news to my parents. I expected they'd be upset. They were. One evening after milking cows, still avoiding Dad at all costs, I sat down to supper. Mom teased Dad about having to walk Isabelle down the church aisle the following year. That was my cue. I ventured, "Dad, you'll never have to walk me down the aisle because I've decided to be a nun." He glared at me, snatched the car keys and stormed out of the house swearing, "Not a cent of inheritance for you! *Not a damn cent!*" Mom slumped over, covered her face and sobbed before she shuffled off to her bedroom. I was left alone, just me, a plate of cold food and my decision.

Obedience

The entry date for Holy Names candidates was the same day every year in Montreal: July twenty-fourth. I was thrilled by the thought of going far away for two years of training. In order to pay my train fare, I worked at the Canadian National Railway fishing lodge at Minaki in the wilderness of northern Ontario where I had waitressed the previous summer. Mr. Pascoe, the manager, his wife, Ali, and their two sons, Wray and David, were as gracious as the pristine setting. When the time came to announce my departure, I found it difficult to tell people why I was leaving. Mr. Pascoe said, "Yvonne, the Montreal train makes a whistle stop here at Minaki. We'll all be out here to wave you on to Montreal and the nunnery."

During my final week at home, I believed I was saying good-bye forever to family and friends, blue jeans, tractors, cows and curlers. I decided that just once I had to fly. Marjorie Kork, a neighbour and friend from primary school days, joined me. We negotiated with the pilot of a nearby crop spraying company for a half-hour in the air. Once aloft, I pointed out the yellow Leroy tractor below where Isabelle was harrowing a freshly ploughed field. The little plane took a nose-dive and we swooped low over the tractor. I waved at Isabelle and saw her duck. We climbed quickly and returned to base. Isabelle was so angry at the scare I had given her, she didn't speak to me for hours.

On the nineteenth of July, 1959, Dad drove me to the train station. Mom came along and so did Anna, my new sister-in-law, who supported my decision. As we left the farm, I looked neither left nor right fearing the same fate as Lot's wife: she turned into a pillar of salt for looking back on her burning city. I was determined not to look back in regret at what might have been.

At the train station, I met two other women who were also joining the convent. Each of us carried a small metal suitcase containing black stockings, a dozen handkerchiefs, and some undergarments—plus a Bible, the first I'd ever owned, because up until then, the Church did not encourage Bible reading. When it was time to board the train Dad was nowhere to be seen. I didn't look for him and wondered *why this show of driving me to the station.* He hadn't paid me that much attention in his entire life. Leaving Mom was wrenching. I felt I was abandoning her to prolonged servitude. She wiped her eyes often but remained very dignified. I promised her that I'd write. I hugged her with a mixture of anger and hope—anger that she didn't resist Dad's tyranny, and hope that as a nun I could do more for her than I had as a daughter. I believed that prayer would be more effective. Isabelle's future was with Connie Bossuyt, so I didn't feel as torn leaving her.

When the porter shouted, "All aboard!" we three future nuns quickly crowded into a compartment where we laughed and wept and laughed some more. The porter came to check our tickets. He scrutinized each one closely before handing them back. With a quizzical look he mumbled, "Hmmm . . . deaconesses, eh?" As soon as he was out of earshot we doubled over with more laughter. "I forgot about that label on my ticket. I bet

he has never seen a deaconess with earrings and lipstick before,"
I wagered.

Soon the train sped past our farm. I could see the black roof of
the barn and realized this was good-bye to farming for me. I felt
sad—for a few minutes.

It was 9:30 P.M. when the train pulled into Minaki Station.
The Pascoes were there, as were a few dozen friends. Some
handed me train letters and flowers. Others just stared. Was it
shock or amazement? Was I being heroic or foolish, I wondered,
as I waved good-bye.

It took us two nights and two days to reach Montreal. *En
route* we decided we would make this last fling fun by taking a
room at a posh hotel. We went straight to the stately Laurentian
and threw ourselves down giggling with excitement on the beds
in the air-conditioned room they gave us on the tenth floor. The
next day we took in Belmont Amusement Park and then danced
until dawn on a moonlight tour boat. By the time we trudged up
the steep hill to our hotel it was a cool 4 A.M..

The sailor I had danced with most of the evening and into the
night had invited us to tour his battleship the next day. We did.
When he asked for a date, I informed him that I couldn't because
I was joining the convent the next day. He stood, frowning,
blinking, and shaking his head.

The day I entered the convent was sultry and hot. For my last
meal I chose the most exotic and most expensive item on the
menu: lobster. It was messy but scrumptious. The deadline for
stepping across the threshold was 4 P.M., so at 3:45 we hailed a
taxi to the Holy Names Mother House on the upper slopes of
Mount Royal. After paying my share of the fare, my worldly
wealth amounted to twenty-seven dollars. Once we reached the
top of the gigantic stone stairway leading into the seven-story
building, I stood, admiring Montreal below. When we faced each

other, we burst out laughing and sobbing simultaneously. Finally, I took a deep breath and pressed the doorbell exclaiming, "Here goes, girls!"

We were ushered along a corridor the length of a city block to a sewing room. I was handed a bundle of black clothing with my name pinned to it. Off came my colourful street clothes. On went the black Oxford tie up shoes, the ankle length black dress, and the black cape. The last and most significant item was the black veil. That was hard for me. I had never liked covering my ears or my hair.

By nightfall, seventy-two of us from various parts of Ontario, Michigan, Manitoba, and Quebec were assembled in a huge room with a high ceiling and a glistening hardwood floor. I thought, *perfect for square dancing.* My veil kept sliding back—disheveling my hair and scraping my ears raw. The cape restricted my arm movements, and the long skirt proved hazardous on the endless staircases. The garb was all very irritating, as well as hot. But then, Africa would likely be hot too, so I endured it all with good humour for a great cause—salvation of my soul and the opportunity to help others.

Soon the Director of Postulants had us seated in alphabetical order using our last names. Letourneau was to my right, and Marleau to my left. Both were in their mid-twenties with several years of teaching behind them. They proved to be exceptional journey mates.

And thus began my training: up at 5:30 for prayer, then Mass, meditation, Gregorian chant of the Divine Office in Latin, and finally, some gruel and coffee for breakfast. The rest of the day was filled with spiritual reading, manual work, study of the vows, history of the Church and the Order, as well as Bible courses, French classes, and choir. I was excused from the latter because I could not produce a single note. Dad's snickers resounded in my ears. Every time I sang, Dad glared and asserted as an absolute and indisputable fact: "You can't sing. Here listen to this." He would proceed to sing an incomprehensible Flemish tune. Soon after, I sang only when driving a roaring tractor. Being excused from choir gave me time to read about Africa.

Life was simple. We each had a curtained cell in a dormitory that held all seventy-two of us. There was no television, radio, newspaper, or magazine, just hours and hours of work-filled silence. Once a month, we had a one-hour family visit or were allowed to write a letter home—the intent being to detach us from worldly concerns so we could concentrate on devotion to God. Great stress was placed on recognizing priests as God's messengers.

In contrast to the simplicity of daily life, were the religious feast days—awesome, with flowers, incense, and sublime music that transported me to far off places—all in the service of God of course. Invariably, there would be a salad or ice cream with dinner. In the afternoon, we would sometimes hike up the mountain to a huge public cemetery, and in the evening we put on skits or taught each other dance steps.

Constipation became my normal state, and my monthly period didn't show up for nine months. Rarely, the nurse would give me a laxative. She seemed to think there was nothing to worry about. Although I lost a few pounds, I was sleeping better than ever. The snake dreams were slowly retreating. I attributed the constipation and lack of period to the absence of exercise and the lack of fibre in my diet.

Every day, we had two one-hour periods of recreation—after lunch and after supper—when we walked up and down the asphalt driveway and chatted. Several of us managed a volleyball game from time to time. After each game, I had rips to mend in my skirt.

What kept me there at age twenty? I held the conviction that convent life would only get better. Soon I would be out there teaching and then—Africa. I felt part of something greater than myself, part of a team with a mission to free people from both spiritual and economic oppression through education. My life had a goal, a meaning. I belonged. Somewhere in the fourth month I realized I no longer woke up frightened and exhausted from the snake dreams—what a relief.

After six months, I moved to a new stage; I became a novice. Sixty-three of us knelt at the altar that February morning. The Bishop solemnly declared in French, *"From this day forward you shall no longer be called Yvonne Maes but Sister Nathalie Mary,"* and handed me another bundle. This was the proper dress or "holy habit," coif and all.

I chose the name Nathalie because it was my mother's name. It sounded strong and dignified. I hoped in time I would see Mom as also strong. I wanted to believe her life had value, that she didn't deserve Dad's degradation. At the time, I could not have known that she and Dad were somewhere in that enormous chapel modeled after the church of Mary Major in Rome. In a way, I was disappointed they had come—somehow this moment lost some of its heroism for me by virtue of my parents having witnessed it. Mom wept quietly and smiled when I told her I had asked for her name on purpose to honour her life. Visiting with them was painful in the large formal parlour. I couldn't even offer them a cup of coffee. The new, stiff habit seemed to cut me off—to separate me from lay people, even my parents. They claimed they were simply visiting Clarisse, who was in the Gaspe, and they happened to come along to my ceremony.

By the end of my two-year training, our ranks had thinned to forty-five. We pronounced vows of poverty, chastity and obedience for three years.

Poverty in those days meant having only two black habits, and holding all property in common, even to the point of calling objects like a pencil "our" rather than "my." Whatever I earned or received was to be handed in. This included chocolates and roses. The basic concept behind all this was not to be destitute but to share whatever one had, and to hold all goods in common much like the early Christians.

Chastity, at the very least, meant no marriage. At most, it included selfless concern and care for others. My life as a prairie daughter had prepared me well for the selfless part. Was there anything else for women raised in the 1950s? If there were, I certainly had not heard of it. Part of me still wanted a family of my own, but my dream of service in Africa overshadowed all that. One of the Holy Names customs forbade us from holding a baby or the hand of a child. This seemed out of step with the dictum to show care.

The hardest vow for me to grasp was obedience. The Church taught that the ultimate authority for any life was individual conscience. At the same time, they stressed that conscience be informed by Church tradition and scripture. While the Holy Spirit lived in each of us, the mother superior, through the bishops and ultimately the Pope, had divine inspiration on her side. Subjects were expected under pain of sin to obey, except in matters of conscience. Therefore, no superior could ask me to miss Mass on Sunday. A guidebook from the middle ages told of early monks who were ordered to plant cabbages upside-down, and that their compliance sanctified the action and the monks too.

I sensed that obedience would cause me turmoil someday. I imagined my difficulties would involve political issues and that an oppressive government would be the sanctioning body. I never imagined that a sanction would spring from my Order of nuns. I did not know of a single woman sanctioned by Rome. What brave thing could I ever do to warrant government or religious sanctions? Yet, the feeling persisted through more than three decades. I held a strong belief in the common good, rather than the individualism of the day. This belief made obedience palatable. Whenever obedience weighed heavily, I reminded myself of the limitations my sisters, Clarisse and Isabelle, faced in their marriages. I thought I had some freedom even with my vow of obedience—a freedom they did not seem to have.

Theilhard de Chardin, a famous Jesuit scientist and theologian, had been silenced by Rome in the 1950's. He agreed not to publish his writings. I felt anguish for him yet admired him at the same time. What I did not know until later was that he had given his manuscripts to lay persons who privately circulated the documents and had them published as soon as he died in 1959. I managed to read most of them in the early 1960s and found them inspiring.

∴ ⋆ ∴

In August 1961, at the age of twenty-two, I applied to pronounce vows for three years. I informed the authorities that I wanted to go to the foreign missions, preferably Lesotho, Africa, as soon as possible. Already I could see myself mingling with women in colourful Basotho blankets, carrying water on their heads, and boys herding cattle in the mountains. The superior responded with, "Not until your perpetual vows, Sister Nathalie, when you are more mature." That gave me five years to prepare. I believed I would learn much from the veteran nuns, and together accomplish great things as women and as a Church. Where else would I find such a tremendous team with such a worthwhile cause?

On the train trip back to Manitoba, I once again spied the roof of the Maes barn. By then, Mom and Dad had retired to Langley,

B.C., and Oscar and his family lived on the farm. I felt I no longer had a home other than the convent. Lorne had married shortly before, so there was no going back to past dreams of marriage. Whenever I crossed the Assiniboine River, I could picture my former self on the riverbank shouting at the ice floes and I'd heave a sigh of relief. I wasn't shouting anymore.

Back in Manitoba, I taught thirty-six wriggling third grade students at Holy Cross Elementary School in St. Boniface. Fortunately, the principal told me that children weren't born wriggling. Soon discipline became easier, and I learned to compensate for my poor singing voice by telling colourful stories. I began to enjoy teaching.

Meanwhile, it was strange to be at Holy Cross and not be able to visit my Aunt Martha who lived close by, as I had done before entering the convent. Her children attended grades one and two. With her usual straight-forwardness, she asked, "Yvonne, when are you going to get rid of those blinkers?" Though she never favoured my joining the convent, she kept her resentment to herself.

Once for a family get-together, I visited Oscar on the farm. The barn, with its curved roof and peak at each end, looked much smaller than it used to. There were just a few calves inside. The chicken house had become a storeroom haunted with memories of Dad coming after me. The yellow brick house looked as sturdy as ever, but had shrunk to the size of a play house. Gone was the coal stove and the hand pump. Things had changed, and so had I. That evening, I returned to the convent content with my lot and eager to gain experience for Africa.

During that time, Clarisse was in Labrador City and seemed far removed. Albert and Maurice were both still in Manitoba, but I had few ties with them. Isabelle called us together from time to time, but we were, in truth, a scattered, loosely knit family that was fast drifting even further apart. That fall, Isabelle dropped in for a visit, beaming as she held her three-day-old son, Randy. She brought along a chocolate cake so we could have a party. A few tugs of motherhood pulled at my heart strings as she walked out the front door with her precious bundle.

We were fourteen in the convent, and for the first time in my life I had a private bedroom with a sink and running water. The following summer, I registered for teacher training along with sixty lay people. On the first day of class, we were handed a current events test. I was so angered by my lack of knowledge, that I complained immediately to my superior, so she lifted the ban on newspapers. When the test results came out, I had the highest score! I never told my superior. That was the first of many, many school holidays spent as a student. I usually managed a week of retreat and a week at the summer camp: swimming, cycling, and hiking before starting the next school year.

In 1965, I was assigned to St. Mary's Academy, my alma mater, to teach high school and head the athletic club. The students were lively and ready to learn. They were eager to excel in class and in the gym. By the third year, I found my stride and bonded with my grade ten homeroom class of forty-two girls right from the start.

A lot of things were changing in convent life in the aftermath of the Vatican Council. We could revert to our family names if we wanted. We could replace the blinkers with a simple short veil and cut the habit to just below the knees. The day I appeared in this new modified habit, one of my students burst out crying, "Oh, sister," she wailed , "I liked your long outfit." Others gawked and exclaimed, "We thought you wore roller skates the way you glide. Why, you have regular legs and ankles!"

Sixty nuns lived and worked in the building. I brought in the first male coaches, which earned me mixed reviews from my colleagues. Once, I was refused permission to coach the final matches of the volleyball team because *"It's night time and the game is across the city."* That inspired my first protest letter.

Journal, March 1966, St. Mary's Academy
Those 3000 bishops sat in St. Peter's for three years prying open the windows of the Catholic Church, and I still can't leave the grounds to coach my volleyball team at the provincial finals! Will that protest letter to the superiors jeopardize my chances of going to Africa?

Although I spoke up and protested from time to time, I had no serious doubts that convent life was for me. I was preparing for Africa. Meanwhile, I enjoyed the orderliness, the self-questioning, the studies, and the times of prayer. When loneliness struck, I would accept it as part of every human life, as a search for the ultimate—God. When wearing black felt boring, I would remind myself that some people had no clothing. Monotony was simply a challenge to develop an interesting personality, I thought. I turned difficulties into challenges.

∴ ∵ ∴

On a sweltering summer afternoon in 1966, I pronounced vows of poverty, chastity, and obedience forever at St. Mary's Cathedral in Winnipeg. From that day on, I champed at the bit for an assignment in Africa. Although I spent two more happy years teaching high school, my heart was already in Lesotho. I could see the thatched roofs, smell the cooking fires, and hear the African drums.

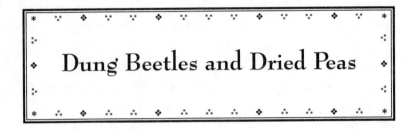

Dung Beetles and Dried Peas

On July 14,1968, I boarded the CNR coach in Winnipeg heading east. I could hardly believe it—finally, I was on my way to Africa. I had longed for this day since 1959 when I bade farewell to Lorne.

Some of my former students waited with me at the station. They waved white handkerchiefs in a cloud of good-byes as I gleefully climbed aboard. A few miles outside the city limits, I spotted the black roof of our dairy barn. A lump of uncertainty, doubt, and relief swelled within me. Although glad to leave, I wiped away a few tears as the homestead disappeared on the horizon. I wondered if I would ever return.

Two days later, the train pulled into Montreal where I spent two weeks anxiously awaiting flight arrangements. I spent some time catching up on events with Sr. Lise Marleau and Sr. Constance Letourneau from my entry group, and a few days at a Holy Names holiday residence by a lake near the village of St. Sauveur. The first evening at the lake, the superior called me in and informed me I had already broken several rules—I wore knee-high nylons, taken them off on the dock, put my bare feet into the lake, and then stretched out on my back to gaze at the clouds. I was enraged at the pettiness of it all, and told a fellow

Manitoban. She shrugged, saying some people just like to make rules so they have something to complain about. I was sure Africa would not be this petty and left alone by bus the next day. I decided to walk up the mountain to the Mother House. My shoes were new and soon my feet were blistered, but I kept on with the uphill climb. It took me three hours. As I reached the majestic front door of the Mother House, I heard my name over a megaphone. This was far different from nine years earlier, when I first stepped over that threshold. Some old friends from Manitoba had dropped by to say good-bye.

The nun in charge of outfitting me for Africa made me a new skirt and bought me a purse. The skirt had shallow pockets and the purse was too small to hold the plane ticket. Fortunately, she knew how to pack parcels for overseas. Together we packed the baseball bats, gloves, and balls which St. Mary's students had given me for my new school, in Africa.

My departure was late in the evening from the new Mirabel Airport, a few miles north of Montreal. A contingent of friends waved me through the gate to board my first commercial airline flight. The next morning, I landed in Amsterdam with a twelve hour layover before my flight to Johannesburg. A bus took me into the centre of the city, and from there I walked canals, admired tulips, and came upon a real organ grinder with a live monkey at the Rijk Museum. Finding a lavatory proved a nightmare. Eventually, in desperation, I opened a green door marked WC and came face to face with a man. He stepped aside and I marched in. So this is Europe, I thought.

That night, I flew over North Africa reaching Brazzaville for a fueling stop early the next morning, From the windows of the plane, I could see strange trees, their palms blowing in the breeze. Flight attendants came in and sprayed us with a fine mist from a big canister before we were allowed a stretch-break. As I stepped to the tarmac the heat hit me like a wave. It felt over-powering. Vendors at the tiny terminal pushed very close to entice me to buy trinkets. I couldn't understand them at first until I realized they were speaking French. For a brief moment I panicked and wondered if I should just turn around and go back to Canada.

I reached Johannesburg by mid-afternoon and had a wait of three hours before my next flight to Bloemfontein. I sat watching my two suitcases and clutching my too-small purse and my too-big ticket. It was bitterly cold, and night fell in the blink of an eye. When scouting for a toilet, I found Vrou Blanke and knew I was deep in apartheid country. By the time I landed at Bloemfontein, my two week euphoric high had been brought down by fatigue.

Two Holy Names sisters welcomed me and proceeded to drive the four hours (on the wrong side of the road!) to Peka, Lesotho. The moon was full and as shiny as a new dime. I craned my neck gawking at the small villages silhouetted in the moon-light. Squat *rondavels*—mud huts with thatched roofs—dotted the valley. Through gaping doors, I could see tiny fires burning inside. I rolled down the window, and the cool night air took my breath away. Far off in the distance I heard drums thundering an ominous steady beat. One of the sisters answered my question before I even asked.

"Witch-doctors," she said matter-of-factly.

I rolled up the window and slid back in my seat, thrilled, frightened, and completely speechless.

Later, in Peka, I lay awake for hours shivering under heavy wool blankets. At dawn I was jolted out of near sleep by howling dogs and church bells. I soon learned that these dogs always howled and sometimes hail clouds scattered when the church bells rang.

Within seconds I was dressed and at the door. There before me, bathed in morning light, was Africa—well a pin-point of Africa. It consisted of a few eucalyptus trees in the foreground, and the strangest sunrise I had ever seen. It seemed to sprout from the hillside. I squinted and looked more closely. I chuckled when I realized it wasn't the sun, but a clump of trees full of pinkish yellow blooms—a mimosa tree. At my doorstep in the sand was a jug of hot water for morning ablutions. I placed it on the washstand not wanting anyone to think I hadn't washed that morning. I stepped outside again and watched a flock of sheep clamour by, bleating as they went.

Once they passed, I spotted a few sisters in veils beyond the eucalyptus. The sisters were wrapped in multicolored blankets and were walking toward the church. They entered and I followed. I sat in the back row. Soon a hymn which started simply, transformed into a spectacular four part harmony just as the priest stepped up to the altar to begin mass. It seemed as if the congregation and the Church were welcoming me to Africa. I felt special and my eyes brimmed with happy tears.

∴ ❖ ∴

My posting was to a teacher's training college at Mazenod, a village along the main road about sixteen miles south of the capital, Maseru. This was a fertile agricultural area with rolling plains and low buttes. Dry river beds crisscrossed the area and became raging torrents when rains fell. Within two weeks I was settled into my new life at the college. Each day started with communal prayer at dawn followed by mass, breakfast, then teaching until late afternoon. Supper was at 5:30. I usually managed a walk afterwards then supervised study hall until 9:00 P.M. The generator closed down at 9:30 leaving me just enough time to read a

chapter or two of some historical novel like James A. Michener's
The Covenant.

On one of my first walks I noticed a beetle rolling a ball of
cow dung up a slope while balancing on its front legs. To get a
better look I went down on my hands and knees. My companions
called it a dung beetle and explained how it stored the dung in
holes in the ground. I recognized it from ancient Egyptian legend
as a symbol of good luck and fertility.

Although I taught in English I knew that in order to grasp
this culture I had to learn their language. Sesotho has prefixes —
eighteen if I remember correctly, although two or three of them
are seldom used. These prefixes are part of the nouns. For example, sotho means brown. Lesotho is the country. One citizen is a
Mosotho. More than one person is Basotho and the language is
Sesotho. Pronouns do not exist so gender is not an issue as it in
the English language. It was easy to make mistakes however. I
remember one day I wanted to say to the girls, "Don't make
noise." But simply by putting an 'a' where an 'o' should have
been, I said, "Don't make love."

There were many new experiences for me in Africa—some
so unique, I could never forget. One Sunday afternoon a netball
(a basketball-like game played by women) player invited me to a
concert her team had organized as a fund raiser. I paid the five
cents admission, had my hand stamped, then sat down on a
bench with my back against the classroom wall. The coordinator
stood in front of a worn blackboard. Every time a new little
group approached her she added their names and the song they
were to perform to the list. When the room was suitably
crowded, the coordinator rang the school bell and called out the
first performers: a troupe called the Queens.

Four black girls assembled at the front of the room. They
started a dance step, then belted out a song in sweet melody. Well

before they had completed their number, a village boy dashed up to the bell ringer and whispered something in her ear. She clanged the bell and the Queens promptly stopped their song and faced the audience in mock disgust. The Emcee announced, "For one cent Thabo requests that he be allowed to stand in the middle of the Queens while they sing."

With his wish granted, he joined the song and dance.

A woman in a blanket hastened to the bell ringer just as the Queens resumed their singing. She whispered something, and then the bell sounded once again.

"For three cents," the coordinator called out, "Lerato asks that the Queens sit down and the Mazenod Brothers come up to sing their song."

The exchange took place with much shoving and laughter. The Queens were barely seated and the Brothers only halfway through the second stanza when a tall man stood.

"The Brothers are requested, for five cents, to face the wall and sing so that they sound like Radio Lesotho." Everyone in the audience laughed. A few bars into the song someone else dashed up to the bell ringer waving a ten cent piece.

"I'll give ten cents to have the Queens come back to finish their song."

This 'concert' continued while the audience became more boisterous. In the frequent exchange of performers, the price for changes got so high that only a combined effort could out-bid the previous wager.

Then a group of my students got together. They had raised a *rand*—about fifty Canadian cents, to hear me sing. I can't sing. I have never sung a note on key in my life. But this was a charity function, and well . . . by the time I reached the make-shift stage I was beet red. I recited *Mary Had a Little Lamb* in a sing-song voice. By the third verse, someone requested that I wear her gloves while I sang. I became a celebrity of sorts, standing there singing (croaking) verse after verse while the netball team laughed along with the rest, thankfully counting their earnings.

∴ ⁖ ∴

Before long, I was involved in community development projects that included the construction of a communal garden, a dam, a fish pond, and several hundred silt traps to arrest soil erosion. The World Food Program provided food for work, the Department of Agriculture provided a tractor, a driver, and a supervisor, while the Church provided me—I was the link.

One day I went to work with the other women, pickaxe slung over my shoulder. Most of the labourers were women but the foreman was a man. After an hour, the women with small children took a break to nurse their babies. After two hours, everyone took a break to eat corn meal from their billy-cans. After three hours, I couldn't move a muscle. I opted out on the pretext that I had a class to teach. The others continued for two more hours. When finished, they had to trek over a mountain to their village, stopping at a spring to fetch water to lug home.

Many times I watched these remarkable women in total awe—big buckets on their heads, babies slung across their backs, small children clinging to their colourful blankets. Where did they get their energy? Furthermore, where were the men? I soon learned that most of the able-bodied men were off in the mines of South Africa and came home for a month each year. Lesotho was a land of women, old men, and children.

After completing two weeks of this development work, a lorry swung by to deliver food. Cooking oil, bread flour, powdered milk, dried peas or beans were the usual allocations. On Christmas Eve 1969, one such shipment was delivered. I had been there observing distribution. Upon my return, I saw a woman with a young child strapped to her back. She knelt at the college gates searching the sand for stray dried peas.

"What happened?" I asked.

"My bag broke," she responded quietly, barely taking her eyes from the ground. "This is all I have for my children for Christmas."

I slid to my knees to help her, and together we picked through the sand.

Some months later, the water storage dam was completed. I was proud of the accomplishment and honoured when the name was unveiled—Sister Yvonne Dam. (To this day I have friends who tease me about "Damn Sister Yvonne") It was the supervisor who had taken a keen interest in me, and had constructed the huge wrought iron sign. I did not return his attentions and wondered why he had this monument made for me.

Although I was very busy with teaching and community work, I thought it was time to do some formal studies of my own. I enrolled, part-time, in the first Master of Education Programme offered at the University of Botswana, Lesotho and Swaziland. Upon completion, my colleague, Sister Barbara and I decided to fill the gap in the high school agriculture course by writing a textbook.

∴ ❖ ∴

All of South Africa at that time was a hot bed of political instability. In 1970 the election in Lesotho had been interrupted with accusations of ballot tampering. Chief Leabua Jonathan, head of the National Party, suspended the constitution and declared a state of emergency by imposing a severe curfew. Gradually the curfew was lifted, but the military presence, the roadblocks and the constant suspicions ebbed and flowed like a seasonal river. We lived under a dictatorship that was reasonably benevolent.

Individual political affiliation seemed determined by one's church affiliation or perhaps vice versa. There were three political parties and three mainline churches. Schools and marriages also adhered closely to Church and party lines. Not only was there an invisible border between Lesotho and the South Africa, there were other invisible demarcations right within the country that cut through families and marriages as well.

Slowly I developed good friendships with Sister Eulalia Leoatla and my hiking companion Sister Barbara Andes. Eulalia and I truly enjoyed sharing a laugh. She was a hefty woman with cheeks like Dizzy Gillespie. She had an excellent command of English and witty word play that sparkled. Once, after one of my amateur archaeology digs I bragged, "Look what I found. It's an authentic tool! It's a *qibi*." By then I had mastered the click that the 'q' required in Sesotho. Eulalia glanced at the brown donut shaped stone coiled in my palm, "Wow! Authentic stool! Did you wash your hands?"

Contrary to Eulalia's little joke, my treasure was indeed a tool. It was a termite hill-smasher, which anthropologists speculate served as a digging utensil as well as a head-smasher. Sister Julienne was envious of my find—she had spent twenty-five years searching for one to no avail.

One glorious sunny day, Eulalia and I walked along a butte far from the college. We came upon a group of men playing *marabaraba*—a complicated multilevel game of stones that represent cattle. In a way, it reminded me of a sophisticated form of Monopoly. The men seemed uncomfortable with us nearby, so we moved off.

"Women are not supposed to play that game," Eulalia informed me as we meandered along the dry rocky path. "It is rumoured that many games serve as a cover for clandestine political meetings." Her cheerful demeanour seemed clouded for a serious moment. We continued in silence. I realized that men in Lesotho, much like men in Canada, did not want women involved in their games: political or otherwise.

We slowed when we heard a song-like voice coming from a nearby village. As we approached, we saw a teenage boy standing in front of a hut chanting a long story for an audience. He wore a sheep skin and a red loincloth decorated with dozens of safety pins. Again my companion explained what was going on. "He is returning from 'circumcision school' and is telling his vision story." Eulalia greeted the villagers and had a brief, friendly conversation. We were invited to join in the celebration by sitting on a bench with the family in front of a freshly smeared, decorated mud hut. Although I knew this was unheard of—nuns participating in a circumcision rite, I saw no harm in being polite and sitting with this proud family. When Eulalia's parish priest learned of this, he was outraged and refused to give her Eucharist at mass.

During my years in Africa, I made annual retreats to local convents to restore my mental balance. In the summer, I planned trips, usually with Sister Barbara, into the mountains. We'd walk down the road with a tent, sleeping bags, a bit of dry food, and a bottle of water stuffed into our knapsacks. We hitch-hiked. Usually it didn't take long before someone would offer us a lift.

On one such expedition, we were picked up by a sturdy Bedford lorry. It was overloaded with ten tons of white flour, and we had to cling to the ropes that straddled the load along with a few men who had also hitched a ride. The heavy truck lurched around mountains and through river beds. Slowly it headed eastward down into Mantsonyane Valley. We drove directly into the end of a spectacular rainbow.

It was on one of these excursions that a woman ran to me as I approached a *kraal*—a pen that held cattle. "Please do not step across the cow's tethering chains," she began as the cattle herded past me. "And see that your shadow does not touch a cow. If it does, she will no longer produce calves or give milk."

I respected the woman's wishes, seeing that this was a serious belief with major consequences. I saw it as a double-edged sword—it restricted all women who deal with cattle, yet was a sign of woman's great power—albeit negative power.

Another time, we set out toward the north end of the Drakensburg Mountains hoping to reach the Oxbow River and even the Kao open-pit diamond mines. We got as far as St. Peter's Mission in the district of Butha-Buthe when a political uprising stopped us. Apparently, when the parish priest, Father Rodney Nelson, voiced his opinion about school ownership, the Prime Minister was annoyed. He whispered something to a well-dressed man who escorted Nelson behind a nearby *rondavel.* Several other well-dressed men followed and roughed up Nelson. When he reappeared he limped and held his head. During the assault, the ringleader had threatened, "You'd better get across that South African border tonight before dark or we'll kill you." Nelson refused to leave and luckily, the threat proved empty. But the next day we had to bring him to the Roma Hospital, a five hour drive away. He drank *en route,* and by the time we reached Roma he wasn't feeling any pain.

The following day, Alphonsus Morapeli, the Archbishop of Maseru, requested that I press charges against the Prime Minister's personal body guards for violating a man of the cloth. I did. Nelson was returned to South Africa, his home. I felt good that I had taken a stand, though I never found out what became of my charges.

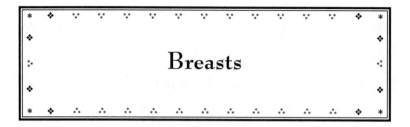

Breasts

In April of 1975, after teaching for seven years at Mazenod, I took a position as a founding staff member of the new National Teacher's Training College (NTTC). Within three years, the seven small Church-run colleges were to be phased out. This meant I had to move to St. Bernadette Convent in Maseru, Lesotho. My parish church was now Our Lady of Victories Cathedral built in honour of the Basotho who fought in WW II. I had a wonderful little corner room on the second floor with a balcony and two windows. For once in my life I had enough doors and window to feel a breeze across my face every night.

The second year I became coordinator of the NTTC internship program. My job was to set up sites throughout the country and arrange placements for student teachers and their supervisors at these sites. By the third year, I had a staff of twenty-seven Peace Corps supervisors and over three hundred student teachers in twenty-five sites. I loved traveling by Land-Rover, horseback, and small airplane. Except for one trip across the mountain ridges from Thaba Tseka to Mashai, I didn't like the days I spent on motorcycle. On that trip, however, I saw a herd of twenty wild horses race up a mountain slope and I spent time chatting with a crew of women working on the glorified bridle path—euphemistically called a road. I tried to imagine their lives: rising before dawn, packing up some cold *papa* and the baby, then walking over a mountain range to the work site. All that for an allocation of food from the famine relief section of the World Food Program.

On one visit to a remote site, I was accompanied by a young Peace Corps officer from New York. It took us well over two hours to reach the school on foot. When the school children heard my Sesotho name they broke out in the Madiepetsane song and dance. We soon forgot how cold we were in the unheated classroom. On the steep trek back it rained a cold drizzle. Halfway up a mountain my companion complained, "Oh, what I'd give for a city sidewalk!" I looked at him dumbfounded. I couldn't imagine anyone preferring cement over earth.

In this job I saw first-hand the grinding hardships faced on a daily basis by primary teachers. Each teacher had as many as a hundred and twenty students, and as little as one piece of chalk per day. Still, they were eager to teach and the students enthusiastic to learn.

By 1979, Sister Veronica Phafoli had earned her Master's Degree in English. She had a heart for leadership. We were the same age and despite the fact that we were from different ends of the earth—she had survived growing up in Soweto—we shared a great deal. That year, she was appointed the first black provincial superior of the Lesotho Holy Names Sisters. One day she asked if I would take the post at Mabathoana High School as headmistress and manager rolled into one. Every day for three years *en route* to the NTTC I had walked past Mabathoana High School. It always gave me a good feeling. The name literally means *mother of the little brown people*. I liked that. Although nervous, I felt confident I could do a commendable job, so I accepted the offer.

That night, I dreamt that I had thirteen breasts. The following day during my tour of the school, I learned it had thirteen classes from grade eight to grade twelve.

I wondered about the significance of breasts in my life. I was in my late thirties and my breasts were often painful, especially just before my period. Over the years, I had four biopsies on lumps in my breasts, but every one came back negative. At that time, seat belts had just become mandatory in all vehicles. Invariably, the belt cut across my breasts and either increased the pain or set off a sexual arousal. It was around then that I rediscovered masturbation.

This time I experienced it as a marvel, though it did have some negative aftermath. Each time I touched myself I thought God had done an incredible job creating me as a woman—as a sexual being. Masturbation was a very personal and intimate experience, an affirmation of the uniqueness of my body from everything else in the universe. It was like the joy I felt each time I squinted at the sun and saw thousands of tiny rainbows in my eyelashes. The universe was full of wonder in those moments. I was alive and could feel—not only for others in a spiritual and emotional sense—but I could also physically *feel* myself, touch parts of my body. Me.

However, after each time I masturbated, I went through days of worry—apparently the Church fathers considered this a sin, a very serious sin in fact. I couldn't imagine why. People don't get hurt by touching themselves in private. I read what little I could find on the subject. Church teaching focused on the wasted semen argument—a very male oriented defense without any scientific basis.

Two friends told me of their experience with masturbation and how they sensed it was sinful because it was selfish. I didn't follow or accept that line of reasoning. It was years before I learned that many people masturbated while fantasizing about having sex with specific partners, or while looking at women's underwear in magazines. A deviant few, I learned, masturbated to pictures of children. My sexual fantasies centered around being held by strong, tender arms. I never saw anything deviant in that.

I read books on celibacy and talked to friends. The trend since the Vatican Council was to promote friendships including those between men and women that were not genital but nonetheless affirming. There were stories of such friendships throughout history such as Claire and Francis of Assisi. The pitfalls in these friendships included the danger of secrecy and sexual activity. Should that happen, one was to seek help and either rededicate to celibacy or leave the religious order and marry. A few of my friends decided on the latter and left the order. Few of those marriages lasted more than a couple of years. I concluded that the adjustment from convent life to marriage would be too risky for me, so I resolved never to leave for a man and, if I should ever leave, to take two years before making any big decisions.

Once settled in Maseru, I joined a Christian discussion and prayer group. I met a married, charismatic, Anglican clergyman with a tremendous following in Lesotho and Southern Africa. I thought he would surely be able to guide me through some of my issues—my fear of God, my incestuous father, and my sexual attraction to men. At first he was sympathetic and helpful. Before long he suggested we "hold hands positively" as a way to experience healthy affection. This led to his kissing me and I felt helpless to stop him. I feared I would hurt his feelings if I rebuked his advances. He believed his actions were part of what the hundred-fold God promised those who served the church. The next time we had a few minutes alone he fondled me. My body thrilled to his touch but my mind went numb. How could that be? I avoided him totally after that. The experience left me utterly confused. I began to wonder if my no touch/no kiss sexual boundaries were outmoded and outdated. If this renowned, married clergyman could praise this sexual activity, perhaps I was narrow-minded and needed some liberation.

Holding hands and fondling was one thing, but the possibility of sexual intercourse was beyond my imagination. There was absolutely no gray area there. And secrecy was an issue I wanted to avoid. Whenever I was going out, I always made sure other sisters in the convent knew where I was going and with whom. I never allowed secrecy into my friendships. I told myself to be patient and honest. I reasoned that Rome was not built in a day. Understanding celibacy and being comfortable as a celibate woman in my own skin was not something that would happen overnight.

To complicate matters even further, the psychology of the day disparaged celibacy and questioned whether anyone who was not sexually active could be whole. This worried me despite the many examples of celibate women and men throughout history. And the women I lived with—weren't they both whole and celibate? Still, the question gnawed at me until my late forties as my hormones struggled to be heard. Perhaps it was my innate biological clock ticking loudly—telling me to get pregnant and propagate the human race even though it was clear that people were propagating just fine without my help.

Poverty was causing me some turmoil as well. By the seventies, I received twenty *rand* per month for items such as stamps, stationary, toiletries, books, dining out, and clothing. When I stopped buying pantyhose I was able to manage—barely. I could never really afford a new book or a real meal out, and when I learned that the seminarians received seventy *rand* a month I was shocked and disgusted. On the other hand, I knew we were living better than most people in the country and my desire to live as poorly as the people clashed with my need for books.

Politically, I was left of centre. I sympathized with the ANC and considered joining, but knew this would meet stiff opposition from the superiors who held to neutrality. A few friends were more politically active and were soon barred from South Africa and Lesotho. As a compromise I helped the revolution in other ways, such as providing support for two socialist Italian priests who had been expelled from Mozambique, even though they lived in a commune and ploughed the fields along side the local people. I felt I was sitting on the fence by not taking a stand and risking prison. My vow of obedience kept me from becoming a strong political activist, however. To this day I do not know if that was good or bad.

What held me together through all this was the strong community life in the St. Bernadette Convent. On my balcony I had an aquarium with two goldfish nicknamed Maba and Thoana. After a hard day at school, I would often talk to my two little fish. They never seemed to mind my venting.

Mealtimes with the sisters were fun. On feast days we would prepare something special and sing, dance, or play cards. Once, on my birthday, Sr. Cletus Maria prepared a surprise for me. When I entered the dining room for breakfast, I spotted a large galvanized zinc laundry tub on the table and a birthday card. In the tub, floating on blue wavy paper were two colourful paper fish labeled Maba and Thoana. But there was also a new book I'd been hankering for—a gift from those who were as poor as I was. It made me realize that though life on the outside appeared greener, life on the inside wasn't so bad.

∴ ⁙ ∴

The staff of Mabathoana included twenty teachers, a lab assistant, two librarians, a maintenance person, and two cooks. Every year, I received several hundred applications for admission to grade eight. The sheer numbers bewildered me. How could I choose some kids and not others without feeling guilty? This selection process became the bane of my existence as an administrator for the next eight years.

In January, at the beginning of each scholastic year, the new grade eight students showed up for their first day of secondary school. I remember how amazed I was each time I faced the new recruits. In a country where schooling is not a right but a privilege, I could not fathom how parents turned out such squeaky clean, uniform-clad children, day after day, after paying school fees and buying books. The minimum wage in Maseru at the time was four *rand*-fifty—about three dollars per day. Some families had four or five children attending school. It never ceased to astound me.

My first year at Mabathoana, I assembled all one hundred sixty-five grade eight scholars in front of my office. I welcomed them to the school, and asked them to follow me to the grade eight block of three classrooms in a separate section. I lead them across the soccer field feeling abashed yet proud of the spectacle it created. I imagined it must have looked like the biblical picture of the good shepherd leading the flock. All one hundred sixty-five lambs sprightly marched behind me without a bleat.

As I neared the classrooms, I realized they were already filled—with older students. Somehow I had ended up at the grades eleven and twelve block. I tried to act as if I knew exactly what I was doing. I gulped down my dismay, and prayed for some clever inspiration to get me out of this mess. I stopped and my flock stopped too. They stared at me with big brown eyes waiting for an explanation.

"Students," I began bravely. I had to enunciate each word carefully for they were not yet accustomed to my Canadian accent. "These are the grade eleven and twelve classrooms. Some of you have older sisters and brothers in there." They peered around but remained perfectly quiet. I continued, "If you study very hard you'll be there someday too. Do you agree?"

"Yes Mother!" they responded with eyes the size of wheelbarrows. I silently emitted a sigh of relief. "Now, turn around and we'll go to your classrooms."

"Yes, Mother."

❊ ❖ ❊

In 1984 I took three months leave to go home. The long voyage caused me much anxiety, but I wasn't afraid of crashing or missing my plane or getting lost. I liked the adventure, the food, and the foreign cultures. My problem was I couldn't protect myself from being groped and manhandled particularly on the long overnight flights. The first time it happened I was scared speechless. What kind of a sicko would grope at a nun on an airplane? I also wonder, now, why I didn't stop him the instant he put his hand on my thigh? I remember feeling shocked and dirty. I didn't want to cause a scene, so I wiggled and he finally stopped touching me and removed his hand.

After that occasion, I decided to travel without my veil thinking perhaps it was a perverse attraction for some men. It made no difference. I was still molested. When I reached New York, I sat beside a couple of obviously experienced female travelers. One of the women worked with the UN and traveled extensively. I told her what happened.

"Twice now during overnight flights, I've woken up with a man's hand on my thigh. I feel angry but helpless when this happens—as if I've invited their advances because I have a female body. The first time it happened I was in my veil. This time, well . . . could you tell I am a nun?"

The UN worker shook her head. Her eyes were knowingly sympathetic.

"I'm scared it could happen again," I admitted shamefully. "I have two more nights of flying ahead of me when I return to Africa."

She smiled and offered some sound advice. "Sister, you don't have to take that. Just tell the flight attendant that you're uncomfortable or you don't feel safe and they will gladly change your seat. Personally, I watch out for men who won't look me in the eye or won't carry on a conversation. They seem to be the sneaky ones with 'Roman' hands and 'Russian' fingers. What I suggest is communicate with whomever is next to you as soon as you're seated. If they won't speak to you or if you get even a whiff of suspicion, ask to change seats."

I sat there, incredulous, that someone would actually do that—change seats. I couldn't—I felt guilty even imagining it. What if I hurt their feelings? I would never have moved away from my father. That wasn't tolerated in my world.

On the next night flight across Africa, the man on my right would not chat or look me in the eye. There were three empty seats in a row up ahead. It took me more than an hour to muster the courage to move. I agonized over moving—it made me feel guilty. It brought back unpleasant memories.

Those memories became reality when I arrived in Canada to visit my parents. Even as an adult I still avoided my father. When I reached their home in Langley, B. C., I deliberately wore the bulkiest sweater I could lay my hands on. I was forty-four years old and I didn't want my father to notice my breasts. It was awful. In the sweltering discomfort of a British Columbia heat-wave I bundled up as if it was winter. Just being near him brought back old fears and sick confusion. I knew that I could not confront him because I still did not have the words. He was ninety-two and hardly able to hobble to the bathroom or hold a coffee cup. I hoped that someday I would be able to tell some-one—someone who could clarify what had happened to me and offer advice—maybe even a solution. In the back of my mind I made a little note—I'd be brave and seek professional help some-day. But for now I'd do as I always did, I'd hide, keep quiet, and be thankful my avoidance techniques worked.

It was during this visit that I first saw Mom wearing a wig. I learned from Clarisse that Dad resented Mom spending money at the hair-dressers, and that he complained about her gray hair, saying it made her look old. It infuriated me to see Mom once again succumbing to Dad's tyranny.

The state of the house was shocking. From floor to ceiling it was cluttered with junk. There wasn't a chair to sit on or a free corner to put my suitcase. I stuffed it in front of the stove and slept on the sofa. After two days of sleeping in the living room, I was ready to leave. Luckily, my brother-in-law, Steve, phoned and asked if I wanted to visit them. Did I? Clarisse came that afternoon to fetch me. A few days later I returned to say good-bye to Mom and Dad. I knew I would never see Dad again. His hair was still black with only a hint of gray at the temples. I managed to kiss him on the forehead and smile—all the while wishing I was ten thousand miles away or better yet, not born at all.

From B.C. I went to Manitoba where I raised funds for a new high school at Abia near Maseru—an extension of Mabathoana. I took time to walk along the Assiniboine River and reflect on something Laurens van der Post once said: that eventually one must return to one's own culture to work out life's meaning. I gave myself three years to finish up in Lesotho at which time I would return to Canada permanently.

Isabelle organized a reunion of the extended family to help with my fund raising. Aunt Martha raffled off a doll, and various parishes and convents contributed. When I counted the pennies I had $25,000 to take to the Canadian International Development Association in Ottawa for a matching 4:1 grant to build fifteen classrooms. Soon I was on my way back to Africa via Amsterdam, where I met with the board of the Dutch Catholic Bishops charity organization. They decided to designate funds for buildings and equipment for practical courses such as wood-work, needlework, cookery and metalwork.

My last stop was Itegem, Belgium for a quiet few days with my aging Uncle Louis and Aunt Fanny. I questioned them about my family history and also about the war years. Uncle Louis was a pious man: he maintained the traditional practice of praying the *angelus* before the noon meal. By then even my Holy Names Order had dropped that prayer. In chats with him I sensed he was terrified of death. He offered me a few poems he had com-posed. These confirmed my suspicion; he felt deeply unworthy and feared facing God his Father. The fact that this devout man in his eighties dreaded facing God confounded me. I could see myself in his shoes and did not like the picture. I needed to make some drastic changes or reach old age as fearful as Uncle Louis. As I wandered along the nearby Nete River, I promised myself that I would seek out help to face my darkest terrors. I didn't think I'd find anyone to help me in Africa and figured it would probably have to wait until I returned to Canada.

Father Goodall

By 1985, I had acquired far too many jobs. I was pushed to the limit with the Headmasters and Headmistresses Association, the Lesotho Teachers Association, the Regional Council for the Lesotho province of the Holy Names Order, and, of course, the two schools where I continued to teach as well as administer and supervise construction. At times I felt that no matter how hard I worked, I could never catch up. It was like the Manitoba gumbo on the old kitchen floor—as fast as I scrubbed it off, it reappeared. I was tired and frustrated, mostly at myself, for not being able to say no to work.

My anger at a male God grew as I looked around me at the overworked women of Africa struggling daily just to keep their children alive. I began to have too many questions—questions about my faith, my fear of death, and my own life's work. Was I really making a difference or simply propping up the *status quo?* Was I ever going to get relief for my questions around my vows? I wanted to live life to the fullest which included the struggles. Pain and questioning seemed to be central to a full life, but maybe I was shirking. Why the failures—almost once a year—in my no touch rule? Why the resentment at the meager budget we received—I had just learned that the boys in the seminary received seventy *rand* a month to my twenty. Furthermore, Nelson Mandela was still in prison, and apartheid seemed to be entrenched as firmly as ever. The international boycotts were hurting the ordinary people more than the white politicians. I needed reaffirmation and time to focus. I didn't want to admit it, but I was getting burned-out.

Sister Francis Allison realized I was in need of renewal. As a senior sister she booked the two of us for a ten-day guided retreat at Durban, in South Africa, starting July 1, 1985.

I had never participated in this new form of retreat, where there were no sermons except at Mass. The retreatant had four private one-hour meditations as well as a daily meeting with the retreat director. These half-hour sessions were designed for spiritual guidance, one-on-one meetings to deal with serious issues vital to the retreatant.

I had many issues I felt were vital. I felt cowardly for not confronting my Dad on his molestation. It bothered me greatly that I was still such a coward in so many areas of life. I thought discussing my feelings with an experienced professional would help me recapture my faith and understand myself better. The retreat sounded like it was just what the doctor ordered.

I drove from Maseru to Durban while Sister Frances navigated. It was an enjoyable trip and we took our time. We found the Dominican Retreat Center at The Bluff on Brighton Beach—a beautiful white section of Durban. The sisters welcomed us and showed us to our rooms then invited us to tea on the verandah. It was warm and humid compared to Maseru. Monkeys chattered in the banana grove that bordered the lawn, and I was feeling very positive about the upcoming retreat. Some twenty sisters, all white and from various parts of South Africa, joined us for tea on the lawn.

I relaxed and nibbled on coffee cake while trying to catch a glimpse of the monkeys in the distance. Suddenly, the calm atmosphere was alive with exclamations and excited laughter. Several sisters clustered around a tall, dark-haired man in a light blue suit. He wore a see-through black shirt with the collar unbuttoned exposing a hairy chest. The pointy tips of his thick-heeled shoes were trimmed in gold. I wondered who he was. My gut tapped out a warning—the same kind of warning I often felt on airplanes. I remained seated and watched. He had lots of female friends. Sister Frances, who sat next to me followed my eyes. She whispered, "that's your retreat director."

I felt my jaw drop. Sister Frances laughed. "Oh Yvonne, lighten up. This is the eighties! You need a good, experienced director."

"I thought I'd get the Sister director?"

She rolled her eyes. "You know the women in the Church don't have half the experience the men have. A priest can help you with your dilemmas—personal and spiritual. I want you to have a wonderful retreat. You have so few chances to do this."

At supper that evening I was introduced to the man in the blue suit. His name was Father Frank Goodall. He was charming and sat beside me. He had an infectious smile. "I read on my list that you are a Holy Names Sister from Maseru," he said.

I nodded politely.

"Just last week I met your ex-provincial, Veronica Phafoli," he added.

Again I nodded.

He stood. "I'll see you in my office at eight tonight with the others in my group so we can set up the timetable."

At eight o'clock I sat with six others. We introduced ourselves and then checked the timetable. We were to start in earnest the following morning and continue for eight full days. The time would be passed in total silence except for sessions with the director. Each of us had to sign up for half-hour daily appointments. I took the four-thirty slot. Before leaving to return to my room, Goodall gave my shoulder a little squeeze then rubbed my neck for just a second. He smiled at me. Nervously I smiled back. I felt both affirmed and confused. The touching bothered me. I didn't know if it was standard practice for these new retreats or something more. I convinced myself to be brave for a change and ask.

The next day at my at four-thirty appointment I asked Goodall, "Is it normal to touch someone like that on the shoulder and neck?"

"Oh no!" he confessed. "That kind of behaviour would soon get around the retreat houses. But I think you are ever so special—a real missionary. Just look at you, surviving the isolation of Lesotho. And your accomplishments through all this are extraordinary."

I felt honoured, even thrilled. But still confused. Politely I smiled, then listened as he proceeded to tell me about his Irish roots in Belfast and his compulsive overwork. I learned his brothers were involved with the IRA, and I felt privileged to hear these stories. However, I didn't get much chance to tell him how my retreat was going. At five o'clock he told me he'd write out some scripture topics on a sheet and slip it under my bedroom door. He did so.

At the following session I told him about the abuse I suffered at the hands of my father and that I couldn't muster the strength to confront Dad before he died. This angered and depressed me. My story did not shock Frank, as everyone called him. I had not told this to any authority figure before. His reaction was comforting. I felt safe in revealing my fears of the male God, of burn-out, and of my ordeal returning to Canada. Once again, he had not prepared scripture passages for me and once again he said he'd deliver them later that evening. This time he knocked. I was knitting. He handed me the sheet of paper and whispered, "Yvonne, if you ever think of leaving the order, I'd be interested."

I simply shrugged my shoulders and shook my head. "I have no intention of leaving the order," I assured him. I didn't tell him that I knew nuns who had left to marry priests. I thought they may have found themselves going from the frying pan into the fire. I had promised myself early on that I would never leave for a man. Still, I was attracted to Frank: he was caring, knowledgeable, and a challenge. Would I be able to figure him out? I liked that kind of challenge in friends.

At our next session, I nervously asked if it was normal for him to come to my bedroom. He assured me that as retreat director he indeed had access to all the retreatants private quarters. He went on to explain how he had been up late the previous night with a sister suffering from a panic attack. I felt he was a dedicated priest giving his time unselfishly to anyone who needed it.

I quickly realized that Frank talked more than I did at our sessions. I felt honoured that he trusted me with his intimate life stories, but at the same time I wasn't getting on with my issues. He told me more about meeting Sister Veronica Phafoli, and how she struck him as a pushy woman. He said, "I don't like pushy women."

Veronica and I had been friends for a long time. We had drifted apart somewhat—after she became the Provincial Superior. This gossip from Frank put a further wedge in our friendship.

One night, clad in my long housecoat with a towel draped around my neck, I saw him amble toward me as I headed for the shower room. I could not escape without showing my embarrassment, so I braced myself and walked on. As he sauntered by he whispered, "My office is just beyond the shower room. You could drop in for a visit after you finish."

Though clenched teeth I forced a grin and quickly walked on. Once again he had my head spinning with confusion. I did not accept the invitation. Although part of me was lonely and wanted someone to talk to, another part said this was far too risky and unprofessional.

As I showered, I wondered again if this was the way these new retreats were run? It certainly was different from any retreat I had ever been on. I wanted to ask Sister Frances but dared not for two reasons—one, the rule was silence, and two, I was embarrassed by my naiveté. Perhaps Frank was just the new, friendlier retreat director type and I was just paranoid and jumping to conclusions. I reasoned that perhaps it's just his friendly Irish personality—his way of teasing and putting retreatants at ease. I scrubbed my hair so long and hard my scalp began to hurt. I felt guilty for feeling suspicious. I chastised myself for being ungrateful and judgmental.

On the fourth day at the end of the half-hour session, Frank suggested we go for a walk on the beach later that evening. He said he could give me the reading suggestions then. I felt perhaps now he was tailoring the retreat to meet my individual needs since he had taken up most of the allotted time on his issues.

It was winter in South Africa and darkness fell by 5:00 P.M.. On the beach we sat at the bandstand. The area was lit with floodlights and a dozen or so white people milled about. After a few minutes Frank showed me his hip holster where he housed a neat little pistol.

"Sometimes, things can get rough," he warned. "I was attacked once in East London after dark so now I carry a gun." He tapped the dark leather pouch like some brave maverick. I glanced at it then looked away, stunned.

We watched the waves of the Indian Ocean thunder and crash over the white sands. After a few moments we took a stroll up along the beach. As we walked, watching the waves pound in, he took my hand. It felt strong and protective still I wondered if this was right—proper. I feared I'd be criticized for being either judgmental or pushy if I yanked away. He had already told me how much he disliked pushy women. As I pondered my uncomfortable feelings, he pulled his hand away slowly. I affirmed that all he was trying to do was make me feel cared for. I felt guilty for willing him away, while at the same time, wanting his affirming touch.

"You are unique," he said calmly as he wrapped his arm protectively around my shoulders. This time I tried very hard to relax and enjoy his company.

"You have a remarkable life story. You've come through so much; your father's abuse, the political turmoil in Lesotho, the stress of living in a different culture." He smiled at me. "Yes, you are a real missionary." I smiled back and felt that my suspicions of him were unfounded. He was just a good man. A priest who understood and could grasp the struggles I faced daily. Sister Frances said this would be a great retreat. Her advice about having an experienced professional seemed to ring true.

As we continued on down the beach he told me a story about a man and his secretary on a business trip. Apparently, as they walked on a beach one night, some thugs held them up at gun point and took their valuables. Then, the muggers forced the couple to perform sex as they watched. It was a frightening story. I felt safe however with his gun and his closeness there to protect me.

I shared with Frank how all my life I hated being a woman. I admitted that I envied the rights and privileges of men, and that I wanted to do the things they did. I confessed that many of my endeavours were to prove my worth to men. I then admitted, fatalistically, that being a woman in the Catholic Church certainly wouldn't help me overcome this feeling.

When we reached the door of the retreat centre, he stopped. "Yvonne," he began solemnly. "I need to tell you my history. Remember I told you I had back trouble at the age of twenty-five from football injuries? Well it was a risk I took—the operation I mean. I was in hospital for a couple of months. No one came to see me, no newspaper, no phone, nothing but pain. A nurse took an interest in me and soon there was a daily newspaper. One night she crept onto the bed beside me. Her uniform slid up as she slipped under the sheet—perfume and all. She wasn't a virgin."

I felt terrible that a nurse had taken advantage of him sexually. He was in such a vulnerable position as her patient. I hugged him good night and thanked him for his honesty and openness. I felt I was keeping limits on the affection without being frigid. Being available to care for others in a self-sacrificial way was a credo dear to all sisters. Our congregation customarily paid special attention to priests because they lead such hard lives and represent God Himself. We were constantly reminded of that.

With each meeting, Frank opened up to me more and more. He told me some very private details about his past. He needed me to listen—to be caring and compassionate. I was. He described himself as a loner—the Clint Eastwood type. He admitted he found some women difficult, saying they were nags and hardly feminine. I worried that he would find me a nag if I talked or complained too much about my life. I curbed myself in order to retain his good opinion. After all, this priest seemed to have chosen me as his special confidante. I felt honoured.

I silently battled with an unpleasant anxiety that crept like a shadow into my thoughts. I still didn't know where I stood on certain issues, yet I was afraid that if I crossed his invisible line or overstepped his undefined boundaries, I'd be added to his list of pushy, nagging women. I made every effort to be cheerful, refined, affirming, non-judgmental and to speak non-assertively.

Two days after the beach walk, Frank came to me and said, "I'm going out for supper with my nephew and his family. I'll be back early. I'll drop in for a visit with you afterwards." I figured he'd want to talk about the things that would come up during his family dinner—things he couldn't share with them or anyone else. Again I felt honoured. I looked forward to his company, especially during the long hours of silence and meditation. I waited, fully dressed, until 11:00 P.M.. When he didn't show, I decided to go to bed.

Moments later I was pulled from near sleep to find Frank next to me on my bed.

"Shhh," he said, "or someone will hear us." I wriggled back against the wall with my hands over my breasts: like in the days of my father. My mouth went dry and my heart thumped wildly as he stretched out over the covers beside me.

"I bet you're glad I've kept my pants on," he teased. He then added, "Supper was great! We watched a World Cup football match that I had on tape. Sorry I'm so late."

A few minutes later he was gone. Then I couldn't sleep. My head swam with dizzying confusion. I knew he felt we had a special relationship, but I was taken aback by his comment about leaving his pants on. And the fact that he actually stretched full length on my bed beside me! I wondered again if he was this friendly with other women. He didn't really do anything wrong. I began rationalizing. I convinced myself that since Frank had directed hundreds of retreats for women, he knew what he was doing. Besides, the other retreatants seemed to respect him. They all seemed to hang on his every word and his homilies at Mass. I blamed myself for overreacting and for being a frightened old woman. In each of the relationships I had with men, we had talked about our boundaries. Frank did not seem to talk about boundaries—he seemed to act. Frank seemed to be shooting down all the safety blocks that surrounded me like targets at a shooting gallery. He was pushing fast and hard and he wasn't really talking. Despite that, I chastised myself for being too judgmental.

Though the Mountains May Fall

On the second to last day of the retreat, Frank whispered to me at morning coffee, "How about meeting me in my office just after lunch. Time is so short and there is so much to talk about."

I agreed that we needed to talk. I wanted to clarify what this relationship meant to him. Was his treatment of me normal? If so, why was I so paranoid about his closeness and his innuendoes? Perhaps if I were open with him he would explain himself. I was troubled with this because he seemed to push the sexual boundaries further and further. I was more confused about male and female interaction now than I was before I came to the retreat. I could accept some physical closeness, including an embrace, a touch on the shoulder, a squeeze of my hand, but I wasn't clear what Frank wanted. I badly needed to know his ideas on this subject in order to feel safe.

Hoping he would bring up our relationship for discussion, I went to his office. After just a few minutes he suggested we step into the adjacent room—his bedroom. He was nonchalant about the request so I figured he must have pictures and memorabilia to show me.

Instead, he hugged me. I was wearing my gray wool skirt and within seconds he had unhooked it. I froze. I didn't know how to push him away or say no without hurting him. Was there a way to show my appreciation for his friendship yet stop him from doing this? I was afraid I would seem ungrateful and unrefined. How could I get out of this without alienating him and his validation of me? I felt trapped.

There was a stone in my throat and a toxic fog in my brain. I knew this was it—sex—intercourse. He commanded in a benevolent tone but commanded nonetheless. Never did he ask what I wanted or how I felt. As he caressed me he talked non-stop, saying things like, "Oh how wonderful. Just as God wants it for man and woman."

Screaming voices of confusion dueled within me. I was ashamed at how his caresses stimulated my entire body. It felt so wonderful. It felt so wrong. I mustered every fiber of courage within the fog and fear to mutter, "I don't want to get pregnant."

With no hesitation whatsoever, he replied, "Oh, don't worry. Trust me. You won't get pregnant."

He was efficient and gentle. My body and mind seemed to become separate entities. I felt passionate waves of sexual pleasure that I, a forty-five year old virgin, never knew existed. Despite the physical coercion it was a pleasurable sexual experience with an orgasm for me; but psychologically it would prove cataclysmic.

Dazed, I dressed quickly. All the while Frank talked. I had no opportunity to express myself. He exclaimed, "Oh Yvonne, we are so good and our systems work perfectly together. You'd think we'd been doing this for twenty years. We could write a book."

Afterwards, Frank explained that since childhood he hadn't masturbated. I wondered what that had to do with me. He said he had the ability to control his fluids. He then added, "Some men are careless with their pre-orgasmic fluids but I've taken care of all that so you won't get pregnant."

That entire "visit" lasted about twenty minutes. As I left he said, "Yvonne, tell me you are the happiest woman in all of South Africa."

Foolish me, I nodded, because my body was happy. But my soul was devastated. I had betrayed God. I had betrayed myself.

I left his room and walked straight outside into the streets of Durban. In a mindless stupor I walked and walked. Somehow I kept putting one foot in front of the other. Waves of suffocating guilt choked me. I couldn't believe what had just happened. I beat myself up inside saying, *What have I done?* and *Why did this happen?* I figured I must have caused it, but how? Couldn't I see what I had done wrong? Frank was the retreat director and I was supposed to trust him totally. I did. I was obedient, a good nun—and now this. I wondered if I would have felt better if he had threatened me or raped me at gun point. But I entered that bedroom on my own two feet. Did that mean I wanted to have sex? He didn't ask, he just acted. He talked incessantly with barely a space for me to interrupt. Sisters are expected to be modest in speech. That was a custom written in the old Holy Names custom book. Interrupting someone was anathema for me. I had jumped in the moment he stopped for a breath. He'd whisked away my concerns about pregnancy as trivial and inconsequential. He knew what to do. How was it he knew so much about pre-orgasmic fluid? I had never even heard of it. And where had he learned so much about sex and the female body? Was I just one of many, or was what we just shared a very special event? No matter what the answer, it was definitely an event that would devastate my life: shatter my dreams, and take away my spirit. My virginity had been threatened by my father and by the Air force officer on that cold and lonely road. I knew what they were after, so I was able to stop them. I never knew what Frank wanted, and I was under *his* authority. His agenda was open to anything.

I tried to compose my thoughts. I needed to talk to him calmly. I didn't know where I'd start and I was afraid approaching the subject would make him angry. Some sniveling little part of me desperately needed his affirmation, and I dreaded his anger. I loved him and I hated him. I hated myself for loving him and needing his affirmation.

Every few minutes, my mind returned to the thought that I could be pregnant. Sheer panic caused beads of sweat to form on my forehead. I recalled one young sister who was seduced by a taxi driver. He left her pregnant and stranded on the street. Priests who fathered children in Lesotho were required to pay a flat settlement to the woman's father, but their ministry went on as usual. Not so when a sister became pregnant. She suffered major hurdles. I knew two sisters who left to raise their children. I knew of only one sister who took a leave of absence under a shroud of suspicion, secretly gave the baby up for adoption, then returned to the convent.

What would I do? I actually would contemplate an abortion, but saw no way I could possibly carry out such a thing. The entire situation could have horrific consequences. It slammed into my entire future—my life. Being a nun—obedience, poverty, celibacy? What did they mean now? Would God ever forgive me? Would I ever forgive myself?

Hours later, I found myself still walking as if in a dream, a traumatic dissociation. Several monkeys chattered as they hopped from banana tree to banana tree along the paved road down to the beach. The waves pounded the shore much as my heart pounded in my chest. It was then that the nausea of my childhood started up again. It crept up and down between the pit of my stomach to the back of my throat. I didn't know where I was, but I knew as long as I followed the coastline I'd find my way back. It was getting dark and cold. I knew that if I missed supper, Sister Frances would surely go looking for me. So would Frank. I dared not create a scene, so I headed back unable to focus on anything but moving my feet—left, right, left—one step at a time.

That evening I couldn't stay in my bedroom. I feared Frank would come, climb into my bed and repeat the sex—no questions asked. I knew I would not have the strength to stop him; I could no more hurt his feelings or refuse his advances than I had my father's. In a trance, I went to the chapel and sat at the back. A few sisters came and went, but no one took notice of me wrapped in a blanket. It felt safe—as safe as any place I could think of. It was public and sacred. I focused on the presence of Christ in the tabernacle. First I prayed that Christ would forgive my shameful weakness and my broken vows. I had failed. Then I began to doubt Frank had controlled his ejaculation and what he called pre-orgasmic fluid. How was I to know whether he was telling the truth or not? Then I began pleading—a frantic bargaining with the Lord, admitting I could face anything but pregnancy. I begged God to punish me by other means—illness, irate parents, difficult teachers, anything but a baby. I simply could not face raising a child on my own with no money, no family, no husband. I would be too ashamed to contact Clarisse or Isabelle, so I would forever be alone with this child. Waves of nausea came and went. Each time I leaned forward ready to vomit.

I continued to pray for divine guidance. Where was this personal God I had believed in all my life? *I need you now!* I prayed. I felt utterly torn inside, from my womb to the roots of my hair. Part of me never wanted to see Father Frank Goodall again.

Another part of me wanted him to come sit beside me, put his strong arm around my shoulder and apologize. I wanted him to help make it better. I wanted God to whisper it was all right. But Jesus was silent and remote. I had never felt so totally alone in my entire life. I stayed fixed to the seat long into the night, waiting. I became vexed at Jesus for not answering me.

If I were pregnant, I realized with a sickening blow, Frank could easily deny having fathered the child. As the night dragged on, I felt worse instead of better. I longed for the sunrise, but when it came I wanted the night again. I didn't know how I would get through the day.

I arrived late for breakfast. There was only one free place at the table and it was next to Frank. He beamed proudly at me then whispered, "Wifey, how are you?"

I was appalled at the term and the joviality in his voice. Did he feel this was a game? A sick joke? My nausea made it impossible to swallow anything solid. I gulped down a mouthful of strong coffee. All I could do was ignore him—it was silence, after all.

That day was the last full day of the retreat. He came to my bedroom and suggested we go for a drive at lunch. He said we could sneak off under the pretense that I had to get petrol before leaving tomorrow. He also hinted that we needed to talk.

We drove along in silence until we found an embankment overlooking the ocean. Once seated on a blanket Frank said, "I was wondering last night as I prayed how this all happened between us. I realized that one thing just led to another and before I knew it I was undressing you. It was so natural and good, not out of lust—but from the purest of motives."

I sat stunned, watching the ocean waves in tune with the waves of nausea that moved incessantly from my stomach to my throat. *He* wasn't feeling any nausea.

He kept talking. "I haven't been this happy for a long, long time," he rambled. Then he suddenly began to sing, *"She was fat and pink and pretty . . ."*—music from the Broadway hit *Oklahoma!.*

When he paused for breath I audaciously blurted out, "How come you know so much about sex?" I hugged myself into a ball anticipating an angry retort.

"Well, that nurse I told you about, remember? She had me for two months and she was no virgin!" he responded without a moment's hesitation.

I thought he must have been a fast learner, but I didn't dare say that out loud. I needed him on my side in case I was pregnant. I was not about to provoke his anger.

"I'm afraid that if I am pregnant you'll claim it isn't your child. You could say that you don't know what I do in Lesotho." I spoke through a mist of numb airwaves with no energy or life. There was no rancor or blame, just my dead voice.

"I'll have a blood test. Anyway, I'd leave my order and take care of the child if it came to that," he commented with some concern in his voice.

"What about me?" I asked.

"I'd take care of you too, if you'd have me. But trust me—you aren't pregnant." At that he launched into another song and I launched into more nausea. Perhaps he'd had a vasectomy and didn't want to tell me? His voice had an edge of anger in it, and I backed off fearing he would accuse me of being as pushy as Veronica. Despite his assurance, I was not at all convinced that I wasn't already pregnant.

"Be not afraid, I go before you always, come follow me and I will give you rest." When he stopped he exclaimed joyously, "I haven't sung like this for years. This is wonderful."

I didn't think it was proper to burst his bubble, so I sat quietly and looked at the ocean.

Later, as we drove into the retreat centre he said, "I'll write a quick note to Veronica. She'll be expecting it when she learns that we met. That will keep her off your back."

I wondered why Veronica would be on my back? He implied that she was demanding and possessive, and he needed to keep her happy. Again he made me feel sorry for him having to pacify a nagging woman. I felt concerned that she might be jealous of me. They could be friends if they wanted, I was not interested in exclusive friendships with anyone. So, on top of everything else, I was confused by his need to write Veronica.

That afternoon at our scheduled half-hour session, the first thing he said was, "I cannot hear your confession Yvonne, but I take responsibility for everything that happened until you can get to confession."

It relieved me somewhat that he finally seemed to take this matter seriously. He cared for my spiritual welfare, and I got the message that he realized having sex was wrong—a serious mistake. I assumed he meant that it would never happen again, that we could have an appropriate celibate friendship from here on.

At a penance service that evening, the entire group assembled in the chapel. The service opened with a popular hymn about biblical Ruth and Naomi: *Wherever you go . . . Wherever you go, I shall go, wherever you live, so shall I live.* Another hymn, that brought me to the verge of tears, was *I Will Never Forget You.* I mumbled along with blurred eyes and choked on the second verse:

Would a mother forget her baby? Or a woman the child within her womb? Even though they forget, yes even though they forget, I will never forsake my own.

I believed Frank had selected these hymns as a message to tell me he would always be a true friend and supporter of me.

When the time came for confession, I was glued to my back row seat. There were only two priests and one was Frank. I recalled something a nun had said when I was in grade nine at St. Mary's back in Manitoba. "If you aren't sure something is a sin, then give yourself the benefit of the doubt." How could I have even a fluff of doubt. I had full sexual intercourse—the true joining of two bodies. Who was I kidding? Was I above the law? A little voice inside me argued that I had not come to the retreat for sex. I had not come to the retreat to get myself pregnant. How could my intent be so different from my actions? I sat totally mute with my own conflicting thoughts.

At our last session, Frank gave me an article by Patrick Carroll, S.J. called: On Becoming a Celibate Lover.

"This could help us grow and mature," he said.

I glanced through the article. The first paragraph read,

"The longings of their human, sexual natures will arise, confusing good and healthy relationships. This will happen when least wanted, least expected. Because they are not Jesus they will fail, as they try to be celibate lovers. But these failures can at least be Christian failures in the right direction, a falling forward rather than a falling back, and we can learn from them and go on."

I was actually relieved to believe that this mistake of ours could be rectified. There was hope in all this despair after all. Everything could truly be for growth as Frank so often told me. Long before I could finish reading the article, he went on with, "I realize women sometimes share intimate parts of their experiences with other women. I don't think we can do this in our case. Our union is that of kindred spirits, very special. This has been a unique bonding that nothing or nobody can take away. A once in a lifetime experience of closeness and wholeness. I can't imagine sharing that with anyone else. I expect that you feel the same."

"But what if I'm pregnant? Frank I am scared," I admitted. "I want you to phone me on July 29th at 4:30 P.M. at my school office. By then I should know for sure."

He straightened his shoulders and huffed out a sigh, "All right, Yvonne, but you are worrying for nothing." He didn't seem pleased with my request.

The following morning, I loaded the car, and waited for Sister Frances Allison to bring her suitcase. We had a long uphill drive back. Frank was in the yard and handed me an envelope for Sister Veronica. He then asked one of the other sisters to take our picture. He held me so tight and his hand was so close to my breast that I blushed with embarrassed. He joked about this being his Clint Eastwood routine. The other sisters chuckled politely and watched as I forced a big, fake smile and stood next to him like a trophy. The only outward resistance I showed was to pull away a few inches but I dared not embarrass him in public. I was disgusted with myself. I must have done something to make this happen.

As I drove off he called out, "Yvonne, don't forget *Though The Mountains May Fall.* Remember that whenever you need to."

Was he making a promise to stand by me?

Sister Frances and I talked casually about the retreat as we started out of Durban.

"So tell me Yvonne, you had the most open and experienced of the three retreat directors. How was he?"

I just smiled and lied through my teeth. "Good. He was very experienced." I wondered if I told her what really happened would she believed me? Would anyone believe me? If the Order ever found out would they help me? Or would I be forced out quietly so as to avoid scandal? News like this would disrupt the whole place, and nuns don't cause disturbances. Nuns cooperate. Women, like our namesake the virgin Mary, listen and obey. We nurture, we forgive and we forget.

Before we reached Brennen Pass through the Drakensburg Mountains, my vagina started to itch badly. I wriggled in my seat. Soon after, I had a terrible urge to urinate. I stopped at several service stations to use the washroom. The itch, the urge to urinate, and the nausea grew as hours passed. There were times when I couldn't see the highway clearly. I chatted on with Sister Frances trying to maintain a semblance of sanity. But my mind was elsewhere. It groped with another sick possibility besides being pregnant. My vagina had never itched before. How in the world would a nun get tested for possible venereal disease?

Listen and Obey

With all my washroom stops it took us twelve hours to reach Lesotho. At supper I met Veronica. As soon as she learned that Frank Goodall had been my retreat director, she became agitated and demanded, "Didn't he send me a note?" Immediately I went to fetch it for her. She asked about him often. When she realized I knew a lot about him she remarked, "Yvonne you didn't make a retreat. You shared life stories with Frank!"

She was right and I felt guilty. But I also felt Veronica was too insistent the way she kept quizzing me. Perhaps she was as pushy as Frank claimed.

The day after my return, I called Father Gregory Brooks, a kind, capable Dominican priest, to hear my confession. His response was, "Yvonne you have sinned by loving too much. I don't know if you should ever see him again."

I left more confused than relieved. Just what did *loving too much* mean? I concluded that I was responsible for the mess and therefore also responsible for the cleanup. Why was Brooks doubtful that I should ever see Frank again, since there was still the pregnancy panic and an infection to deal with. Father Brooks never asked about such consequences. Looking back, I am shocked that he didn't put the responsibility directly on the retreat director. The sickening feeling that had started when I walked the streets of Durban, did not subside despite making peace with God. The experience of confession was so self-blaming that I have not been to confession since.

Frank phoned as requested on July 29th. I was safe. The call was brief. He sounded hurried and impatient. I did not tell him of the infection, my relief at not being pregnant was so great. I felt that I needed to show him some gratitude for protecting me.

But the pain from the infection kept me awake several hours every night. I began to fear AIDS as well as venereal disease. At lunch time I would sneak into the school library and read anything I could find on these topics. There was precious little except that venereal diseases could be latent for many years. I puzzled over how Frank could have caught this—in my naiveté, I thought he might have a latent venereal disease caught from the nurse years earlier!

When the pain moved up to my right ovary, I rehearsed telling a doctor that I was raped while at a conference in Durban. The word rape choked me just thinking about it. I didn't even want to say retreat, that would have felt disloyal to Frank.

When I finally told Dr. Mlotjoi, she responded compassionately saying, "Sister Yvonne, it could happen to anyone—even me. I'll treat it as vaginitis. Some antibiotics should clear it up."

The itch decreased but the pain on my left side and in my vagina endured another three years.

Puzzled and searching for answers I asked myself many questions. Was I in love with Frank? I answered honestly—yes. But I'd fallen in love before. I was in love with Lorne and kept my head. What had failed this time? I wasn't attracted enough to him to want to marry him. Why ever had I gone to bed with him? Or more accurately, allowed myself to be taken to bed? I still did not see it as rape.

I had read a bit about Freud and his theory that daughters sexually desire their fathers. That struck me as weird. It certainly had not been my experience of my father, but then when Freud talked about our unconscious and subconscious desires, I began to doubt myself. Perhaps I had wanted sex with my father and perhaps I had wanted sex with Frank subconsciously. I knew I wanted his affirmation and I appreciated a touch on the shoulder. But sex? That wasn't even in the ballpark.

In mid August, 1985, Frank sent me a poem:

FREEDOM — RESURRECTION
Snow drop innocence almost
we met in joy
in Him.
Pray Mary's love
not Magdalen's now.
Father, if
your gift I shadowed or disturbed
To her 'Rabbuni' give Risen joy
to me healing and newness.
FRANK GOODALL

Her faults were mine—her virtues
were her own.
LORD BYRON

Why the reference to Magdalen? I couldn't make sense of the poem until I read the letter. He claimed to have information, but not from anyone at my house, that I had talked about us. He concluded with, *"I could never trust you again. I am not angry just sad. Goodbye."* I felt judged, condemned and discarded without even a hearing. Veronica and I lived in the same house. Sister Frances was the only other person who knew Frank and I had told her nothing. I wanted to ask Veronica what she had written about me to Frank but felt that questioning her would make her more curious and insistent. I would likely have to come clean with her—tell her the whole story. That would be going directly against Frank's express wishes. I would indeed be unworthy of his trust. It was all so complicated and emotionally draining. For two weeks I did not sleep. I would lay awake for hours and finally get up and write pages and pages. Sometimes I broke the lead of my pencil I wrote with such anger. Other times I was explaining, even pleading for a hearing.

Furthermore, I had made a bargain with God that if I wasn't pregnant I could handle anything else. The anything else was proving heavy—first the infection, and now total rejection.

After three weeks of rage, nausea, and pain in my ovary, I decided to write Frank. I wrote simply, "I did not tell anyone. Why are you judging me as untrustworthy?"

Two months passed with no response. Then a short note saying only, "I am not good at writing. We must meet to discuss this. Sorry I came to a quick conclusion." He enclosed his timetable which listed a retreat at Lydenburg, Transvaal, just at the time I was traveling up to Kruger National Game Park. Sister Frances Allison was only too happy to include a visit to the retreat centre where Frank would be.

When we reached Lydenburg, the six of us from Lesotho were treated to a lovely lunch served by a sister whose eyes followed Frank's every move. She had the saddest eyes I have ever seen. After the meal, while the others toured the place, I followed Frank for a private talk. Instead of finding myself in an office, I found myself in a bedroom—his bedroom. There were two chairs. Frank started right in with, "I'm sorry I jumped to some conclusions without checking. Nothing has changed, Yvonne."

I sat crying quietly feeling both relief and disappointment. I had regained his approval but I had no grasp of why I had lost it in the first place. "What do you mean nothing has changed. You said good-bye, didn't you." I whispered not daring to make it sound like an accusation.

"I just told you it was a mistake and I have a lot of building to do to make up for the way I treated you. I misinterpreted something that was written to me. But that's in the past now." He talked on about how special our friendship was to him for his growth and maturity. He never disclosed who had written, and of course, I dared not ask. He then asked about my schools and the political situation. I was so glad to get any form of apology that I was willing to let the issue drop.

He asked me to step into the next room. It was a bathroom. Immediately he hugged me and fondled my breasts all the while explaining the purity of our friendship. He kept repeating, "You are a queen among queens. Our union was so pure! So good! Don't ever forget that. Promise!"

I was in that same trap again as in Durban. I never seemed to learn. I wished I could flush myself down the toilet. Once again I had walked into this with my own two feet. After that incident, I quit praying the rosary. For years I had honoured Mary as a woman of compassion and courage. She dared to stand at the foot of the cross when her son was crucified. The angel Gabriel had come directly to her and not to her father. That was unheard of in earlier scriptures. Besides, she had questioned God on how she could bear a son since she knew no man. What about Joseph?

Gradually it occurred to me that the Church promoted the image of Mary as the woman who 'listened and obeyed.' That felt more and more like a clever manipulation by the patriarchy to keep women obedient to men. She was honoured for bearing a boy. Would she have been honoured for bearing a girl? I began to notice that statues depicted her with her head slightly tilted— a sign of submission. The statues of Peter and John did not show similar submission. Mary. Madiepetsane. It made no difference, they began to disgust me with their sniveling servility!

Sister Frances Allison had initiated a project to provide some sisters with an opportunity to experience England as well as upgrade their teaching. In June of 1986, Frances and I visited the UK to set this up. After making the arrangements, we had a few days for ourselves. Frances wanted a day at Canterbury and I wanted a day at Stonehenge. We managed both.

Stonehenge was a twenty year old dream come true for me. I was not disappointed. While driving around the back of the stone circles, I stopped to gaze and noticed at my feet a rock crudely shaped like the head, neck and shoulders of a woman. I called her my goddess. She reminded me that women have been and always will be strong.

Some weeks after my return to Lesotho, Frank phoned me from Cape Town saying that he would be passing through Bloemfontein the following week and insisted that I meet him there. I hesitated and then replied that likely there would be rooms available for both of us at the cathedral rectory.

"No, at a hotel," his voice boomed authoritatively. "Honourably of course."

I said I'd have to think about it. He ended the call abruptly.

Once again I felt he was insulted and hurt because of me. I couldn't trust him. I wanted to, but I couldn't imagine myself comfortable in a hotel. I came up with a safe alternative. I decided to invite him to Lesotho—my territory— where I could surely protect myself and have better control of the situation.

Father God

Frank visited me in Maseru in September 1986 for six days. The three resident priests took him into their rectory. I continued my school work, so except for evenings we had little time together. I felt that unless he were willing to tell me his expectations up-front, I had no choice but to spend as little time with him as possible.

Shortly after his arrival, I approached him with a very delicate topic. I braced myself and explained, "Frank, the day I left The Bluff, I started having a vaginal infection. I'm worried that you have a latent VD. You must have caught it from your nurse." I believed most sincerely attributing the infection to any other behaviour was to judge Frank and prove to him beyond doubt that I was a judgmental woman—a state worse in the eyes of God than sexual sin.

He stammered for a moment, "No, ah . . . you're wrong, Yvonne." Then his usual authoritative voice returned, "I don't have VD. You must have caught that infection from a toilet seat somewhere on your travels." The next day he said, "I have a visa for South Africa. It shows I am clear."

I knew that my South African visitor's visa did not require a VD test but thought perhaps his residence visa was different so I made no further protest.

From day one of his visit, Frank spoke of Veronica chasing him. She did seem abrupt with him but also appeasing. I could not figure it out. I felt that I was doing the same with him.

There were a whole raft of issues I felt tense about—from the sex at Durban, to his judgmental good-bye, to his lame excuses. I wanted a pat on the shoulder from time to time—fully dressed, but what did he want? He wouldn't talk about his expectations.

According to Frank, Veronica demanded time from him that he did not want to give her. One day in a matter of fact tone he said, "I guess you know who wrote me the letter that upset me so."

"Veronica?"

"Yes."

"Why did you say the person did not live in my house?"

"Oh, that was to protect you from discord."

He still didn't tell me what she had written that upset him. His evasions irritated me. He'd lied and that was that. For a fleeting moment, I even wondered if Veronica had ever said anything. He had simply chosen to discard me. Immediately I felt guilty for thinking such a disgusting thought. Why would he lie to that extent? I concluded that Veronica must have written some simple comment like, *"Yvonne seems to know a lot about you."* and he'd let his oversensitive nature jump to false conclusions. I did not feel any particular anger at Veronica. She had been as fair with me as I had with her. We were both ambitious nuns. We both resented some of the restrictions the congregation imposed on us. There was an unspoken rivalry between us, especially in the areas of education and political awareness. I both respected and feared her.

That whole week Frank seemed irritated with me for keeping him at arms length. I felt too unsafe to spend much time with him alone in private. When I'd leave him in his room at the rectory he was abrasive with me. Was his disclosure about Veronica a way to make me jealous? Was he trying to appease me so I would cuddle and fondle him or allow him to do so to me? Why couldn't this be discussed openly between us?

My way of coping was to assume the blame. I must be misleading him. I must be giving him mixed messages somehow like Veronica had in her letter. But then maybe he was making false assumptions. Part of me knew I was not very experienced in all this but then why was he? Another part of me said that if there was a false assumption on his part, then I must have given him grounds for it. I dared not ask for fear he'd label me stupid.

After meeting some of my friends Frank exploded. "Why didn't you tell me you have all these male friends?" I stood dumbfounded while he raged on. Had I committed some terrible sin by having male friends? Did he think I was having sex with each one of them? When I finally found my voice I mumbled, "Well . . . there was no "Bluff" experience with any of them."

Some time later I ventured to ask, "Why were you upset that I have male friends?"

"Oh, it was something I had to think through." He clammed up without explaining further. Had he given up the idea that I was having sex with these other men? Did he realize how preposterous that was once he thought it through? I banished the thought into oblivion as judgmental and sick.

That Sunday night I needed to wait at school for two busloads of students to arrive back from their field trip to the mountains of

Qacha's Nek. The buses had left on Thursday morning and were late returning. The trip took twelve hours in dry weather, but it was raining heavily, so the roads would be slippery and rivers over-flowing their banks. One of my biggest worries was not necessarily the roads but the bus drivers. I knew some drivers drank on the job. A few parents phoned and I assured them I would wait up for the students and bed them down in the classrooms for the night. Some parents came to the office to wait with me. I asked Frank if he wanted to join us. We sat around an asbestos heater drinking cocoa. Frank was wonderful company; he ingratiated himself with the parents.

It was cold as well as damp. When we were alone for a few minutes he bent down and rubbed my cold legs. It felt wonderful to have someone wait up with me and care for me. Again he flattered me by saying, "You are a real missionary. Look at you! Up all night dealing with worried parents."

By midnight the buses still hadn't arrived. Shortly thereafter everyone left the school and went home to get some rest. I kissed Frank goodnight: he'd kept boundaries and I felt in control of the relationship.

At 7:00 A.M.. I spoke over the mission transmitter hoping to make contact with the teachers. The static from the rain was so severe that I couldn't get through. Around 11:00 A.M.. the buses lumbered into the school yard. They had had a harrowing trip. At Qacha's Nek, one driver was drunk and became extremely irritated when the teachers suggested they wait until he was sober before leaving. At his angry insistence they boarded the bus. During a short stop this same driver became enraged, took out a long barreled shotgun and fired it into the air several times. Because of the rain they were forced to sleep over at a school.

Meanwhile, it was Frank's last day in Lesotho so I took the afternoon off and we hiked up to God-Help-Us-Pass for a picnic.

The sun had come out and the world felt fresh and bright after all that rain. The Pass had a beautiful waterfall, picturesque villages, cattle, sheep, goats and their shepherds. It was a favorite tourist spot. I felt sure that out in the open air Frank would not try anything. After a climb and a picnic we sat on some rocks near the falls. Out of the blue, he commanded, "Yvonne take off your pants! Not both legs—just one will do. Quick now." Stupid me, I did exactly as told. I simply obeyed. It didn't occur to me to just say no—to refuse his express command.

The pain of his penetration seared my entire body. I focused on a rock high up on the mountain. I focused with total concentration so that I could tolerate the pain. I did not wince. I did not cry. I did not ask him to stop. To do so would have angered him and likely prolonged my agony. God had not helped me at this Pass but then perhaps I had not helped myself.

Finally he withdrew and I dressed quickly glancing around to make sure no shepherds were in view. I sat rocking myself in a trance wondering how long the pain would continue. Meanwhile he chatted on and on, "never lust or orgasm, but the purest of motives, as God wants it for man and woman."

I heard only blurred words. I felt neither lust nor orgasm. How he separated lust from sex stumped me. There seemed to be some hair splitting going on in his reasoning. He seemed to demand both without respect and without integrity. I never did find out how sex between a nun and a priest could be anything other than lust or perhaps the need for power—at least for one of the parties.

After a few minutes we went in opposite directions into bushes to urinate. When I returned to my pack-sack, two small shepherd boys appeared along one of the trails. After the appropriate greetings I offered them oranges. They accepted politely with both hands and then giggled as they scampered off peeling the oranges. Just then Frank returned to the scene.

"Did they see anything?" he asked with a frown.

Assuming he meant, had the shepherds seen me urinate I responded, "I doubt it. Anyway they have seen that before." I had been modest and covered myself in any case.

As we trudged down to the truck, he said, "Yvonne, that must have hurt. I have red spots on my penis."

Did it hurt! What an understatement. Still, I was grateful that he even noticed suffering was possible on my part and I felt he realized this was all wrong, all for his benefit and not mine. I presumed that he had some painful blood blisters on his penis. I was glad that he too had suffered at least a little. Only years later did I come to realize that it was my blood on his penis, not his. This enraged me. Why did God give women so much pain when the very men who perpetrated the pain felt none? It wasn't fair.

Frank flew out the next afternoon. Veronica and I took him to the airport and watched him walk out on the tarmac to the waiting plane. At the base of the loading ramp he turned around and waved to us. We waved back. We could stand side by side and wave at this man but we couldn't talk to each other about him. The wedge that Frank had driven between us by his need for secrecy and loyalty grew into a chasm.

Our friendship never came right again. Years later, when I faced the reality of Frank's abuse of me and could break the secrecy, Veronica was on her deathbed. Her death at that precise time shook me. Had she lived a little longer we might have been able to set things right and I might have had incredible support in my struggles to come free of this abuse.

In December 1986, Frank left South Africa for a sabbatical in the UK. From his residence at Clapham he sent an audio tape:

. . . memories of The Bluff, then that reconciliation, are beginning to erase the misunderstandings at Lydenburg. The glorious week in Lesotho where we shared so much and our intentions were so right and so good. We did show our affection. Never planned and always borne of the purest, most sensitive of sources. So I introduce this tape by saying I love you in the best possible way, non-threatening, non-possessive. . . . As regards some cards I may send, they may seem a bit intimate physically but they are not intended that way. It's just illustrating our closeness at a deeper and higher level.

I was not at all convinced that he was as non-threatening and as non-possessive as he made out. However, I preferred to dwell on the positive, so I ignored those parts of the tape that confused and angered me.

Shortly after he sent me a Gallery Card. A slender naked women stood with her back to the photographer. What was he saying to me? Not wanting to judge him I concluded that he was simply telling me that I was attractive. I took a photograph of him and placed it over the top edge of the postcard and took a picture. The result was a naked woman positioned as if walking past Frank. Would he understand that admiration is one thing but distance is essential? I wanted a hug from him from time to time. I loved him. I loved several other men and women also. As with the others, I wanted to share life experiences, insights, politics, and jokes. I never dreamt of running off with him. Furthermore, it didn't have to be sexual. There were boundaries that I could discuss with others. Why did these fail utterly with Frank?

My chronic overwork and the nausea created by this secret left me abrasive with my staff and the sisters. I was not doing well any more. I knew I needed some time to slow down and evaluate myself, so I let everyone know that I intended to take a long sabbatical starting the middle of 1987.

Meanwhile, in December of 1986, just after the last grade 12 examination on a quiet Sunday afternoon, I learned that the military junta had murdered four people, one a staff member of mine from Mabathoana High School. Not a single representative of the government attended the funeral. I felt I made a public stand against the military rule by walking behind those four coffins. I felt strong. I was fulfilling a life dream by standing up to an unjust regime. My life was on track at least in that area. It was far from on track in the area of Frank and celibacy.

Not a month later, I had another opportunity to make a strong political statement. It all centered around an innocent twelve year old boy. In January 1987, I refused admission into grade eight to some two or three hundred applicants. One of these was the son of the leader of the military junta. After posting the list of those admitted, I left to do some business in town. When I returned to the office, I found several teachers excitedly scanning the newly released grade ten public examination results. They fell quiet as I entered but did not look up except for Mr. November, the deputy headmaster, who said, "Sister Yvonne, the General wants you at headquarters right away."

I laughed and said, "Oh yeah, me . . . go to those headquarters!"

"Yes, that's the message from his personal bodyguard."

At this all the teachers looked at me in silence. The deputy continued, "He sent a Land-Rover to pick you up. He wants to talk to you about the admission of his son. The soldiers waited here and walked around for a while and then left giving me orders to tell you to go up as soon as you come in."

"They were soldiers in camouflage suits carrying guns—two Land-Rovers full!" added another teacher.

I marched straight to the office of the secretary for Catholic Schools to report the situation to him personally.

"This is unacceptable," he exclaimed. "Yvonne, I want you to go into hiding for a few days while I address this with the Archbishop and the Minister of Education. Don't go outside and don't speak to anyone from the government!"

Two days later, I was called to the secretary's office to receive an official apology from the Minister of Education. The apology included a clear message that I was to admit the General's son.

I learned very quickly that apologies are not very satisfying experiences. Frank's apology certainly hadn't satisfied me. Perhaps apologies were just another form of manipulation to get the same end. I felt judgmental just thinking this, so I blocked out the possibility that Frank might be manipulating me.

During these months, I stopped attending daily Mass. I used excuses like fatigue or work, but the real issue was my growing disgust at the prayers. The Credo started, "I believe in God the Father almighty, creator of Heaven and earth and in Jesus Christ His only Son. . . ." I particularly detested the words almighty and father. Priests were almighty and fathers. The military government was almighty and all male too. Removing myself from daily mass alleviated some of my anger at the male domination, and it left me with more emotional and physical energy—though both were in limited supply.

My sisters, Clarisse and Isabelle, called me in late March to say Dad was dying. I didn't have the will to be there at his death or go to the funeral. I had said my good-byes to him. I had no more to add.

On the outside I functioned reasonably well, but on the inside I was definitely crumbling. I couldn't understand why I needed

Frank's support and affirmation so desperately. Why this steel bond of loyalty to his secret? This mess of incomprehension grew until it clouded my whole life. I had bargained with God that I could handle anything but pregnancy, but I hadn't allowed for this deep disgust and confusion. My life was a meaningless melee of nameless pain. What was the root of it all? Why did I keep running faster and faster yet ended up nowhere? This treadmill of deceit and overwork was killing me. I had to jump off, even if it meant breaking my legs. So, I finished my projects, wrote the final reports, and left for a sabbatical quite sure I would never return to Africa.

JOURNAL, MAY 15TH 1987

I need to face this almighty rapist Father God. It's all wrapped up with this male church and male head of the family. I've been refused dignity in marriage and in church. In politics as well. Robbed and raped by every institute simply because I was born female. Can I come to terms with this? Do I want to come to terms with this? Not if it means submission. I leave Africa at the end of May. Beyond that is sheer emptiness. Miles of dull nausea and blank eyes.

Hawkstone Hall

On May 30th, 1987, Sisters Theresa Habaka, Theresa Lebesa, Sylvesteria Bushman, and I had flown the entire length of Africa and into Europe as far as Heathrow Airport outside London. As we landed, a war rage within me. I had asked Frank for his help. On the one hand, I hoped he would meet us and be our personal guide since I didn't know how to get to Hastings. But on the other hand, I felt I shouldn't have asked for his assistance. Would he misinterpret it as a come-on, a request for sex? I wondered if it would ever be possible to get anything right between us.

I wanted an honest open friendship with him in which we could share ideas, problems, and humour without the entanglements of sexual activity. Why, I do not know. I felt that there had to be a logical reason for the relationship. There had to be a way to fix it. It worked with other men. If a boundary was pushed, there was a discussion and the boundary was put back. I was determined to make this happen with Frank. But could I? He was so different from the other men I knew.

I wondered if I was intrigued by Frank because he was such a challenge, or was I playing super-woman—feeling the need to straighten out the world? Yes. It was my duty to right what was wrong. I had no power, but I had a strong sense of duty. I felt both inadequate and completely responsible.

Frank was there, waiting for me and my entourage. He stood at the far edge of the milling mass—a swarm of multicolored travelers descending on London from the four corners of the earth. After introductions, he led us to the upper level of a red double-decker London bus. Once seated, I handed him a package that Veronica had sent. He opened it immediately with some annoyance and pocketed the contents.

Not ten minutes out of Heathrow, I noticed Sister Theresa Habaka clutching the frame of her seat. When she started to turn green I asked her what was wrong.

"I'm scared!" she confessed. "We drive right into the top of trees. Branches hit the window every time we turn a corner. I'm afraid a branch is going to smash my face."

We moved to the lower level and faced the rear of the bus.

At Charing Cross we stopped for a snack and then a walk along the Thames. It was a misty, soft London afternoon full of promise despite my fatigue. We eventually found a bench facing an obelisk. When I read the plaque I was incensed. "This is Cleopatra's Needle," I said to my companions. "Some marauding British colonial lifted it from North Africa!"

The others looked at the tall granite statue complacently. I don't think they shared my sentiment.

Around Frank I was very tense. He also seemed nervous. I wanted to show him I cared, that I wasn't angry. Could I do that without sending him a mixed message? When we crowded four on a single bench, I made sure I sat next to him and I squeezed his hand for a moment. Later, I stretched, putting both arms on the back rail of the bench so that one arm was around his back and the other around Sister Sylvesteria. That seemed to drain the tension out of both of us. I concluded that humans need some physical contact. I just wasn't sure if Frank could come to a similar conclusion about the limitations of such contact.

As we boarded the train for Hastings, he wished us good-bye then invited me to Hawkstone Hall, in Shrewsbury. I was disappointed that he had not invited me to meet his sister who lived in London. I sensed I would have been safe in her home; certain he wouldn't try anything with his sister near. Hawkstone Hall was a retreat centre with many rooms and many strangers. I was not at all sure I would be safe there.

Once the student sisters were settled into their "Teaching of English as a Second Language Course" I set off for a three-day visit to Hawkstone Hall. With a large dose of trepidation, and an even larger dose of the chronic nausea, I battled different scenarios as they popped into my head.

Hawkstone Hall was a large, old, rural manor house converted into a centre which provided renewal programmes that lasted three months. The forty or fifty participants were all middle-aged nuns, except for two or three teaching brothers. Participants came from various parts of the world.

When I finally reached Frank in his office that evening I announced, "We have a lot to talk about." I was determined to make it clear to him that I did not want sex as part of our friendship. He asked me how the sisters were doing and then proceeded to do the talking—non-stop chatter about his seven years at Hawkstone as a young seminarian. He described himself as an oyster who seldom emerged from his shell. He must have been on one of his rare forays that evening—out of his shell and acting very much like he did during the sessions at the Durban retreat. By the middle of the first evening, sitting in his office listening to him, my spirits began to sink. There was no way I could get my concerns out in the open. He was not listening. My old patterns of listen and obey, support the priest, the genteel woman who never

angers another, held me fixed like a fly in a spider web. I was
stuck there and I knew it. I could barely concentrate enough to
nod and smile from time to time. He was so humorous, so
affirming of me that I dared not upset him. My only hope was
that in the intervening period he had learned to control himself
and limit his sexual activity. I thought my reticence—my distance from him on the couch, would give him the message that
I was not interested in sex. No such luck. Soon he edged closer
until he had his arm over my shoulders. Maybe his arm would
stay there, comfortable but not sexual? Again, no such luck.
Part of me felt like obedient Mary, part of me felt like seduc-
tress Eve.

He elaborated on his crowded schedule, his inability to say no
to sisters who wanted to see him for spiritual direction. He complained how the other priests shirked this responsibility so that
most of it landed on him. He needed my empathy. Once again I
became his care-giver. All my desperate plans to force him to talk
about us seeped away like water through a sieve.

Everything I said to him he turned into a joke. Trying to pin
him down to discuss our relationship was like trying to pin a cor-
sage on a sprinter after the race had started. When he pulled me
onto his lap I still hoped he would stop. Couldn't he see my discomfort? Why didn't he ask? When he loosened my skirt I
switched into total self-blame.

My mind whirled with the same conflicting voices I'd fought
with at the airport. Why hadn't I spoken up sooner? It's too late
now. He'll really blowup if I resist. Why did I come here? I came
on my own accord didn't I? Stupid! Stop! Why?

After that I simply survived. I turned everything off and
became emotionally numb. I felt myself drifting off to the top of
the long drapes. I'm sure he never noticed I was gone. Did he
even care? From my perch on the drapery rod I told the body

below: *"It's okay Yvonne. As long as you don't get pregnant you are okay. He believes this friendship is a gift of God. You just don't understand. Someday you will. If you weren't the good woman he deserves he wouldn't be doing this."*

And once again as at The Bluff, my body responded to his touch; my body betrayed me while my mind hung in shreds on the drapes waiting for it to end.

"You are so wonderful. Our systems are in sync better than ever. Now, turn over and push up you pelvis. That's it," he ordered.

I'd seen cattle mate in this fashion. I don't know how it felt to a cow, but I felt sickened—reduced to something so animalistic. It was very painful and I felt like screaming. When he finished I dared to ask, "Did you mean that to be anal?"

"Oh, did I get the wrong opening?" he replied flippantly. "Well now we know that works also." He combed his dark wavy hair in front of the mirror while I dressed quickly and left.

That night I drifted into a stupor. When my mind returned to my aching body, I consoled myself by thinking, *well at least he didn't ejaculate and I wouldn't have to worry about pregnancy.* As if that was any consolation. I believed him because to doubt what a person says is to question their integrity, and I did not do that as a good nun. Still, there were moments when I felt panic at the possibility of pregnancy.

The next morning he showed me a small, flat box saying, "A woman sent me these in the post. I don't know what to do with them." Inside was a pair of lacy black bikini panties. I was shocked. How could any woman be so crude as to send such a thing to a priest? I offered to get rid of them and tossed them in the garbage bin in back of the manor.

Inexplicably, I felt sorry for him—Poor Frank, bombarded by women chasing after him. I wondered if he thought *I* was chasing after him. I began to worry. Why were things so compli-cated and so sexual between us? Perhaps I was fooling myself. Perhaps I really did want the sex. Maybe I subconsciously plotted this all the time. Why else was this happening to me? What other reason was there preventing me from telling him to stop?

Just before leaving on the third day I confessed with a quiver-ing voice, "I feel I have lowered my standards and you might think I am seductive." I was too frightened to say that I also thought he lowered his standards.

"Yvonne, you have high standards and the very best of per-sonal values. You haven't lowered anything. Everything we've shared is from the purest of love. We are kindred spirits and have only good intentions. Just remember that when doubts come." He had developed a booming, authoritative voice as a priest. It served him well when microphones broke down. He seldom used the boom on me but the authority was very familiar.

Feeling dismayed at the way he had dismissed my concern as totally unfounded, I tried another route to make my point. "I don't think many priests live celibacy," I mumbled.

His eyes flashed. He moved forward in his chair and barked at me, "How dare you! I work with a lot of priests and I think they do live their celibacy. I've worked with priests all my life and I see their struggles. I know!" Every muscle in his face was taut. I had merited both his boom and his authority that time.

I dared not go any further although I wanted to ask, "well what about you?" I wanted to bring up my pregnancy panic and the fact that he sodomized me. My immediate concern however was to get away from Hawkstone Hall in one piece.

I left that morning for London where I met my old friend, Sister Eulalia Leoatla. When we toured the British Museum for a look at the Rosetta stone and the Egyptian mummies, she asked if these were more of my authentic stools. I could laugh with her.

I was safe with her. I just wished I could tell her what I was going through. I needed to talk to someone.

∴ ⋁ ∴

A month later, I found myself flying over the North Atlantic heading toward Canada. I stared into space—a complete blank before me. I had no idea what to do next. I'd be going back to Manitoba, but then what? I couldn't see anything but blackness before me. Physically, there didn't seem to be anything wrong with me except for the sharp pain from time to time in my right ovary. Emotionally I was a wreck—in intense pain. The constant nausea was a psychosomatic disorder. Nothing mattered. Nothing was important. Nineteen years earlier I had gone to Africa full of energy, seeking adventure and willing to contribute to education. Now I had lost my energy, lost all taste for adventure, lost my virginity. And I wondered if indeed I really had contributed to education at all. I questioned my purpose in life. I had lost my dream.

Self Portrait

Once back in Canada, life seemed to have lost all meaning. In the mornings I'd find myself lying quietly waiting for the bray of a donkey or the long drawn out cooing of a laughing dove. Of course, I'd never hear them, just silence. At noon I'd walk outside and find my shadow on the north instead of the south. I felt upside down. Everything, from pallid white faces to billowing drifts of snow felt strange. I was a fish out of water.

I had no energy. I had no purpose. I slept twelve hours a day and still felt too tired to eat. Walking down a corridor was a chore. The nausea was chronic and my right ovary caused spasms of crippling pain. The infection I developed after my first encounter with Frank Goodall seemed worse than ever.

I had chosen to live at St. Mary's Academy, in Winnipeg, with some twenty elderly sisters until I could decide what to do next. The superior, Sister Vera Hoelscher, was a friend from my Lesotho days.

The thermostat inside the convent seemed stuck at 30° Celsius. My skin was clammy and my nausea plump around the clock. I felt like I was suffocating. I pushed my bed next to the window. All winter I kept the window open with my head propped as close to it as possible. It was the only way I could enjoy even the tiniest whiff of fresh air on my cheeks. Getting enough air seemed to be a constant concern. When I did feel a breeze on my face, I would hold myself in a fetal ball and believe there was a God somewhere. Sometimes I dared to call this God 'She' but each time I did I winced; how dare I challenge centuries of tradition? Who was I to tear those beliefs to shreds when I couldn't even live my own life properly—I couldn't even clean up my unhealthy relationship with Frank. I was such a hypocrite.

My sister Isabelle lived on a farm just twenty minutes away by car. She did her best to revive me. She'd invite me over for meals and arranged meetings with old and new friends alike. She took me shopping for street clothes and for material so I could make my own. I found a sewing machine, and made a few blouses for myself. These activities became monumental projects.

Was I pining away for Lesotho? Very much so. Was I so burned-out that this was normal? Perhaps. Was I facing too many adjustments at once? Likely. I had a thorough medical checkup. There was nothing wrong with me physically.

"Vera," I asked one day. "How long will it take before I feel comfortable again in Canada?"

"Oh, that depends," she answered. "I was in Lesotho ten years, and I'm still not all back yet and it's been seven years. I'd say the same number of years as you were away."

"Nineteen years!" I groaned. I couldn't imagine.

During my first months at St. Mary's I pushed myself to attend daily mass in the chapel. Before long the sexist stories and language of the scripture readings revolted me. I then went to mass only on Sundays. I considered seeking out spiritual direction or counseling, but felt I could trust neither man nor woman. I feared women would blame me for having "an affair"; as for men—now I was afraid of them too. I did not trust myself to be alone with a male counselor or spiritual director. Besides, if they were Freudian thinkers, I'd be in for more blame. I spent enough time blaming myself.

My provincial superior was solicitous. "Would you like to take some renewal programme? Here look at these brochures." Every brochure pictured a middle-aged women listening attentively to a middle-aged man, likely a priest. I rejected that offer.

In February Sister Eleanora died. She had put a human face on history for me when I was in college. At her wake we were handed tattered photocopies of prayers which were used at each wake for each dead nun. My eyes filled with tears. It felt so generic. After fifty or sixty years of dedicated service this is all Eleanora got from us.

The next day I learned she had been a qualified teacher at sixteen and entered the convent at twenty-four. While teaching full-time she had completed her master of science through part-time studies and was then denied doctoral studies. I didn't learn why, but most likely there wasn't enough money to go around and some younger sisters needed basic teaching certificates first.

Not two weeks later, Father Jensen died. He had made political science come alive for me. At his wake I was handed a sheet freshly photocopied with his picture as well as his favourite hymns and scripture quotations. I noted that he had three doctorates.

While Sister Eleanora never got a day off to study, her peer had been given years and years to improve himself academically. While she was out teaching by day and studying by night, he had been simply studying. Comparing these two lives lead me to conclude that nuns had far too many duties. This enraged me, but I did not allow myself anger. I sincerely believed that anger was thoroughly wrong—especially for women. So I turned my anger into depression and helplessness which increased my nausea. I was slowly committing suicide.

All along, I had anticipated that as I understood life better I would somehow get beyond this sickness. Instead, new awareness seemed to do the opposite. I felt like I was stuck in quicksand. On the farm we once had a cow that got stuck in mud. Dad tied a rope around her neck and pulled gently with a tractor. Eventually she became unstuck but was so damaged he had to slaughter her. Was death going to be the only way I would get out of my mire? I often wished I would go to sleep and never wake up.

By April, 1988, my fatigue was still so great that I had difficulty just walking around the block. I'd wonder if I'd have the energy to make it back to the convent. I had found a programme of studies in Chicago that interested me for the fall term, and I agreed to guide several more sisters through studies at Hastings that summer.

England presented a major dilemma; should I let Frank know that I would be in the UK? I figured this trip would probably be my last across any ocean. This was likely my last chance to face Frank and straighten things out. To see him was scary. Not to see him was cowardice. I chose to tell him I was coming.

He invited me to Hawkstone. I rehearsed being decisive yet gentle, strong yet feminine. I found even the rehearsal futile. Decisive and strong seemed diametrically opposed to gentle and feminine. I had to be gentle and feminine or suffer his dreaded negative labels.

On a hot June afternoon I reached Hawkstone Hall weary from worry. He said he was busy for some hours, so I took a nap hoping to strengthen myself for confrontation. Before I dropped off to sleep however, he showed up at my door. He came in, and within minutes was lying beside me, tugging at my clothes. Once again I battled the feeling of betrayal. Was it Frank or my body that betrayed me? I had taken the train myself to his place so it must be me. My mind went numb with paralysis and submission.

When he left, I thought of packing my bag then and there and walking the many miles to the train station, but I knew I didn't have the strength to walk that far. Perhaps I could phone a taxi? But finding a phone, a phone number, proper change, and sneaking off without being seen would be impossible either in the day or in the night.

Thoughts of *Tess of the d'Urbervilles* kept creeping through my abyss. She had been raped and betrayed. Eventually she fled to Stonehenge where she slept on the cold, stone Druid altar. I could see her stretched on that altar in the moonlight. Was she a priestess like the Druids before her, or was she a victim of abuse? If only I had her courage, I too would have fled to Stonehenge. But I couldn't even pick myself up, let alone flee.

In two and a half days Frank had six or seven sessions with me. It seemed non-stop. I do remember however, having lunch in the large dining room with the high ceiling one afternoon: there were forty or fifty women around and a few men. One woman came over to Frank. He stood up, hugged her, then lifted her off her feet swinging her around in several complete circles. Was he showing me he had lots of female friends? Was he plain boisterous and macho? I felt disturbed that he made such a show and wondered how the woman felt. Was she taken up by him and caught in a web as I was? I pushed this out of my mind as an evil, judgmental thought.

At one point he put on a video for me. It was story of Yentl, a Jewish girl who dressed as a boy in order to go to school. He said, "I can't bear this cross-dressing." He then left the room.

To avoid pain during one of the sessions, I suggested a position I had seen in Hindu temple art; it did not involve intercourse. Frank seemed irritated at my passivity, so I thought my initiative would reduce his irritation and eliminate my pain at the same time. He joked and chatted a lot. He was definitely evasive about anything beyond the present moment. Years later, he used my initiative then as proof that I was an equal and willing partner in the sexual relationship. I suspect many people believe his version as the truth, and mine as fabrication to bring down an innocent priest.

The last evening the sex hurt so much that I begged Frank to stop. He refused whispering in his authoritative tone, "No, not just yet." He finally said, "I have to withdraw because I'm about to come." Then he remarked rather off-handed, "Your pain must have been caused by a hair."

A hair! Could a hair cause such pain? I thought he was being ridiculous. Then I blamed myself for being so naïve—perhaps hairs do cause women pain?

He then proposed to take some pictures of me with his Polaroid camera. I could not oppose his suggestions. I had tried to stop him just a few moments earlier and failed.

"For remembrance!" he insisted. He snapped one of himself kissing me. I though that would be the end. Far from it. "Now, Yvonne, you are so beautiful that I want some of you alone. Including some close-ups."

By then the "hair" pain had subsided, but my stomach revolted. I heaved and almost vomited. To survive I left my body. I let my mind float away to the far corner of the ceiling. There, I just pretended everything was okay. I kept telling myself I would survive and it would be over soon.

Early the next morning, he came to my room with the developed pictures. "I examined these photos last night," he quipped as if talking about some inanimate object. "I think you need medical help. Look here. You have a blister just inside your vagina." I simply nodded and looked away, too disgusted to open my mouth. I wondered how in the world I would ever go to a clinic; I was too ashamed. Part of me was glad he showed concern about my health, but at the same time it was a superficial concern—he had caused the abrasion in the first place.

During those three blurred days I recall participating at a mass with Frank at the altar. They sang the hymn, *Lay Your Hands Gently.* I wanted to believe that he had a gentle hand and never meant to hurt me in any way. The morning I left I stammered like a terrified fool, "Frank, ah, ah, er, sex was not, ah , was not part . . . was not on my agenda."

Without a moment of hesitation, he responded flippantly, "Oh Yvonne, I had an open agenda. I left that up to you."

This utterly stumped me. I took it to mean it was all my fault, my doing! Would he have accepted a no? Even after all this I preferred to take the responsibility on myself leaving him worthy of my respect and trust.

As he stepped over to take my suitcase he patted his genitals and said, "All that is yours, Yvonne. I don't need it. It's for you!" Revulsion rose to my throat. I kept silent afraid even to nod or shake my head. If I nodded I would be accepting his genitalia. If I shook my head he would be enraged.

He then handed me a letter saying: "This is for the train."

At the Wellington train station we shook hands quickly and he strode off without a backward glance. I had the distinct feeling that I was already history. Once on the train I opened the envelope. It contained two Polaroid pictures. The first was him kissing me and the other was a close up of an erect, fully engorged penis. On the back in ink, he had written, "Self-portrait." I stuffed the pictures quickly into the envelope and sat stark still wondering how I would get rid of the abominable "self-portrait."

Shortly after reaching Hastings, I hid in the farthest corner of the convent yard behind a grove of trees. There I burned the "self-portrait" and cropped the other one leaving only his hand on my shoulder. I wanted his comforting hand, his gentle affirming touch. I didn't want his penis! I never did.

I looked at his cut-out hand on my cut-out shoulder. This part was safe and must be the real Frank—the man that had given such promise to my missionary life back when I first met him on the Durban retreat. He meant no harm—did he? I convinced myself that he just got carried away and I never did enough to stop him. Once again I beat myself up inside, believing I was to blame.

That summer, I substituted nature walks for my breviary prayers which had been my daily inspiration for over twenty-five years. In my free time I walked the public footpaths of Hastings, Rye and Battle. I didn't pray. I couldn't, the conventional prayers were full of the male God and male stories. Before I left Hastings, I received a letter from Frank. It had a short note and a postcard of a long penis, the tip just penetrating a vagina. The two people were photographed sitting astride one another and leaning back. I burned it too.

In July, I crossed the Channel for four days to visit my Aunt Fanny and Uncle Louis. They were like caring parents to me. Uncle Louis shared more of his poems, and once again they described himself as a man afraid to die, afraid to meet God because he had not been perfect. I commiserated with him; I too feared God and death. I too had failed. It shattered me to think of reaching my uncle's age of eighty-eight and still fearing God. I knew I had to use my course in Chicago to destroy my image of the male, rapist God. I had to create a new God for myself; a loving, personal Creator who would never set traps for me. I knew what I had to do during the next year at the spiritual leadership course in Chicago.

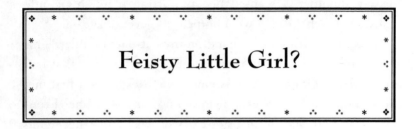

Feisty Little Girl?

That fall, I attended the Institute for Spiritual Leadership programme in Chicago. It was ideal for me. The training in spiritual
direction included looking at our own issues. As my director I
chose Pat Coughlin, a Benedictine. Her knack for listening with
her mouth wide open gave me the impression that she didn't
care what people thought. I liked that. She reacted with spon-
taneity to my comments. I liked that too. This was my first experience of long-term counseling. With her there was none of the
ambiguity of the Durban retreat. I felt safe. I wasn't taking care
of her in the counseling sessions. That was amazing and entirely
new for me.

I shared a third floor apartment with three other women, all
nuns. Between us we spoke ten languages and had lived in almost
as many countries. Though I continued to sleep long hours, I
never missed class or assignments and I managed to do my share
of the housework.

After two months, I attended a Chicago Symphony Orchestra
concert. Seated high in the balcony, the musicians were pinpoints off in the distance. By intermission I was exhausted. I
began to panic, wondering how I'd manage the two buses home

without collapsing. For months after that I was afraid to attend any functions.

By November 1988, five months after the self-portrait and donation of his genitals, Frank had not sent me a single communication. I felt both used and abandoned and risked asking in a letter, "Is the physical relationship all you wanted?" At Christmas I received a small card signed only "F" and nothing else. That angered me so much that I picked up the phone. As soon as I identified myself Frank growled, "What's the matter?"

"I want to know why you haven't written to me?" I responded meekly.

"You're lucky you got a Christmas card! I almost didn't send one," he hissed.

"What have I done to make you so angry?"

"What have you done! You judged me as having lesser motives. I do not take kindly to that! I was just giving it all a rest," he snorted.

"I felt like you didn't care. Not a sign of life all those months. I don't understand your silence." Despite being angry at myself, I sobbed. "And Frank, I burned that 'self-portrait' you gave me."

"Right! You just don't want *any* part of me, do you?" he shouted.

"That's not the reason." My head spun, confused by his logic.

"Oh really!"

"I burned it because I travel a lot and I didn't want that photo getting into other hands." It wasn't the real reason, but it was the only one I could think of that would pacify him. I couldn't tell him the truth—that it disgusted me.

"Okay, okay, I'm sorry about my abruptness," he said switching to a conciliatory tone. "I'll write soon. This is all a misunderstanding. We can work it out. We are very different people.

Just remember I'm the oyster who isn't good at expressing how I really feel."

When I hung up I felt like I'd been shaken against a wall and then propped up with pillows to recover. I could not understand why I was being blamed for asking a question.

I received a letter from Frank written January 5, 1989. It went:

> I'm sorry about the frank exchange before Christmas. Almost certainly it will be for deeper understanding and growth. Some things were clarified, and the words clearly were spoken from pain; for you, the pain of seeming neglect,—for me, the pain of being accused of 'lower motives' in our relationship. . . . I want you to know what is important for us. . . .

I reread the last line wondering how he knew what was important for us yet I didn't. I read on, wondering how he would define "our" world for me.

> You were miles high above all impact and importance and, for me, our meeting was a 'coming home', a discovery of something that had been lacking in my life. You were full of character, freshness, and life: my whole being responded to you. For me it was as great a shock and surprise (as for you) that we blended, entwined, fused together physically in so short a time. That union was not an end in itself but an expression of every part of us wanting to share—mind, heart, laughter, knowledge, life!

This was not my interpretation of the events—he had not seemed shocked or surprised in the least!

Whenever I think of you, it is not primarily of a physical setting, although that experience is part of the whole love-story.
When we lay together in that closest possible union of man
and woman, my awareness was of being taken into the life
centre of this wondrous girl—taking her into my life-cen-
tre,—awareness beyond the physical entwining . . . I was in
AWE and stunningly enriched . . . For me, the coming
together, the deep friendship was like being part of an
exquisite symphony, part of a delicate piece of art; it was the
exhilaration of the mountain top when on a clear day you can
see forever, the innocent freshness of a spring morning, the
rich warmth of a winter log-fire.

What a bubble of revisionist romance and poetry he lived in!
Yet, I didn't burst it. Why? Why couldn't I act out against him or
just ignore him altogether? I reasoned that what I wanted from
him was what he had promised me during the early sessions in
Durban. I wanted to get over my guilt, my father, my anger at
this male God. I wanted *that* retreat director who had taken me
in—trusted me enough to share his personal stories, showed me
tenderness and compassion. I began to realize that *that* person
was not *this* person.

With Pat Coughlin, I shared my anger and my image of the
rapist father God. She encouraged me to draw. I sat in front of a
large piece of paper with crayons all around me, and could not
formulate an image much less pick up a crayon. I felt that nothing would ever encapsulate my rage adequately, nothing would
ever express it properly. I waited, aware of the perspiration
beading on my face.

Gradually, a San cave painting I had once seen came to mind.
The central figure was a *tokolosi,* a small trickster, with a hoop
around his torso. There had been a controversy at one time

involving scholars and lay-persons alike as to whether the hoop was a willow branch or his penis. The trickster grew in my imagination until he was as tall as a man. I knew what I had to draw next. But could I do it?

"You have some nerve doing this!" I thought to myself. I had to make a choice—cower before my rapist God or draw this image. I started slowly by drawing a sturdy black pole in the middle of my paper. After a long pause and a deep breath I drew with fury—a crude sketch all in black. When I finished, I plunked down the crayon. I was exhausted but leaned back and examined my artwork. My trickster was not *tokolosi,* but God. I had tied Him to the pole by His own penis. I grabbed the red crayon and added squiggles of pain flinging out of the *tokolosi*-man-god.

Then I was overcome with terror! Would I be struck blind for drawing this? I covered the picture and rolled it up in a ball for a long time, waiting. When I got up I took a pen and wrote, "God is bigger than my anger!" on my wall. Some days later I pinned the drawing to my wall and walked an inch taller. I still could not dance or shriek. But I was standing.

My next step to inner freedom was a letter to Pope John Paul II regarding his newly issued pastoral letter, *The Dignity of Women.* In my early days as a missionary, I had thought that the Church offered women an alternative to marriage in the form of religious life as a nun. Gradually I had come to believe that both vocations were part of the oppression of women. I studied this papal letter hoping for evidence that some changes in this oppression were in sight. Over and over Pope John Paul II affirmed how wonderful women were as "mothers" and "virgins" as well as "sisters" and "daughters."

The text was filled with the word "man." A few times the text said "man and woman" but nine-tenths of the time the term "man" was used in a context that was ambiguous to me. Each time I met this word I reread the paragraph in order to figure out if "man" meant "male" or "humankind." Each time I was forced to stop and ask myself, *"Am I included or am I not!"* Why did I have to ask *if* I were included when my brothers never had to ask?

I came to the realization that my life was like a track meet; by the time I got to the starting blocks the gun had long been fired and the men were miles ahead. They'd always beat me because I had to check first if I was allowed to race at all.

The Pope had written in the final pages that Jesus came on earth as *". . . 'son of man,' true man, a male."* Therefore, argued the Pope, women cannot represent Christ as priests; only males can do that.

Something fundamental snapped within me. What was he saying? That if I didn't have a penis, I'd never be part of the race? According to the Pope I was not a true man, a male. Had Jesus come as a male or as a human being? From this letter it seemed clear to me that because I was female I wasn't good enough to represent Jesus. The wound this letter caused still seeps puss.

My first draft response filled twenty-three pages—single-spaced. I wrote until my fingers throbbed. Ultimately I condensed it to three pages ending with the couplet:

> *Jesus set women free*
> *Until Rome got hold of the key!*

I sent it off and celebrated with a few classmates. Some months later I received a postcard from the papal nuncio in Ottawa saying the Pope had received my letter. Nothing else. I had expected more. I dreamed of a personal letter accepting my arguments and a promise of change. How naïve of me. Why did I keep hoping?

⁙ ⁙ ⁙

In Chicago, during a class presentation, someone asked, "Is it ever possible that a director and client have a sexual relationship?" My heart raced and my breathing stopped. No one picked up on the question. I looked around dazed. The silence gave tacit affirmation to the question. Regrettably, I thought that perhaps Frank was right—our union was from God. The term sexual abuse had surfaced during the programme, but only in reference to child sexual abuse and rape. There was no talk whatsoever of adults being sexually abused by professionals let alone by spiritual directors.

Chronic nausea plagued me that entire year. I had recurring snake dreams after my uncle died. He had mauled my breasts one day at a family gathering just before I left for Africa. The night I learned of his death I dreamed I had a little girl clasped tightly in my hand. The following morning I wrote:

> I dreamed I clasped a little girl in my left hand. She fought to get out but I tightened my grip and clamped my right hand over her. Her kicking and screaming exhausted me and my hand loosened an inch. She escaped. I was terrified she'd run away into the forest and I would never see her again. I loved her very much. Well she didn't run more than a few feet before she turned around and started to dance and sing. She invited me to dance with her.

Reflecting, I realized that I had clamped a hand around myself. I refused myself freedom to breath, dance, and sing. I drew a picture of this scene and pinned it on the wall next to the rapist god tied to a pole.

Sometime after that, I wrote Frank of my anger at patriarchy and the short shrift I'd been dealt as a woman. Despite all his commiseration with me on this issue, I did not think he grasped the devastation it caused me. I sent him a copy of my letter to the Pope.

20th May, 1989 Frank wrote:

... You bet I'm aware of your anger ... in a simplistic way; forget the past & healing of memories: the future is not here yet: and in the present 'accentuate the positive, eliminate the negative.' You remain trapped in your own anger if you keep knocking your head against the immovable. It is simplistic— but the truth lies in there!

I felt patted on the head like a puppy. *"Good little bitch. Sit. Stay."* He was not dealing with reality. His solutions were too simplistic for me to swallow. Too cliché. The old forgive and forget. He continued:

That's why any thought of the physical is of the deepest and highest sources ... all incorporated into my being in a memory of stupendous, soul-shattering experience ,— to be treasured until my dying day. You understand?

No. I did not understand! Obviously he expected me to agree or be further patted on the head for my stupidity.

At that time I completely gave up all attempts at attending mass except on Sunday. I studied the wording of the sign of the cross—"In the name of the Father and the Son and the Holy Spirit." The literature in both French and English spoke of the Holy Spirit as male. The entire Trinity was male; three males make one God. I have not made a sign of the cross since. When I see others bless themselves I cringe but say nothing. Do they realize what they are declaring about women and men and God?

In the summer of 1989 I wrote Frank in a carefully worded letter explaining how difficult it had been for me to say what I needed during the Durban retreat and after. I explained how the theology of Mary, "the woman who listens and obeys" had harmed me—drained me of all rights and needs.

A six page letter came dated September 22nd, 1989:

Your letter arrived yesterday. At least you feel the freedom to write what you are experiencing and I'm happy that you trust me with that confidence.

I will come back to some of the content of your letter, but—gosh—I never realized in Durban and Lesotho that you were so 'indecisive and dependent' as you now reveal. You appeared to me as a very decisive and independent educationalist; but presumably I did not listen with enough sensitivity to the person behind the school-head . . . I really could help you come to terms—with the fact that not all men want to bully or rape or dominate you:—certainly not me! In fact, darling, I was very uncertain and insecure with you. Initially, because of your education and general knowledge, which— at that time—I felt was wider than my own.

It is true that I was quite neutral about our sexual sharing. After all, I came to Lesotho for some days, and the only time we were intimate in that way was by the river-bank on our day's trekking. And that was a very mutual, unplanned, and spontaneous union.

I could barely believe his view of the river bank episode. Did I really want that pain? I must be masochist. I had risked telling him of my fears and doubts and this is what I got for my efforts.

In the fall of 1989 while finishing some Master's courses in pastoral studies at Loyola, I participated in a therapy group for survivors of childhood sexual abuse. Eight women survivors showed up every Wednesday night. I feared telling my story because it looked so minor compared with the stories the others shared; my father had only molested me that once, the hot panting down my neck and strange hugs did not seem much in comparison with rapes and threats of physical violence. When I finally whispered, "Dad grabbed me in front of relatives, pulled me down on his knees, groped my breast, saying, "she will be a big breasted wife for somebody," I heard a little gasp from one woman. That little gasp still reminds me that someone recognized this as horrible. In the feedback period, one survivor commented, "I see you as a feisty little girl." Oh how I wished I had been feisty and bitten Dad. But even in 1989, forty years after the event I could not imagine biting him. Will I ever be able to imagine being that disobedient?

For six months I lived in a one room apartment in an old Chicago hotel with a dear friend just across the hall. I didn't know anyone else on the floor, but I had seen the back of my next door neighbour once as he entered his room.

At 6:00 A.M.. one Saturday morning music thundered through my wall. By 6:30 I had rolled myself in my sheet and plugged my ears. I tuned in to the BBC on the short-wave radio to block out the screeching jazz from next door:

In Pretoria, today, women were beaten, charged, and detained as they marched on the Union Buildings protesting the apartheid system. The permission they had obtained to convene and present their complaints to the government was revoked just a few hours prior to the scheduled time of the presentation. Bus companies were denied permits to transport the women to Pretoria but they came anyway.

How could I stay here rolled up in a ball while other women braved imprisonment for their beliefs? But then they were fighting for their loved ones. I felt it was wrong to protest for my own needs.

Then, as if the blast of jazz from next door were an alarm clock, I woke up. I realized that if I didn't start standing up for myself, I'd always feel oppressed. I knocked on the wall with my fist. The noise continued unabated. I stepped over to the mirror and combed my hair with rough jerks. As I tied the belt on my housecoat, I rehearsed how I would knock on the door next to me and how I would not say "please."

Once in the corridor I could hear the thump of my heartbeat reverberate from the dark narrow walls. I knocked so hard my knuckles hurt. There was no response so I knocked again.

"Who is it?" responded a male voice over the radio blare. I hadn't anticipated this response. When I recovered my wits I simply asked, "Would you turn that radio down?" without the please.

"No problem," he answered, and that was that.

Then came deafening silence. My body shivered as I returned to curl up in my bed. It was so simple; just ask and you shall receive. Why had I made a mountain out of a mole hill? Why hadn't I simply told Dad to stop panting down my neck? And Frank to stop forcing sex during our visits and into his letters?

Not once in my year and a half in Chicago had I revealed to Pat Coughlin or the survivors' group anything about Frank Goodall. I was so bound by his secret that even seeking help without disclosing his name was out of the question. I would be disloyal and therefore a bad, unworthy woman. When I look back on that period of my life I see myself as the sacrificial lamb led to slaughter without a bleat—as if I had no right to protest at the honour of being chosen for a special relationship with this man of God. I could be sacrificed—I was just an offering. Wasn't Jesus presented to Christians as the sacrificial lamb offered for the redemption of the people so the Father would forgive us our sins and permit us into His friendship? Jesus had not protested his lot and I had taken on that same approach. I could protest to help others but not to help myself—that I believed was a grave mark of selfishness in a nun. I could be many things, but selfish was not one of them.

The Shoemaker's Children

The morning I left Chicago for Manitoba, fourteen women in Montreal were murdered. They had been killed because they were women. We learned that the man who killed them believed women should not be engineers. The funeral was presided by twenty-three priests, all males, and in the entire service no mention was made of the cause of the massacre.

In the dead of Winnipeg winter, I started training as a volunteer with Klinic, a crisis centre. This gave me experience in dealing with abuse of all sorts usually from the victim's point of view. I came face to face with victim-blaming and revictimization by the justice system. The complex dynamics of abusive relationships became clearer as I dealt with rape victims. The term *professional abuse* had still not appeared in the vocabulary of the day, so I still had no words for the way I felt about Frank Goodall.

In the spring of 1990, I moved to a convent in St. Boniface. The three sisters welcomed me and so did the Seine River that flowed nearby. I soon discovered the little river had a long uninterrupted path along the bank and was home to ducks, beaver, turtles, and fox. It was along these banks that I sat and wept the first time I deliberately missed Sunday mass. The previous week, the priest had said on the occasion of Mother's Day that women are like a book with blank pages; a mystery. I was not amused. Would he like me telling him that men are like the blank pages of a book? Apparently men do not need to know much about women but the reverse is unacceptable. Each Sunday I returned from mass crushed by the language and the images that excluded me as woman.

That August, my mother died suddenly of a stroke at age eighty-three. I had never been close to her and resented that she had stayed with Dad and let him control her all those years. We buried her in the same plot as my Dad and in the same Swan Lake graveyard as my four grandparents. The six of us siblings met the next day to go through the last of her belongings. I found my grade four report card and noticed that I was first in class. I had beaten my twin brother. Shame swept over me—had I humiliated Albert? Then I felt anger at myself; why shouldn't I be first? Had the society and the Church drilled this into my soul so deeply that I could not eradicate it? Was that perhaps why Mom had stayed with Dad so long? Was she unable to eradicate the same messages—that a wife must be lesser and accepting? She had rebelled but with little success. I was having no more success than she had.

In September, I landed a full time job training twelve members of the Hollow Water community to be sexual abuse treatment workers. They were dealing with victims, offenders, families, and the community as a whole. This was a fast learning curve for me, and I felt both exhilarated and depressed by the learning. I enjoyed the participants for their courage in facing these painful issues, and found I had a lot of energy when I was with them. Through that experience I came to accept my mother's submission but not my Dad's need to dominate.

One Monday morning I left Winnipeg for Hollow Water at 5:30 A.M. It was -37° Celsius with a very high wind-chill. Furthermore, it was pitch dark and the van was so large that the little heater hardly dented the cold. The warmth of the Hollow Water group made up for the three-hour drive as did the truckers at the cafe in Pine Falls where I stopped for a quick coffee.

I shared my new experiences of the healing programme with Frank in a letter.

Nov. 29th, 1990 he replied:

You write/shout at me as if being a man meant that I am guilty of lechery, rape, child abuse, beating up my wives and women, kicking my grandmother, brothel frequenting, female groping in the subways,—to mention only a few of my lesser activities . . . The male 'willy' or penis, or cock, need not be a weapon of greed or abuse or violence—but an instrument of loving union, of loving procreation, of a whole lot of intrinsically good things.

The ferocity of the first part of his letter jolted me. The tone changed toward the end and he became affirming again. I figured that the affirming part was the real Frank so I overlooked his shouting. It never dawned on me that this could be a confession—it felt more like a kick in the stomach.

Months later, he wrote from Erdington, Birmingham:

11TH MARCH, 1991
All the generalizations about Man do not apply to me, I'm perfect. You know that I listen to and read all your intelligent statements and all your 'ravings': I agree with a lot of it, but not all of it. But, I'm not really judgmental. . . . Phoebe (Paul to Romans) first woman officially to hold office, Olympias in

Constantinople in 4th century, Clothilda, Queen of the Franks, and Radegund—ordered religious life in 6th century, etc. These girls were ministering with great ability . . .

Girls! I raged. Clothilda was a woman not a 'girl.' How dare he call these apostles girls! I suspected these stories had been lifted directly from a text. He continued:

"*Also, my shadow wife from Canada.* . . . He signed off, "*The shadow husband.*"

I had told him I did not accept his "wifey" comments. He persisted despite my protests. Did he think he was honouring me? I felt degraded.

His next letter dated, July 16, 1991, had Castlebar, Co. Mayo, Eire, as the return address. Enclosed was a photograph showing him with his arms around a sister, the headmistress of a school in Zimbabwe. He listed a full page of characteristics using the Myers Briggs personality type coordinates:

In a sense, I don't give a fuck where you are on the development levels, except that it causes you pain, and anger, and suffering. When I first knew you, you were in the top half, now you are in the "unhealthy" and have no peace. It matters to me. I'm the one who cares.

He was defining me as unhealthy and labeling me as intolerant, vengeful and arrogant. I was waking up. He needed me to stay weak and unwell.

He closed that letter with:

Our unions were about this:—an entering into your being, to be part of you, and you of me,—as time stood still, the act illuminating the walls of the skull and the ecstasy of the senses,—an enriching and enlightening—an act of growth and beauty. Never for us, dear woman, an earthy pelvis jerking to register on the pleasure scale. I love you immensely and unchangeable. Frank.

He flipped in each letter from rage to support. Strange how when I expressed my thoughts or told of my own experience he labeled me as unhealthy yet he could write about sex as eloquently as that classic British womanizer, Byron.

Early in 1992, he sent a picture of himself at a Christmas party in Littlehampton, Sussex. A nurse had her arm around his shoulders. On the back he wrote, *"PS I've still got something left."* In part he wrote:

> I do not allow myself to have any special friends; my life is trouble-free in that area (although it may sound unhealthy). The photo is 'teasing you'—nursing staff Christmas dinner at Littlehampton, after I gave a sisters tridium and a nurses Day of Reflection.

How would he react if I suggested to him that having no special friends was indeed most unhealthy?

✵ ✵ ✵

Early in 1992, my brother Maurice became very ill with a recurrence of cancer. I had just finished my contract with Hollow Water and was co-facilitating a male batterers group as a volunteer with Evolve in Winnipeg. Fortunately, I was able to spend some good days with Maurice and his family. He went through excruciating pain, yet never complained. One evening I told him of my fear of Dad. He responded ever so gently by saying, "Oh Yvonne, Why didn't you tell me. I had no idea."

I said, "There was nothing you could have done. Mom did her best."

We buried him near my parents.

That same week I flew to Labrador on the invitation of Sister Marjorie Moffatt to see if I'd like to work there for a few years with abuse issues. Sister Marjorie was a Holy Names Sister with lots of creative ideas. She introduced me to an Innu woman, Rose Gregoire, who lived nearby. Before long I felt close to Rose—she was a woman to admire; a warrior of my age and inclinations. We were about the same height and weight. She had a ready smile and long hair that she tied back. Women and children in need came to her house all hours of the day and night. I liked what I saw in Sheshatsheit—the Innu community where I'd be living. I was offered a two year contract by the local bishop, Henri Goudreault.

In August, I moved from St. Boniface to Labrador and started work with victims and offenders. I was glad to get away from the city and out into the black spruce forests among people who lived close to the land. One of my first Sundays there, Rose invited me to go blueberry picking. She went prepared for a boil up—an open fire tea party near a stream.

"Just like in the movies—only I forgot the pork and beans," joked Rose as we sipped tea.

"Yeah, and with real Indians," I added.

We both laughed.

That winter, I attended a training programme in Halifax on Clergy Sexual Abuse by Reverend Marie Fortune, Director of the Center for Prevention of Domestic and Sexual Abuse in Seattle. There I was introduced to the dynamics of abuse by professionals—particularly clergy. I also got hold of some litera-ture on the topic. I read Peter Rutter's *Sex in the Forbidden Zone* with eyes like saucers. The idea of holding the person with the greater power (usually a male) responsible for breaking sexual boundaries made sense, but that is not what I had been taught over the years. Except for violent rape, it had always been the responsibility of the woman; and even then there was doubt because she might have caused the rape through some form of provocation like wearing a short skirt. I spent time at the train-ing with a woman who told me of her abuse by a Lutheran cler-gyman. Despite all that, I still did not acknowledge that I, too, had been used and abused by a priest in a position of power.

On Saturdays, I baked bread and watched it rise near the wood stove that warmed the house I shared with Sister Marjorie. One such Saturday, I watched this process while writing Frank. I wondered if pregnant women felt the same mysterious awe I felt while watching bread rise. Were they fascinated to feel a child grow inside them? Any thought of pregnant women now came with fear and panic. It never used to. I used to look at expectant mothers and smile. I could only imagine how wonderful it would be—knowing as a nun it would never be something I'd ever experience.

I poked my finger in the bread dough and it slowly deflated. I was suddenly enraged. It wasn't fair. As a woman who practiced celibacy and kept her virginity into middle-age, I shouldn't have this memory of panic and fear. I decided to tell Frank—gently of course. I wrote, "The bread dough rising reminded me of the times I thought I was pregnant and how I panicked." I dared not be any more explicit. I hoped however, that he would read between the lines.

We had a house cat then, named Frankie. He used to crawl on my lap or on my chest whenever I read. It struck me that Frankie felt safe in body contact with me—safe enough to purr, yawn and roll on his back. He knew I would not strangle or crush or pinch him. He knew I would respect his needs. It occurred to me that children should have that same right to freedom from abuse—they should be safe in the lap of their daddies, uncles, mommies, and grandfathers. I decided to formulate an analogy with the cat so I could get through to Frank without provoking his anger. Surely if I put this into some positive example he would grasp that I wanted to feel as safe and free of sexual activity with him as the cat was with me. I wrote that I wished he was curled up in my lap. After sending off the letter I feared he would misinterpret my analogy as an approval of sex. Was I inviting trouble in my attempt to be heard? Would I ever be able to speak plainly?

Looking back on this, I recognize the insidious effects that Frank's lies and need for secrecy had on me—I could not trust my own judgment and dared not ask for help because of the secrecy. The dilemma created more dysfunction and perpetuated my victimization.

.* .* .*

Meanwhile, I was running into some severe problems in the community. I reported a member of a prominent family for sexually abusing a thirteen year old. When the man was jailed, some people signed a petition to have me removed from the village. I also reported a priest for sexually abusing parishioners. The bishop did not follow his own policy regarding the priest.

JOURNAL FOR 16TH APRIL, 1993
Just wrote Frank a sarcastic letter saying:
So, you say you are weary of my 150 references to abuse per letter? Gee, I wish I was weary of your 150 phone calls

and letters. You seem to pay more attention to your big toe than to me. You dash around the world saving everyone. Then once every 4 or 5 months you donate me 5 minutes of your time between trains.'

I couldn't think of a way to end this letter. I wanted him to listen to me; to see that *he* sexualized everything and that I was fed up with that. I thought perhaps if I expressed a sexual desire, he'd be shocked. It was contrary to all I'd been telling him these years so it ought to wake him up. At least then he'd ask what I meant instead of telling me what I should think. So I concluded with,

"I lust after you! Now swallow that with your crispy corn flakes. Asshole."

I drew a stick man with one foot raised and head bent looking at his big toe.

A few weeks later a card arrived from Frank, dated the 15th April, 1993. The cover showed two teddy bears standing facing each other. The caption said, *"I don't always like you"*. Then inside, *". . . but I do always love you!"* The teddy bears were then embraced in a full body hug. Only the arms and legs of one teddy were visible and around the two floated a sea of little hearts.

Underneath the bears Frank wrote:

No, he's not raping her!—(it is possible to have a warm, heart-to-heart cuddle). i.e. without wanting to put 'it' in. . . . The woman/person baking bread—makes me love you more and more. Now that love has nothing to do with 'penile penetration'. There is another area of living where there is no sexual abuse, incest, wife-beating. There are normal, happy couples, loving and supporting one another, and making sacrifices for each other . . . you should visit them some-time—to get a better and balanced view of our poor world.

Why this aggressiveness? Why the reference to rape? Why does he think he knows more about normal life than I do? How dare he preach to me! I phoned him. His first words were, "What's wrong?"

"You seemed so upset in your teddy bear card. Why?"

"Because you shout abuse stuff at me until I feel I'm to blame for it all!" he shouted.

We had a heated discussion in which I admitted that I didn't know where he was coming from. I was tired of all the avoidance to what was really going on between us. I told him that I felt used and abandoned.

"Honestly," he replied in a gentler tone. "I'm on the move too much."

"You were three years at Hawkstone Hall, in one place," I retorted.

"Oh, I wasn't mature then," he blurted too quickly.

He had an excuse for everything. He continued, "Well, I'm glad you called; I'm getting engaged next week to a red-head. Seriously, I've started a letter to you. It tells you my feelings."

"Good," I responded thinking finally we'd deal with reality. I took a big breath, relieved.

About ten days later his promised letter arrived. It was six tightly written pages, and began:

Dear Ms. Maes,
I would be less than honest if these 'reflections' were not written and forwarded to you. My fault has been to emphasize the positive side of my ambivalence to you, odio et amo! In recent years there has been a growing surge of anger towards you that you should 'pound' me every letter with diatribes about male domination, incest, abuse etc. You just go on & on, although I've acknowledged my awareness

and pain about what has happened, historically,—and I've told you that I work now patiently with and for women in the atmosphere of changing church and society. You just never listen.

I want you to know a few things:

i.) I'm supposed to be quite intelligent and I've been observing your performances (personality) over the years. You are so unhealthy, and unhealed. You really are!

ii.) I'm a 'mean bastard' when I'm annoyed, and if anyone else had written all that stuff to me, and got all that mileage' out of our relationship, in a cruel and sneaky way, I would have blasted them. (Now please note— until now I only have blasted men—otherwise your myopic view of 'any activity' becomes anti-woman.) Good memories gave me patience until now.

iii.) How dare you insult my intelligence and professional experience by continually lecturing me on 'Women's Rights.' I work with professional women and we discuss the whole area, but in a reasoned, intelligent way. My sister was chief executive of Hammersmith Housing in the Civil Service, the first woman appointed to that level. Do you not think we discuss that area. Two of my best women friends are members of 'Beginning Experience— a support group for divorced & separated. I meet one or the other for dinner in London, when passing through. We are big friends (not sexually): what do you think we talk about? I have a rough enough time trying to live my religious and priestly life, and work for others, under constant strain. All I don't need is this constant, bitter, punitive sound from some woman—who at times seems half-demented in the snow of Canada! You do not make me feel guilty, just very angry at your arrogance.

I've tried answering what you have written. I've tried acknowledging my sad awareness—lately I've tried ignoring it; but the last letters from you are in the same tone. I'll bet you have driven most of your other friends underground. Well, like I'm telling you that I've had enough!! I'm probably the last poor sucker left on whom you can spit your anger.

And, of course, I know the reason for so much of this. I've met a few people who knew you in USA. One female said so rightly: she likes men near but then she punishes them. And, of course, the phone. The give away question was what's wrong? Does it make you feel guilty? That says it all!! Y.M.—the punitive avenger.

If you are so cruel, condemnatory, punitive and lacking in compassion as you seem in what you write, I would question your suitability for counseling and delving into people's lives. You are not healed yourself. You have such anger—how can you honestly deal with men or women?

You have talked tough in all your letters. So please accept this toughness without calling it 'another (male) rejection!' I would deal the same cards if it were a mole or hermaphrodite. You are not the person I met in Durban. And you have become so coarse. What are you trying to prove by using 'shit' & 'asshole'? Do you wear trousers as well? My confreres, my brothers, my divorced friends don't have to use these words, why have you?

You have never acknowledged any fault in the perfect Ms. Maes. It is incredible how you interpret events to suit your present 'platform'. How often have you written 'I was afraid to say 'no' or 'make a choice'. It is a bit ungallant, but don't you remember "another position to try which you saw in a book," or at the riverside in Lesotho, when I hesitated, you encouraged, "those kids have seen it before, don't worry." Who are you kidding? Or is your memory so bad?

Ms Maes you have 'punished' so much that I'm sorry we were ever intimate. You've pushed it so far that I wouldn't honestly want to kiss you now, never mind seek any other intimacy. You do a good demolition job on any friendship. You probably know that from other severed interpersonal fiascoes.

The easy response to this letter is 'rejection', or as 'from a man,' It is neither; it is someone who is telling you honestly where your are at, as far as I can tell. Some of those USA people are sorry for you or laughing at your indignant anger. I'm doing neither; I'm saying this is how I feel. You are never wrong, or imperfect: always the victim.

I have lived 3/4 of my life. I've come down from any ladders of falsehood and pride and found myself in the rag-and-bone shop of my heart. A heart that regrets many things—a heart that has made peace with a compassionate God—and a heart that wants peace to live out what years remain.

If you need to 'punish' try somewhere else. I've just had enough. You wanted to know how I feel; now you know.

> *Regretfully,*
> *Frank*
> NOTTINGHAM. 10.5.93

I sat, shocked. Why did he refer to kissing me—that was not part of his pattern. Perhaps he still had the Polaroid picture of him kissing me. The phrase that startled me back to life was 'half-demented.' Batterers used that in the last stages of controlling their victims; it was called crazy-making; the deliberate twisting of events and words so the victim believed she was going crazy. Was I that abused woman? I had indeed lost two jobs that year—both the treatment centre and the bishop had ended their contracts with me. My work had put me in contact with a grim side of life. Plus a good portion of the village had signed a petition to send me away. Perhaps I *was* going crazy? Was chronic nausea a sign of being half-demented?

Breaking Silence

May 1993 brought warm spring evenings in Labrador. Children played by the edge of the lake. They threw sticks into the water and dogs splashed after them. I sat motionless in front of the window. Goodall's six-page good-bye letter lay scattered about the table like shrapnel from an exploded letter bomb. How could a few sheets of paper contain so much devastation? *"Half-demented!"* The hyphenated insult bounced inside my skull like a smartly smacked Ping-Pong ball. It gave me a dull, annoying headache.

I jumped when someone knocked loudly at the back door. It was Rose—just the person I needed to see. I invited her in for a cup of tea. The moment she sat down, Frankie the cat, made a bed of her lap.

Rose was my sounding board, my rock, my lifeline. She had broad shoulders both literally and figuratively. Though she was a brave woman who spent more than eight years breaking the silence of abuse for women and children, I wondered how she would react if I told her about Goodall. I started thinking of him as Goodall in order to create a distance from him and his need for secrecy. At first, using his last name made me feel disloyal as well as harsh and cold, but I persisted.

"Why do women stay so long with men who abuse them?" I asked Rose, hoping to feel her out before jumping in.

"Well I know here it's because most people don't believe the women. And to make it worse, the priest we had for twenty years told men they should be the boss and told women to obey their men. He then told everyone this is what God ordered."

I shook my head. "Sounds like the same priest my Dad used to listen to. I'm still appalled that so many men think it's their duty, their right, to keep women in line. A little beating now and then just showed how much he loved her, right?"

"Yes, the stage is conveniently set for abuse. Women: forbidden to argue with God, priests, or husbands. No wonder so many believe they deserve the beatings and the rapes."

Rose and I had shared a lot, still I was afraid to tell her my secret. What would she think of me, a nun, having had an affair? That's what I had come to calling it. I had accused myself of having had an affair with Father Frank Goodall. But slowly I was allowing myself to consider the possibility that I might have been abused: it had started on a retreat, after all. It was not consensual, because he never asked. He asked me to keep it secret. There certainly was a pattern. The need to talk to someone I trusted outweighed my apprehension. I nervously pushed the letter towards her after explaining the relationship I was trapped in.

She showed no emotions as she slowly read the six pages. I waited, feeling dirty and exposed with my heart, my soul, my guts, lying wide open. What if she gasped and yelled at me saying it was all my fault? Would I ever be able to pull myself together again?

Finally, Rose spoke. "Yvonne, he's scared of you! He's trying to intimidate you in this letter. You could report him."

Just the thought of reporting Goodall to the police made me gag. Rose fetched a basin from the bathroom and placed it on the floor near me. "My God, how could I? He had so many good qualities. He seemed so compassionate about race issues, women's oppression, life as a missionary in Africa. He even understood why I was so angry at the male privileges that he and his brothers in Christ enjoyed." I began to sob, angry at him, angry at myself. "He said he had an open agenda, and you know, for a celibate man he sure knew a lot about sex!"

"An open agenda? You mean a hidden agenda. He's doing his best to blame you so you don't catch on. He even calls you crazy so you'll blame yourself instead of him." She looked around. "Where's that article you showed me the other day? The one on the torture of prisoners of war."

I darted to my bedroom to fetch the articles I had collected on abuse. Rose picked out the one by NiCarthy on batterers' tactics. She read aloud. "Isolation. Did this Goodall cut you off from others?"

"Yeah, come to think of it he did. He wanted all this to be our secret."

"Secrecy! Oh, of course he'd want that wouldn't he!"

"There's more," I added. "He often called women pushy and nagging. That scared me so much that I never dared cross him." I paused. Scenes of Veronica, agitated and suspicious when Goodall visited me, came to mind. It had only confused me at the time. I had taken his explanation and never asked her for hers. He'd put a deep wedge between us. I retched but could not vomit, realizing how much Goodall had actually managed to isolate me from Veronica. Perhaps she had been as confused and controlled as me. Why had they been so angry at each other? Why did Goodall need to keep her off my back with a note when I left that Durban retreat? I looked up at Rose. "I'm so confused. I just don't understand any of this."

"We live in a weird world, Yvonne," she said with a wave of her hand. "Men are priests, men are lawyers, men are chiefs, yet they're so threatened when a woman asks a simple little question. Here's Goodall writing like he's your victim," she read aloud, ". . . the last poor sucker left on whom you can spit your anger." She raised her eyebrows. "And this comment about the trousers!" She huffed.

I shook my head. "As if what a person wears has any bearing on who they are inside. He wears a long skirt whenever he prances about the altar, doesn't he?"

"Yeah, but when we wear a skirt, we are still mere women subject to him as a man. When he wears a skirt, he becomes the boss sent by God to tell us precisely how to obey him."

"So, by that very logic when I wear pants I should be the boss sent by God to tell men how to obey me." I grinned ironically at the audacity of the thought. "Such thinking would get me excommunicated, wouldn't it?"

"This article says clergy sex offenders seldom have friends. Do you know if Frank had any friends?"

"He used to brag that he was an oyster—all closed up. He even wrote that he had no friends and therefore no complications in his life." I suddenly wondered how a spiritual director could help people in relationships when he prided himself on having none of his own. It was such a contradiction, especially when he had talked about our special friendship. This was getting harder and harder to understand. Why did it bother me so much to call him an abuser, a victimizer? I felt disloyal to this man who had affirmed my life—given my world meaning when I was exhausted and needed to make changes. It was hard to admit that my world had fallen apart in the years immediately after I met Goodall—not before. I may have been burned-out when I

entered that fateful Durban retreat, but at least I was whole—
and a celibate virgin.

Something was stirring inside me. What could I do? For
starters, I could call him Goodall instead of Frank and start
detaching. I had, in fact, broken his secret and was determined to
get to the bottom of his need for secrecy.

So here I was, sitting over the basin, physically ill and still
denying the truth. I could not allow myself to realize that he was
the chief instigator of my chaos about church and vows, let alone
my depression. I had assumed he was a support, a means to help
me come out of my chaos. It would take another two to three
years before I could fully admit that his behaviour and teach-
ing/preaching had gravely distorted my world view and
destroyed the underpinnings of my life.

∴ ∵ ∴

That very week I received a phone call telling me that Veronica
Phafoli had died after a short illness. I was shocked. As I reflected
on our long and rocky friendship, I wondered what had happened between her and Goodall. Why were they always at each
others throats? Could Veronica have been caught in the same
web? Had Goodall abused and victimized her too? With her
passing, I sadly realized I would never know the answer to these
and other questions.

A few days later, I traveled to Ottawa for a weekend with a
dear friend. Marguerite McDonald listened to my story through
my sobs and silences. I felt stupid that I had let this happen to me.
I told her so. At that, she walked to the middle of the kitchen
floor. With one arm jutted out in front of her she whirled about
and pointed in four directions. Each time she stopped she'd
exclaim, "Stupid!" So in the end I got, "Stupid! Stupid! Stupid!

Stupid! It's no sin to be so stupid!" Her antics made me laugh. With this disclosure, first to Rose and now Marguerite, I began to feel a small tinge of wellness. Perhaps this was the cure for my years of nausea? Maybe talking about Goodall to folks who really cared would lead me down the road of recovery.

From Ottawa, I traveled to Kingston for training in sex offender treatment work. It felt ironic—and timely. Tony Eccles and Sharon Hodkinson at the Kingston Sexual Behaviour Clinic had years of experience with sex offenders. During those three weeks I told them my story. They encouraged me to move ahead rather than bury it. They warned me of something I already knew, that if I didn't deal with my personal abuse I couldn't expect other victims or offenders to deal with theirs. In other words, I would need to find another career. I decided the time had come to report Goodall.

The first few evenings I sat alone in my Kingston apartment and wrote letters to people who might help me find Goodall's superior. When I returned to Happy Valley-Goose Bay I had his superior's name, Jim McManus, and his London address. I wrote:

> My purpose in contacting you is to find out what your province has as policy and procedure when you receive a report that a retreat master has had sex with a retreatant? Is it ever permissible for a retreat director to sexualize his contact with a person on his retreat? And what would happen if the retreat master claimed it was consensual? Would the retreatant be seen to have equal responsibility with the retreat master for keeping the professional boundaries? What would be the response if he claims that she initiated the sexual activities or that she is an angry/frustrated woman because he is not continuing to be intimate with her?

I am not sure how you handle such allegations? Would there be an investigation? How would it be conducted? Who would conduct it? Would his retreatants in other countries, other districts be contacted? How would this be done? Who would confront the priest? With what attitude?

I wanted to make sure there was a safe process in place before I disclosed the name or any details of the abuse. Meanwhile, I received several responses. One South African bishop, wrote me saying,

"I fully agree with you about the havoc and suffering and betrayal caused by such people. And it is probably quite widespread." This sounded supportive. But in the same letter he also wrote: *"As you well know, it is extremely difficult to do a great deal about it."*

He seemed to wash his hands of any responsibility as a member of the Church. The next sentence alarmed me. *"But Yvonne, there is always the matter of consenting adults and the possible seductive element from either side. I'm sure your are familiar with the Eamonn Casey case which pinpoints the complexities involved especially immaturity, mixed motives etc."*

I felt not only preached at but betrayed. I was familiar with the Casey case. He was an older bishop, a famous charismatic leader who took in his much younger cousin after a messy marriage break down. What was complex about assigning responsibility in that case? Even if the young woman seduced her famous, powerful cousin, he had the role of protector, not lover. He knew that. She ended up with a fatherless child while he went right on receiving promotions within the Church. This was a poor example to illustrate seduction and consensual behaviour.

In August, 1993, I traveled out of the province to participate in a five-day Training for Trainers of Clergy Sexual Misconduct facilitated by Reverend Marie Fortune. Bishop Goudreault sponsored me for this conference in the wake of massive evidence of abuse by clergy in Labrador. The highlight for me was one comment Marie made about adult female victims of clergy. In retreats with them she asks, *"If this had been the man next door instead of a minister, would you have become sexually involved?" The women invariably pause, then adamantly shake their heads, no."* That night I asked myself the same question. I too came out with a resounding *"No!"*

Somehow, I knew that from a minister I expected an open relationship that would energize me in my service of God and neighbour. I expected to develop a greater sense of mission, of life, a deeper commitment to justice and liberation through my relationship. That's what I expected with Goodall. But the sexualization ruined that. Then, in my vain effort to right the wrong and get back to the original expectation, I twisted myself into a pretzel, wondering all the while how I could have let this happen. Instead of greater energy and freedom serving God, I had experienced years of depression and confusion. No, if Goodall had been my next door neighbour things would have been different. I would have been alert to the possibility of seduction. I would have been able to defend myself—to stand up for myself as with a co-worker. Goodall had been my retreat director not my co-worker, and I had not been liberated but victimized.

At the training, I spoke to several women who had been abused as adults by clergy. Not one of them had received anything resembling justice from their various churches.

En route from the workshop, I visited my home in St. Boniface. The newly elected provincial Sister Rolande Joyal lived there. It never even entered my head to tell Sister Rolande about this abuse. I had decided that I had walked into this abuse as an independent adult, and I would get out of it the same way. Besides, I had never heard of a sister reporting abuse by a priest.

I saw no advantage to involving the sisters: none of them had training or work experience in the area of clergy sexual abuse.

Flying back to Labrador, I stared out the small oval window at the rugged terrain below and hoped that I'd find a letter from McManus when I arrived home. Despite all the warnings by Marie Fortune, and the bleak record of other victims before me, I really believed McManus would provide a safe and fair process where I could tell my story. I also felt confident that the Redemptorists would investigate all the centres where Goodall had lived and worked. Surely, I reasoned with myself, McManus would want to do this for their own good name as Redemptorists as well as the good name of the Church. What awaited me was radically different.

Black Fly Season

After greeting the cat and Marjorie, I rifled through my mail looking for a letter from McManus. There it was. I tore it open confident that the disclosure process was going somewhere. McManus confirmed my suspicion that they had no policy in place for handling an allegation of clergy sexual abuse. He offered his own procedure. I read on with dread.

1) I would state to the person accused that to have sex, as a Religious, with anyone, and especially with a retreatant, is a serious violation of the person's trust and gravely sinful. I would ask him if he agreed with this evaluation.

What was the purpose of this? *Ask* the offender priest? If he disagreed did that mean it was all forgotten because he didn't see any problem?

2) I would then inform him that someone had made a serious allegation against him and ask for his response. I would ask the person concerned to make the charge either in writing or to come and make the charge in my presence with him.

Oh great! The victim was to face her offender in front of McManus and have a shouting match! Was he prepared to be mediator? He wasn't even a neutral agent. My alarm bells were clanging.

3) If the priest accused denied the facts it would then be a question of either believing the one who brought the charge or believing him. If the priest had never been accused of such misconduct before I would have to accept that a serious allegation had been made, but, without further evidence, I would not be able to act on it, on this occasion. This would not be because I believed him rather than her. It would be a matter of due process. A person cannot simply be convicted on the uncorroborated word of another.

So, all the priest had to do was deny what happened and he was off the hook. How convenient. It must have required thousands of years to refine a process so geared to meet the needs of sex offenders.

However, if the person bringing the charge knew of others who could make similar charges, I would encourage her to get in touch with them. If they too brought similar charges I would have to suspend the priest while a full investigation took place. This investigation would be carried out by my Council. If the investigation established the truth of the charges the priest would never again conduct retreats and he would remain suspended from all other priestly duties for a considerable length of time. If he continued to have sexual relations with women he would then be expelled from the Congregation.

I wondered how I would contact other nuns and ask such a delicate question. I had feared something was going on between Goodall and Veronica Phafoli but I just couldn't bring myself to ask—and Veronica wasn't a stranger. Now, it was too late to ask her anything.

4) I would never take the view that the woman must have been the initiator. I accept that a priest, in a time of weakness, may sin, but I could never condone his conduct or seek to blame it on others.

The strong talk of expulsion didn't strike me as having any weight. I had been a nun for over thirty years and had never heard of a priest being expelled for his sexual activities. A priest who challenges dogma or becomes too political might be expelled. Womanizing was a cause for compassion for the priest and an occasion for blaming the woman.

I'd find others somehow. Immediately I wrote to the retreat centre directors at Durban and Lydenburg asking if they had any information that could be of help to me. I also wrote Josephine Bird at Hawkstone Hall in the UK as well as a contact in Zimbabwe plus a few friends in South Africa. I figured I would need a lot of corroborating evidence before McManus would take me seriously. But I had to be so careful. If I went about this too aggressively, he could accuse me of witch-hunting and I'd still be out in the cold.

It was berry picking season at Sheshatsheit, which coincided with black fly season. Black flies are stealthy, annoying little insects that can leave welts the size of a partridge berry. Unlike the mosquito who warns with her buzzing, the black fly creeps into the hair soundlessly, clamps onto a huge piece of scalp, and flies off with a belly-full of blood—mission accomplished. More often than not, by the time the itch comes, the bug is long gone.

As I picked and swatted, I wondered how I could be a black fly to McManus. What would it take to move him into action? I planned my letter carefully yet with rage. There were moments I feared I'd be struck dead just for thinking about a well versed, powerful rebuttal. How would I ever accomplish all the requirements and not sound like some vengeful old woman? It was like wandering across a mine field trying to reach a hospital. I'd never get better if I just gave up, but the problems I faced seeking justice seemed insurmountable.

On 8th September, 1993 I started calmly with:

Dear Father McManus,
I am the victim of pastoral sexual abuse by one of the men in your province. I have gathered my evidence and I realize that between letters and a tape he made for me that I have explicit evidence to prove that I am his victim and that it started while he was my retreat director.

Soon I let go of the niceties and became challenging.

I believe that one victim is sufficient for an investigation so I request that when you receive my written report you undertake a proper investigation of pastoral sexual abuse.

His response was prompt. He said:

I am sad to hear that a member of my Province used, as you wrote, "his authority as director to initiate sexual activity" with yourself. Please send me your evidence.

Nothing is more harmful to the ministry of the Church than the abuse of authority. When this abuse is of a sexual nature it can destroy even the faith of strong people. I trust that your own faith has not been damaged.

Had he even read my letter? There was no indication of an investigation. Goodall could simply deny this was abuse. I began to lose all hope that McManus could be impartial. I felt that he patted me on the head. I was expected to trust him with my story—with my recovery.

That week I spent a lot of time after work walking along a dry creek bed picking berries. The flies were gone. The hours in the bush helped stave off the nausea and the rage I felt at McManus' glib response to my concerns. He didn't even answer my questions—he just told me to send my evidence to him. Then what? I felt his suggestions were simply lip-service and I couldn't tolerate that. I would rather go to the police or to Cardinal Hume in the UK.

I typed out a summary of my story starting with the retreat in 1985 up to the 1993 good-bye letter and showed it to Marjorie. When she came to the river bank scene she looked up at me and said, "Yvonne, *that* is rape!"

Shamefully, I argued that I wasn't sure. She asked me if I had consented. I assured her, "Certainly not! He didn't even ask!" I remember pausing and adding, "who will ever believe me? He didn't beat me up, rip off my clothes, slap my face . . ."

"He used surprise and authority, didn't he? Physically, isn't he considerably bigger than you?"

"Yes but I didn't fight. I didn't want to create a scene by resisting so . . . well, I gave in."

"But you didn't agree. In order to consent you have to be asked. Did he ask, or did he act?"

"He ordered me to pull down my slacks. He never asked at all. But I didn't have to obey."

"What would have happened if you'd have resisted?"

"Oh my, he'd have been very angry, growled at me about why this and why that! He was already irritated because I hadn't given in earlier."

"That's not giving you a choice. A choice means you can say either yes or no and have no negative consequences either way. If there are negative consequences then it wasn't a real choice, it was coercion!"

I listened to Marjorie and, yes, what she said was true. But inside, I still felt like I was to blame. I hadn't fought. I had not wanted to face his anger and condemnation.

"I was a coward," I mumbled.

"Cowardice doesn't make you responsible for your rape. He's responsible. He knew exactly how much surprise and pressure to use to get you to cooperate. I'd say he is very experienced. I think he is dangerous to all women."

I felt supported by Marjorie's encouragement. I could acknowledge that one episode as rape but found the word rape too strong for the other episodes. I wrote McManus on 29th September, 1993:

> . . . will you consider one victim sufficient to conduct a proper investigation? . . . I am reluctant to send it (written report) to you without some definite assurance that a proper investigation will be conducted.

It was trust that got me into trouble with Goodall. It wasn't going to happen with his superiors. I knew what they probably wished for—for me to vanish silently into the northern lights.

McManus' next letter dated 8 October, 1993, was not a condescending pat on the head. It was a vicious attack.

First of all I don't know you, yet you expect me to accept, at
face value, what you submit. Secondly, I would have to submit your report to the person concerned to hear his response.
Thirdly, I would have to search to discover whether similar
allegations had ever been made against this person. The
answer to your question 'will you consider one victim
sufficient to conduct a proper investigation?' cannot be given
until I have completed those three steps. . . .

Since you make very serious allegations against another
person, that person is entitled to the full protection of his
human rights, namely that a person is innocent until he is
proven guilty. To set up an "investigation team" simply
because you submit a report would, in my view, constitute a
breach of this right.

I could not believe my eyes. I had written three credible letters. What more did he want? His first comment about not
knowing me enraged me to the core. My God, I was a nun for
more than thirty years—didn't that give me any credibility? Do
police officers have to 'know' the victim before they'll investigate
a complaint of sexual assault? And what if he did know me?
Would he have taken my complaint more seriously and repri-
manded Goodall without question?

This seemed like deliberate stonewalling. I felt so betrayed
that once again I questioned my own sanity. Perhaps McManus
was right, I was demanding too much. McManus had conceded
one point however—that he would inquire if there were other
complaints. I was suspicious of how useful that would be given

the history of denial and cover ups. How often had anyone dared write an official complaint? Who had ever bothered to investigate such a complaint? More than likely the accused was asked to explain and that was the end of the matter. More than likely the evidence would be destroyed.

Some people may question my suspicious line of thinking. But in Newfoundland where the sexual abuse of boys in parishes and in Mount Cashel had been covered-up for many years, I had good reason to be leery. I had met some of those victims and seen the long term devastation they experienced—no one having believed their story. Would I end up like that?

In my next letter on the 29th October I was very straight-forward:

> How many such additional complaints would constitute a sufficient number to warrant a proper investigation? I hold that one complaint even without a second is sufficient. If I report a car theft would the police hesitate to investigate until there are three other reported car thefts?

Interesting how often sexual abuse needs corroboration. In Pakistan, the victim needs four male witnesses. I felt I was being asked to produce at least four other victims—preferably male—for they would be believed more readily than females.

> I agree that the respondent has a right to be considered innocent until proven guilty. The complainant has the right to be considered innocent of malicious intent until proven otherwise.

Another point that worried me was the thought of having all men, all priests, and all Redemptorists investigate. I wrote,

Normally an agency or institute does not investigate its own members regarding a complaint from an outside person or agency. Yet the Redemptorists are to investigate the Redemptorists. It is hard for me to imagine that I will receive an impartial hearing.

To show him how serious I was about a safe and just hearing, I included,

If a complaint is mismanaged, the complainant has the right to go to higher levels within the church or even to the legal system to obtain an impartial hearing . . . It is my belief that the church should lead, not drag behind the justice system, in protecting the vulnerable.

You said in your letter of 8th Oct. 1993 that, 'To set up an investigation team simply because you submit a report would, in my view, constitute a breach of this right.' (innocent until proven guilty) I am not asking anyone to judge this man guilty. I am asking for a fair investigation in order to establish innocence or guilt. I feel judged by your statement. I feel that your are making me out to be unjust. That is intimidation in my view.

I then proposed two procedures set up by Canadian congregations of priests. I also told McManus that I feared my offender. *"I feel he is a danger to my existence if I report him."* I thought Goodall might still find some way to silence me and perhaps physically harm me. This was probably irrational but my fear would not let up for months. I could not imagine reporting Goodall if he lived in the same town or even the same continent. I needed an ocean between us to have enough safety to report him.

I decided to include a deadline for a response: *"I would like to hear from you concerning this urgent matter by the end of November, 1993."*

With the letter sealed, stamped and addressed I marched across the high steel bridge over North West River to the post office. On my face I wore a grin but there was still a lump of nausea in my stomach. I had put my own needs and definitions first—how unladylike! McManus had thrown paternalistic platitudes at me and I had defended myself at last.

By this time I had shown my story to Father Fred Magee, the parish priest of Davis Inlet and Sheshatsheit. He calculated that I had five sexual abuse charges against Goodall. He also said he felt McManus was handling this very badly. He suggested I establish some credibility by getting a few authority figures to write character references on my behalf.

That sounded like good advice. Fred agreed to be one of my references. He stated to McManus that I had a well substantiated complaint which merited his urgent attention. I wrote to Sister Rolande, my provincial in Manitoba, asking her to be my reference also.

That same day I phoned the Center for Prevention of Domestic and Sexual Violence in Seattle for names of persons in UK who might help me. Reverend Marie Fortune put me in contact with Margaret Kennedy and Jenny Fasal in England. Margaret coordinated a group called Christian Survivors of Sexual Abuse while Jenny coordinated POPAN (Prevention of Professional Abuse Network), also in London. Within the week I mailed both these women my story.

By this time, November had snowed its way into December, and I had no response from McManus. While I pondered my next move, Sister Rolande phoned to tell me that she had contacted our Superior General, Sister Mary Ellen Holohan upon reading my request for a reference. I was taken aback that she had called the Superior General without asking me. Sister Rolande reported that McManus had phoned her saying he was late responding to me because he had been in the hospital. I had included the phone numbers of Father Fred and Sister Rolande in my last letter to him so he used it to assure Sister Rolande that he was not deliberately negligent. McManus asked Sister Rolande the name of the priest I was accusing. She did not know.

Sister Mary Ellen had suggested that I tell her and Sister Rolande my story so they could provide support. I was told that such matters were dealt with between provincials and not a provincial with a member. McManus hadn't seen that as important—perhaps he could intimidate me more easily than he could my provincial. I wanted support, but I wasn't too sure if they would really provide that. Women provincials hadn't fared well against their male counterparts in disputes I had dealt with in the past. I had grave doubts that this would go any better. On the other hand, how much choice did I have? These two major superiors requested a meeting with me. I could hardly disobey.

While preparing for this meeting, a friend suggested I contact Father Doug Stamp, a Redemptorist canon lawyer living in St. John's, Newfoundland. I did and found him supportive. This allayed my fears somewhat knowing that a Redemptorist could admit that a brother Redemptorist had sexually abused. Perhaps there was a chance of some justice after all.

In December 1993, I was subpoenaed as a witness for the crown prosecutor in a case of sexual abuse. The girl was twelve when a twenty year old man abused her on three different occasions. The man had disclosed the abuse to me but then pleaded not guilty in court. He was convicted and taken immediately into custody. This caused shock waves in the community, so much so that by the next day Fred asked me, on the recommendation of

Bishop Goudreault, to leave the community for a few days. For the second time in my life I was forced into hiding.

To be honest, those days of rest were wonderful. I stayed with the Hayden family and went for long walks on the clear ice along the shore of Lake Melville. I even ventured ice skating for the first time in thirty years. I lasted only fifteen minutes before the nippy temperature of -30° C forced me back to the warm house.

On the 10th of December 1993, I flew to Montreal to meet Sister Rolande and Sister Mary Ellen to tell my story. Sister Mary Ellen, a wispy looking woman in her early fifties had her hair pulled back in a lose bun. A shy nervous smile came easily to her face.

The telling proved very difficult for me. Sometimes I would open my mouth to speak and a high pitched screech came out. This had never happened to me before in my life. I feared they would call me dirty or at least conclude that I had consented. I felt I was helpless before a jury with only my words to convince them. They would decide if I had a case or not. The vows of poverty and obedience give the superiors immense power—like feudal kings.

Sister Mary Ellen commented that my story made sense and matched what she had heard about Foreign Born Irish (FBI) priests. They were known in the USA for avoiding friendships with women because it was too dangerous to celibacy. But these same men indulged in short affairs because affairs required no commitment. They seemed to believe that these short affairs were not a serious breach of celibacy—just weakness and passion.

It was reassuring to know that Sister Mary Ellen had some idea of what I was talking about. Sister Rolande told me that she did not judge me and that as provincial superior it was her task to handle this despite her lack of experience and knowledge. I felt relieved to have some help from authorities and thought McManus might take them more seriously than he had taken me.

At this point I felt I had little choice—these were the two most powerful women in my religious community. They held the purse strings, and without their approval I could do very little. Besides, my vows of poverty and obedience made it close to impossible to refuse their help. After some faxes back and forth, McManus and Sister Rolande agreed on a definition of clergy abuse and McManus promised:

> Any alleged abuse or violation of that trust is taken extremely seriously by the London Province of the Most Holy Redeemer and will be investigated fully according to the process drawn up by the Toronto Redemptorists and dealt with according to the demands of canon or civil law.

This was a switch for McManus! He would act on *one* allegation. I had five instances; five charges of pastoral sexual abuse to report. My superiors decided to report only the first instance. I felt short changed and disbelieved. Did they think I had consented to the last four abuses? I worried that if I argued too hard for all five charges, my superiors would find me 'unhealthy' and perhaps even 'half-demented.' Besides I was drained—perhaps I was just a nag after all. So I let go. I acquiesced just as I had with my Dad and with Goodall. I gave up my values in order to preserve the peace and to retain some affirmation and support from people who had power over me.

They wrote to McManus that there needed to be an investigation team, written reports from both claimant (me) and respondent (Goodall), and that if the team found cause for a full investigation that:

> the respondent be suspended from ministry, and places where he lived and worked over the last 10 years be notified of the suspension and the reason for the suspension . . . that each work and living place of the respondent be requested to bring to the investigation team any first hand knowledge and any third party reports of sexual misdemeanors by the respondent . . . that bishops of each of the dioceses where the respondent has lived and worked in these last ten years be notified of the suspension, the charge, and be requested to bring to the investigation team any complaints or information they may have.

To this day, these stipulations have not been carried out, despite the fact that at least one other written complaint was made about Goodall's sexual behavior.

Nuns are generally a servant class to priests. I was not at all confident that my superiors would get any further than I had with McManus. In my years in the convent, I had not seen much evidence of priests listening to sisters.

I flew back over the Labrador wilderness into Happy Valley-Goose Bay feeling that I had another layer of administration and patriarchy to deal with—my own superiors this time. My sense of helplessness was as great as when I had left Goose Bay for the Montreal meeting. I was doing the dance again—two steps forwards, ten steps back.

Into the Fire

For the first time in my life I dreaded receiving mail. Even letters from friends sometimes contained belittling comments and pat answers. The hardest were those with creative versions of *forgive and forget*. A few went so far as to declare, *It takes two to tango.* I went into a down spin each time—licking my wounds for days before my rage would revive me.

Among the worst of the correspondence was from Sister Jacqueline at The Bluff, Durban. It came just before Christmas.

> . . . I was indeed shocked and deeply distressed to read what you had written about Father Frank Goodall. If he tried that on me I would have slapped him right in his face.

I had certainly failed her criteria: slapping Goodall had never occurred to me any more than slapping my father. She dug her mightier-than-thou claws in deeper by adding,

"Even Maria Goretti knew what to do at the age of twelve."

Maria Goretti, was a wisp of a girl from Italy—a heroine of chastity. Unlike me, she had fought off her knife-wielding offender. He killed her anyway.

Over the years I have shocked priests and colleagues by declaring that Maria Goretti was lucky to have died; the rest of us have to live with the trauma of *failing* to fight to the death to protect our chastity.

> . . . I am pleased that you have informed his Provincial and I pray that something will be done about this sad state of affairs. I couldn't sleep for several nights after I read your letter, as it affected me so badly. I am afraid however that I cannot accede to your request to contact others who made a retreat with him as I feel this would be an intrusion into their privacy.

Somehow her concern did not seem authentic. Shouldn't she have felt a duty to contact every single person who had ever been in her retreat centre? Again I saw privacy being used to protect offending priests.

When I showed the letter to Marjorie she said, "Good thing you didn't say anything to her on that retreat. She wouldn't have believed you! And that comparison with Maria Goretti is odious. You have a long road to walk, Yvonne."

Several months later, when I felt strong enough to stand up to Sister Jacqueline I sent her my story plus a copy of *Sex in the Forbidden Zone*. To date she has not responded. I wonder why she is so silent?

A week later I received a letter from the Lydenburg Diocese Pastoral Centre written by Sister Marianne Graf.

> I have received no complaints about him, other than your own. For that reason, I would not know how to go about putting you in contact with others whom he might have abused. I have not kept records of which persons were

assisted by which director. I do not think it would be correct procedure to write to all those persons who were at the centre during all the retreats which he helped to direct.

I shook my head. How could these powerful women just throw up their hands in despair without even an attempt to seek the truth? What were they afraid of?

That night I wrote in my journal:

Discouraged by the responses from the retreat centres. My bishop friend from South Africa hasn't answered. I suspect he's afraid of me. He molested me once and wouldn't want that to be reported now, would he!

I had written him a summary of my story and asked if he knew anything about Goodall. His response was quick and affirming. It was time to confront him on his molestation of me—he's groped my breasts once as I walked with him and several others after supper at language school. He was a staff member. I was a student.

In my letter I thanked him for the support but then asked him why he had groped me. To my surprise he did respond saying he had met Goodall but had no information on him. Then he added;

I see elements of recklessness and self-destruction coming through, things which I have never associated with you . . . the tone and implications, especially of your last letter, were a source of concern to me. You no longer seemed to be the Yvonne I knew or thought I knew . . . you need to bring gentleness and kindness and forgiveness and healing into your life.

Instead of dealing with the way he touched me, he gave me a lecture. Well, didn't *that* sound familiar. I slammed the letter down and stomped around the kitchen in an attempt to calm myself.

Perhaps I *was* reckless and self-destructive. Anyone confronting a priest would have to be. It was proving to be exactly that. Fortunately my rage gave me audacity to write back to him:

> How dare you preach to me about healing, humility and forgiveness! You are not even humble enough to admit you made a mistake in molesting me. I think it is time you practice what you preach . . .

When I dropped that letter in the bright red Canada Post box, I was sure I would never hear from him again: I wasn't that happy little nun anymore—the one he obviously preferred. Had he ever been my friend? All he seemed to want was a nun who smiled and never questioned his groping hands. Some months later I received a last letter saying that he did not remember the incident but that he did not deny it either.

His 'black out' baffled me. Was such behaviour so inconsequential that he had no memory of it? Perhaps it was so ordinary that he didn't remember doing it to *me* in particular? Could it be that way with all men? Are women 'felt up' and groped so often that it's become a tolerated male behaviour? Was I expected to just forget it also? Bury it? Pretend it was something other than sexual harassment?

∴ ❖ ∴

Meanwhile, Sister Rolande received a letter from McManus dated 26 January 1994. I saw this for the first time two years later.

He wrote:

> I was very surprised that the accusation was being brought against Father Frank Goodall. He is a highly respected priest in our province.

McManus then pointed out that the Church statute of limitations was past and so even if Goodall admitted everything there was nothing to be done canonically. However, he would consider a pastoral solution. I knew what that meant—a tap on Goodall's wrist and a pity letter to me. Then, business as usual.

> I am very troubled that Sister Yvonne has been writing letters to places where Father Goodall has worked in the hope of gathering evidence to support her charge against him. I received a copy of a five page letter which she sent to a Sister in Zimbabwe, detailing a series of sexual encounters with Father Goodall. While Sister Yvonne may feel that Father Goodall had forfeited his good name, she is not entitled, despite her hurt, to defame him.

What did this man expect! It was he who suggested I look for other victims in the first place. Now he wasn't pleased to have the truth told.

> She also implies in the letter that she was writing at my express request. This is very misleading.

Interesting how frequently I seem to misinterpret him. Goodall accused me of the same thing, many, many times. Another letter by McManus that I saw only two years later was dated 28 January 1994:

My dear Frank,

Thank you for coming to see me last Monday. I have discussed the full implications of the charge which Sister Yvonne is bringing against you with two Canon lawyers and the Province's civil lawyer at Witham Weld. The civil lawyer told me that you should not leave for Zimbabwe in April. I am, therefore, writing to ask you to postpone your visit until this matter has been resolved. Please inform the Congregations in Zimbabwe that you are not available for retreat work. I must also ask you not to undertake retreats for women until I give you express permission.

Our lawyer says that we cannot avoid an investigation of the charge but he is hoping that the investigation will be held in private. When we know what the process is, we will give you the full details.

I am glad that you can put your confidence in Ralph and discuss the whole matter with him.

With every good wish, Fraternally in Christ.

My gut had told me that McManus would never be impartial with one of his own priests. This letter validated my interpretation.

To Sister Rolande, however, McManus wrote that he had consulted more lawyers.

In the light of their advice, a civil enquiry needs to be held into Sister Yvonne's complaints. The enquiry will take place in private and the rules of natural justice should apply.

A Committee of Enquiry will be appointed by our Provincial Council and comprise Sister Anne Marie Crowley, who is a former Provincial of the Order of Our

Lady of Evron, Father Michael McGreevy who is a respected and senior member or our Congregation and Mrs. Rosemary Gallagher, an editor with Redemptorist Publications and a consultant to the Bishops' Conference on marriage and questions of sexual abuse.

He was dictating new terms, and appointing the panel exactly as he wished. The previous agreement was disregarded and he was making decisions without consulting me or my superiors. It felt like a set-up for failure.

My ire flared when I was constantly referred to as Sister Yvonne, yet the priest was Father Goodall. This infuriated me. I protested this sexist use of names. In South Africa, blacks usually were addressed by their first names and whites by their family names. My superiors heeded my protest, but McManus continued. I guess they never brought it up to him. It was my issue, not theirs.

McManus then outlined his seven points of procedure. The first point stated that I was to send my written report to Mr. Hawthorne and that Goodall would respond within fourteen days and then in twenty-eight days I was to meet the committee along with Goodall.

Mr. Hawthorne will be present to advise generally and in the light of the rules of natural justice.

There would be time for the committee to question both Goodall and myself. Then Goodall could question me and I could question him.

Much of this process worried me. Why did McManus have the right to choose the panel? Why was it private and not public?

Why was Goodall to be present during my testimony? What was 'natural' about this so called 'justice'?

I told Sister Rolande my reservations about having Goodall present as I told my story. I also wondered why there was only one lawyer: theirs. Sister Rolande asked McManus what natural justice meant and why the need for a private civil enquiry. McManus indicated that this was to be simultaneously a civil and canonical hearing:

> King's College which is part of the University of London has been criticized in the media for the way in which it handled an abuse case without first considering legal implications and the involvement of the public authorities.

Fear of the media seemed to be driving this process—not concern for truth.

The Times Higher Education Supplement of October 22, 1993 wrote:

> . . . The college has come in for criticism for trying to handle the matter internally, rather than sending the case to the police immediately. Disciplinary committees in universities were set up to deal with cases of exam fraud, or sexual harassment, not rape.

I knew the Church was *not* set up to hear clergy sexual abuse any better than King's College, yet McManus was attempting to do so on his terms. He was seeking legal and canonical advice while my superiors had not yet seen fit to seek the same. I felt that I was not worth the trouble or expense, but Goodall obviously deserved the best. I had begged for legal advice several times and been shrugged off. My vows of poverty and obedience made it

impossible for me to do so on my own. I felt like a captured creature, chained and gagged with only my flashing eyes and sharp
claws to protect me. How un-nun-like—fighting and standing
up to a priest. I bet they thought my punitive behaviour was a
guaranteed one-way ticket straight to hell. Little did they know,
I was already there.

∴ ❖ ∴

In February of 1994, Bishop Goudreault called a Diocesan congress in Québec City. The coordinator asked me to present a half-
day workshop on the topic of pastoral sexual abuse to the sixty
participants. The room was tense throughout the workshop and
so were the discussions afterwards.

During my days at the congress, I also participated in a three-
way teleconference with Sister Mary Ellen in Montreal and Sister
Rolande in Winnipeg to discuss our response to the last letter
from McManus. The office I used for this teleconference was
freezing cold. By the end of the hour call my teeth chattered—as
much from frustration as from bitter cold.

My superiors told me that they would not use the criminal or
civil legal system *"now or in the future."* I clearly told them that I
would not accept telling McManus that.

I felt I was being pressured into the traditional woman's role
again: like Mary who listens and obeys. They asked me to
reconsider. I wanted to scream at McManus, not appease him.
Was my resistance proving to my superiors that I was no longer
rational?

That night I wrote in my journal:

Even if we never use the legal system why do we have to
promise them—comfort them—appease them? I can not

sign away all my civil rights, my human right! This is disgusting. I am being betrayed by my own.

I returned to Labrador with a very heavy heart indeed.

Early in March, 1994 I flew to Winnipeg to participate in a consultation for Voices for Non-Violence set up by the Mennonite Central Committee. The first evening was a sharing time for the eight participants. A Baptist Minister told how she was being pushed out of her church after she disclosed that a powerful member of the congregation had sexually harassed her. I risked giving an outline of my story and felt immense support from each of the participants. The discussions that weekend included the whole question of fiduciary duties of those in positions of authority. Ernie Epp of Saskatoon spoke to me at break of religious authorities' fiduciary duties to those vowed in their care. For the first time I had words to express my superiors duties to me—these went far beyond food and shelter.

My new awareness did not stand the test at the next teleconference. I acquiesced to, *"We intend to pursue this canonically and only canonically. There is no intention on our part to make use of either criminal or civil courts for laying this complaint."* They did not insist on keeping "Now and in the future." I knew my superiors would let me wilt like a plant without water until I agreed to something of the kind. I warned them:

"This statement of intent would not be accepted as a contract in any legal court of justice. It is only a statement of intent."

Sister Mary Ellen replied sternly, "We keep our word, Yvonne! I take a statement like this seriously!"

In early April I received a letter from Sr. Margaret Mehren, a spiritual director in a leadership position in Southern Africa. She had information that Goodall was known for *"this kind of behaviour"* but that he likely had some counseling so *"was not doing that anymore."* She insisted that civil action served no purpose but rather the *"two superiors should meet."* She continued:

> I am afraid you will get more hurt in the (civil) process. Also a scandal in the church should be dealt with in the church. The press in the USA seems to thrive on church scandals, quite disgusting. I would not want to add to it. After all there are still many good priests. . . . What is more important than making a case is to stop his activities, to make him accept help, and for you: to find healing which is not possible without forgiving—forgiving yourself, forgiving your father, forgiving F. G. . . . Any trace of revenge would be destructive—it destroys oneself, as does resentment, hatred, anger!

More platitudes. And blaming the press. This from a nun with no experience in clergy sexual abuse. Why did she presume the right to give me a lecture. Who was she protecting? I disagreed on every point and wrote to tell her so.

Church leaders presumed to preach "forgiveness" to victims before they even knew the facts. Well this one would hear the facts. I sent Margaret my story. She wrote back to say she did not realize the extent of the abuse and offered to support me. I have not heard from her since. Another friend lost.

Grasping for straws, I came up with a brilliant idea: contact Father Gregory Brooks, the confessor I had gone to after that fateful Durban retreat. I traced him by telephone to Virginia, Republic of South Africa. He told me he was aware of missionaries saying to women, *"This (sex) is for the good of the church."* Brooks offered *"to write my story for evidence provided I send him a copy first so he would not break the seal of confession."*

I danced around the house that day rejoicing. "I did tell some-one! I do have evidence! It's not just my word against Goodall's." I knew that having told someone at the time of the abuse stood up in legal cases and I hoped it would in the Church as well. I thought I had finally broken out of my trap. I had sprung it myself.

On the UK front, Margaret Kennedy and Jenny Fasal told me about a Bishop Budd of Plymouth, who dealt with clergy sexual abuse and was interested in my case. They were having difficulty finding a canon lawyer to look at my story. Finally a Father Ralph Brown agreed to meet with them but on the appointed day Brown did not show up.

In addition, Margaret had phoned Goodall's house in Liverpool and was told Goodall was on sabbatical. My superiors had refused to ask McManus what Goodall was doing but Margaret had an answer with one phone call. Why hadn't Sister Rolande made that call?

Meanwhile, I contacted George Daniels, Archbishop of Pretoria, Republic of South Africa. He made some inquiries only to find that no one would speak with him about Goodall. The net of secrecy and fear was tightening.

After months of waiting for Brooks' letter I phoned him again. He said my information had not reached him. It was dur-ing the first-ever multi-race elections in South Africa so the post offices were jammed. That same week I sent Brooks another packet of my material. To this very day, after giving me so much hope in finally finding an ally, he has not responded after three more requests on my part. Someday I will confront him on this but for the time being I cannot face him. I still feel too betrayed to speak coherently to him on the telephone.

.: ❧ :.

That entire spring of 1994 was difficult on several counts. Bishop Goudreault had informed me that my contract would not be renewed. This was a complete turn around from the Québec congress when he had asked me to provide training for his diocesan committee on sexual abuse.

My relationship with Sister Marjorie, my house-mate, was also deteriorating. She told me that I was using emotions from one issue and putting them into other issues. "You need to take a year off the case and just take care of yourself." I feared therapy. My impression was that it just helped women shut up and accept a subservient role. I was not going to accept or adapt to patriarchy. I feared that therapy might dissipate my rage leaving me a zombie—too dispassionate to stand up to injustice.

One day, Marjorie took a call from my older sister Clarisse when I was out. Clarisse phoned later concerned about me. "Marjorie said you are unhealthy and that you want Frank in jail. You know I think that's exactly where he belongs, but I never heard you say that. What's going on?" Immediately I confronted Marjorie. She denied it all until the next morning when she admitted, "Perhaps I told Clarisse that you need help. And you do want Frank in jail. You want to go to civil court so that means he could go to jail."

"Marjorie! I am prepared to go through that private civil enquiry that McManus is imposing if I cannot get any other." I flung back at her. "I never said I want Goodall in jail. Even if I did want him in jail, what is so unhealthy about that? We expect lay offenders to go to jail but we protect priests! Why?"

"Well if you go civil and he's found guilty then he will go to jail," she commented.

"No Marjorie, civil cases are about damages. Criminal cases are about incarceration."

"Oh, I didn't know the difference."

This was hardly an admission but it did clear the air between us. Nonetheless I felt judged; I felt inadequate and downright evil for wanting consequences for Goodall.

Meanwhile, Bishop Goudreault had spoken to Sister Rolande informing her that I was a scandal—I did not go to church often enough. Did he consider the priest in his diocese who had sexually abused for twenty years a scandal? The priest in question had never apologize to his victims and continued as parish leader. Obviously repentance and amends were not required when the offender was a priest. Was I crazy to think that the offending priest should spend his time making amends instead of preaching justice and compassion?

From the day I reported clergy sexual abuse I was labeled "unhealthy." *"Take time for yourself, Sister,"* had become a byword from the bishop on down.

It was at this time that I came into contact with Ray and Anne Higgins in Santa Barbara, California. I phoned them for information and got some of the best support ever. They had worked with victims of a minor seminary run by Franciscan priests and knew first hand how devastating the process of disclosure could be. Their son had been one of the victims.

∴ ∵ ∴

One splendid May morning, Rose Gregoire and I walked two hours across the glistening ice on the North West River to The Rapids where her sister had set up camp. Without sunglasses I would have been blinded. We found Philomena and her husband, Joachim, at their ice fishing hole near the camp. Philomena cooked up one of her catch on her square tin stove in her neat canvas tent. After a sound nap on the spruce boughs, I watched Philomena and her granddaughter pluck a goose. Philomena invited me to wrap my freezing hands in the goose down. The warmth that crept into my stiff fingers was immediate and soothing.

Soon it was time to trek back across the ice to the village. I felt whole that day. For those few hours I felt I could handle whatever life had in store for me.

Another blow-up with Marjorie came the following day. I overheard her tell Fred Magee on the telephone, "Yvonne is a walking time bomb." It was beginning to annoy me that she wasted so much time trying to have me silenced. When I asked her why she said, "You're going too fast. The people here aren't with you. I called Leslie, your provincial councilor, and told her I'm concerned about you."

I began to think of myself as a mouse in the paws of a lion. As I struggled for my life, Marjorie and my superiors stood behind the zoo fence and sympathized with me, *"Yvonne, you need help! Get some help for yourself. No, don't call the police! No! You must not call a lawyer either. We had a chat with the chief lion. He'll take care of this problem."*

The twists and turns, the deceptions, and the back-stabbing seemed endless. Each day I wondered where the next blow would come from and how I would survive it. That next blow still stuns my imagination. It came from Goodall, and it was the ultimate manipulation.

On April 26, 1994, McManus wrote Sister Rolande saying:

Father Goodall has decided to save further harm, upset and costs being caused to all concerned by accepting his responsibility and apologizing for this to Sister Yvonne Maes.

I breathed a sigh of relief—he's admitting something happened. Anxiously I read on knowing that offenders seldom admit more than the tip of the iceberg.

Accordingly I write to inform you that he admits that his part in the relationship with Sister Yvonne Maes was wrong and harmful and apologizes for this. I can inform you that he has been suspended from retreat work since Sister Yvonne's complaints were made known to us and further, to reduce as far as possible the risk of any such circumstances occurring again, he expresses his willingness to accept specialist counseling and advice, which may influence the decisions to be taken about his future.

So all an offender needs to do is admit something happened, attend a few counseling sessions on how to protect himself from seductive women in the future and, *whammo,* he's back in business.

This apology and information it is hoped will relieve the main concerns you express and bring the complaint to a conclusion, but please let me know if further clarification is desired.

Conclusion! My mouth dropped open at the sheer outrage. A one line apology sent through his superior to my superior and I am expected to drop on my knees in gratitude. Maybe I was even expected to praise God for His goodness to me. Emphasis on *His!* It seemed to me these were God's men laughing at women who dared to expose their abusive behaviour.

McManus didn't even need to offer any therapy for me. Now Goodall was the fair-haired boy because he was saving them all from an inquiry. He could be back in ministry 'saving' women in no time. His supply of victims could be assured by this simple admission of some minor failing in celibacy. Brilliant!

My low-grade nausea swelled until it reached my Adam's apple where it was lodged for days after that news. I could not come to grips with the arrogance displayed by McManus. Was he serious or was this a colossal joke?

Fearing that my superiors might pressure me to drop the whole thing, I drafted a strong response and faxed it to Sister Rolande. I also suggested that she consult Doug Stamp, Phyllis Clarke and Ray Higgins. She spoke to Stamp but not the others.

Sister Rolande watered down my response and sent it to McManus. She made six points in all.

1. Maes needs to tell her story in full to an investigation panel.
2. Goodall needs to write an appropriate apology and then make a face to face apology to Maes.
3. All places where Goodall lived and worked be thoroughly investigated.
4. Goodall is to undergo assessment and treatment.
5. The pornographic pictures Frank Goodall took of Yvonne Maes at Hawkstone Hall in 1988 be destroyed and that any reference to Yvonne Maes in his personal journal be destroyed.
6. The Redemptorists pay the Holy Names $50,000 dollars for therapy and travel expenses.

Overall, this was a fair letter and stronger than I had expected. However, my reservations about the competence of the panel continued to gnaw at me. I decided to let this go rather than irritate Sister Rolande; after all, she had made several good points on my behalf. I should be grateful even for crumbs.

Meanwhile, Sister Rolande would not give me either a refusal or consent to my taking a job in Happy Valley-Goose Bay with

Labrador Legal Services. As a result, I could not look for a place to live or even put an address on my twelve cardboard boxes. I was a puppet on strings held by Sister Rolande. I often wished I would never wake up—just float into oblivion. There were no snake dreams any longer, but often I dreamed that I could not find my clothes.

My first task seemed to be to prove to my authorities that I was sane, stable, and capable of making reasonable decisions about the abuse. I booked myself with a therapist experienced in dealing with victims of clergy abuse in Vancouver. I chose Vancouver because I could stay with my sister Clarisse during the therapy. For once I did not ask permission.

The evening before my departure from Labrador, an adult in the community disclosed horrific stories of clergy abuse. When I boarded the plane the next morning I wondered if I would ever return to these people. I also wondered if and when the church would burn.

A Gift

Clarisse was waiting for me when I landed at Vancouver Airport. It was a blistering July afternoon. My emotions were mixed at seeing her. Although I was relieved and happy, I was also nervous and afraid—afraid that, having not seen me in over a year, she'd find me 'unhealthy' just as the others had.

I was red-eyed from weeping my way across five Canadian time zones, but kept my composure until we started winding our way through the Vancouver traffic. The unfamiliar swish of cars and the claustrophobia induced by the tall buildings overwhelmed me. Before we reached Clarisse's house I blurted out the story of abuse I'd heard the night before—the burden of carrying that alone was too much for me. I was careful to avoid all names, and to stress my reactions rather than the details of the story. Clarisse took it all in, including my rage at the Church, without running a single red light. Once that was off my chest I calmed down.

Soon we were sipping orange juice on her deck overlooking English Bay and Lion's Gate Bridge. We talked into the night to the amazement of her husband, Steve. I'd built up a head of steam like a pressure cooker and couldn't get enough of talking. She did not find me the least bit unhealthy.

A few days after my arrival Sister Rolande sent me a fax from McManus. It started:

> Your letter is disappointing: firstly although you agree it is a positive development that Father Goodall has accepted responsibility and admits that his part in the relationship with Sister Yvonne Maes was wrong and harmful and apologizes for this, it goes on to seek redress against 'the offender' without reciprocating as regards any part in the relationship played by Sister Yvonne Maes.

My immediate reaction—I yelled, "his part!" The implication was that my part was as big and as bad as his. McManus sounded enraged at us: how dare we not be satisfied with the one-line third-party apology! Furthermore, I sensed a strong resentment at our use of the term offender. Good sisters would never label anyone. He continued:

> Secondly, and this point illustrates the importance of reciprocity, your letter reports for the first time, photographs said to have been taken in the UK in 1988. Your new report is of considerable concern because the original report was of events of July 1985, whose definition you proposed and in good faith I accepted. You will understand that a fundamental question now arises as to the presence of Sister Yvonne Maes in the company of Father Goodall in 1988. Since Father Goodall has already admitted and apologized for his involvement, there is now a need for openness about any involvement of Sister Yvonne Maes, especially about what she was doing in 1988. Your new report implies that she traveled to England in 1988 and there met with Father Goodall. Is that correct and if so was she in Father Goodall's company upon

an involuntary basis? If so details of any coercion are urgently required. But if not, before any of the points in your letter can equitably be taken further, there is a need for a full and frank account by Sister Yvonne Maes of her involvement including in particular how and why it was she came to be with Father Goodall at Hawkstone Hall in 1988 in the light of her complaints about his 1985 behaviour . . . If a child and adult are involved, full culpability by the latter will almost certainly be established; likewise where a woman and a man are involved and the latter uses force or violence. Where a woman and a man are involved and the man has the role of director, he may be found principally responsible but that is not to say that the adult woman will be found to be beyond reproach. But where the same woman and man meet several years later, the circumstances of such meeting including whether it was accidental, deliberate but voluntary or coerced, are fundamental to attempting to apportion responsibility.

He was grievously disappointed in me and my behaviour. Was he as indignant about Goodall's behaviour? Apparently Goodall had not given McManus a full and frank disclosure, otherwise McManus would have known about the pictures taken at Hawkstone Hall. Where was the empathy for the victim which he spoke about in his first letters? Obviously this empathy went up in smoke when a name was attached to the allegation. I could not imagine his selecting a neutral panel, let alone carrying out any negative recommendations.

Sister Rolande phoned to tell me she did not want me to send any correspondence with her name on it to outsiders. I had shared several previous faxes with persons who could shed light on the issue. I believed this was my case and that I had at least the right to seek out advice, since Sister Rolande didn't seem to do much of that. In addition, Sister Rolande warned me that I might be charged with defamation of character if I wrote any of this to outsiders. I couldn't believe that telling the truth was defamation. I looked in *Martin's Commentary, 1994* on the Criminal Code of Canada at the local library. I learned that the truth isn't always sufficient except if it serves the public good. I felt my talking about Goodall clearly served the public good.

Then came my first session with the therapist, Cheryl Bell-Gadsby. I tripped into her office barely able to breathe—I was not proud of being a nun, and even less proud of being the victim of a priest. I felt that I was hanging out the Church's dirty laundry for all to see. By the time I left her office an hour later, I could breathe again. Cheryl immediately put me in touch with another survivor of clergy abuse whose story read like a merry-go-round with three ponies called evasion, belittlement, and stonewalling. Hearing her experience alerted me to be extremely cautious about a Church hearing. I decided to keep better notes and to record telephone conversations and meetings from then on.

Every morning at Clarisse's I'd sit for hours at the breakfast table overlooking English Bay and write in my journal. By the end of the five weeks, I had several hundred pages of anger, arguments, poems, allegories, and swearing, firmly down on paper. Sometimes I'd laugh at the outlandish images I created. At other times I broke my pencil in frustration and banged the table with my fists. How could I have been so stupid to let this happen to me? Why did I let it go on so many years?

He loved too much.
Indeed.

Himself
Not me!
For his part—sorrow.

Now Sister, let it go.
After he's Defrocked,
Certainly!

During these mornings in the kitchen, Clarisse kept a safe distance. Until I was ready to share my insights over a cup of coffee, she just let me be. Once, after I had vented away—muttering and sputtering to myself, crying, laughing, snapping my pencil, she cocked her head and said, "I'm so glad Mom and Dad had you. What a gift you are to me!"

Her words stunned me to tears. I couldn't imagine anyone on the planet thinking I was a gift! I couldn't remember the last time I felt that kind of affirmation. I had been fighting this war for so long in the dark, I hadn't stopped to realize how often I beat myself up. I saw a tiny pinhole of light and it was my dear sister who put it there. Maybe I wasn't insane after all.

When I had worn myself out writing, I'd read and read. I started with Judith Herman's book, *Trauma and Recovery* then Phyllis Chesler, *Women and Madness* and Suzanne Sgori's *Vulnerable Populations.* Each book shored up my belief that the systems I lived in promoted sexual abuse and protected offenders. I admit that on many occasions when I wasn't believed or ordered into silence, I had acted hysterically—if you call venting anger and raising one's voice hysterical. When men brawled at bars or at hockey games, were they labeled hysterical? Of course not. All I had to do was raise my voice against injustice and I was called berserk.

My stay with Clarisse and therapy with Cheryl ended all too soon. The five weeks seemed to pass like five days. Because nuns don't often get permission to visit family, I suspected it would be years before I'd see Clarisse again. Our good-bye was a tearful one. She was the best big sister a person could have.

I traveled directly to St. John's Abbey, Collegeville, Minnesota for the second annual conference of LINKUP, an advocacy and support organization for survivors of clergy sexual abuse. I resented the monastic surroundings—too many memories of men in the pulpit and women in the pews.

My first goal on reaching the conference was to connect with Margaret Kennedy from the UK. She had come over for the conference. Although she was younger than I anticipated, she was every bit as dynamic as I imagined. The first evening the auditorium was packed when Sister Joan Chittister stepped to the microphone to give the keynote speech. She started with this story:

On a foggy night in a narrow salt water channel two lights faced each other. One signaled, 'Please move five degrees to the south!'

The reply: 'I request that you move five degrees to the south.'

And then, 'This is Admiral Murphy and I order you to steer five degrees to the south.'

'This is Captain Campbell and I repeat, Move five degrees to the south!'

'This is Admiral Murphy of the Royal British Battleship, Arizona and I order you to steer five degrees to the south!'

'This is Captain Campbell, of the Royal British Lighthouse, Random Point and I order you to steer five degrees to the south!'

Chittister concluded the story with, "Point: not all wisdom lies in rank!" Her excellent analysis of the patriarchal system and how it fails, held the packed hall speechless that evening.

Father Tom Doyle, canon lawyer and chaplain in the US navy, spoke the following day. He described the last eight to ten years in which the Church had been forced begrudgingly to face the facts of clergy sexual abuse yet continued to minimize, deflect, and stonewall the entire issue. I cornered him for a few minute later and asked which canon lawyer in the UK might help me. He shook his head wearily and said in a low voice, "No canon lawyer in the UK will take your case."

"Why is that?" I asked naively.

"Because they would loose all chances of promotion if they did." Then he added, "Don't expect anything to come from a Church hearing. You'll be disappointed."

I heard that same statement over and over from people who had tried. A. W. Richard Sipe, another keynote speaker and author of *A Secret World: Sexuality and the Search for Celibacy* and *Sex, Power and Priests,* gave evidence of massive reluctance by Church leaders to deal with abuse by their own members. I felt that my superiors would be strong and help turn this around—after all, we were dedicated to the liberation of women.

I met Frank Fitzpatrick, survivor of the infamous Father James Porter. Fitzpatrick challenged victims who had signed gag orders on their church settlements to break the silence and even go public. I wondered if the Redemptorists would try that on me. I swore I'd go on welfare before I'd ever sign a gag order.

Immediately after the conference, I flew to Winnipeg to meet with both Sister Mary Ellen and Sister Rolande. I arrived at the provincial office excited to tell them about my therapy with Cheryl Bell-Gadsby and my experiences at the LINKUP conference.

After listening to me for a few short minutes they switched the subject to my life in Labrador. They empathized with the difficulties I had faced there and then for the third time asked me what I wanted. Yet again the same question; *"Sister, what do you want?"* Weren't they listening? I had never wavered or equivocated. "I've told you," I stated once again. "I want to move ahead immediately with my case and I want to go back to Labrador." Briefly, I explained the Criminal Code commentary about defamation. I requested that they seek legal advice and educate themselves on clergy abuse.

Their eyes glazed over. They shifted in their chairs and shuffled their papers.

Then I said, "I'd like to have someone else appointed to handle my case, Rolande. That way you can be my provincial instead of the dual roles of provincial and advocate." They smiled indulgently.

Sister Mary Ellen spoke up then. In her calm detached voice she said, "I think you are vengeful. I think you want a civil suit and, in fact, I think you want to find other victims so that you can bring forth a class action suit."

My brain went into overdrive; she was telling me what she *thought* I wanted. I had never asked to have Goodall jailed, castrated, or even dismissed from the priesthood for that matter. Still, she found it necessary to label me vengeful. If anything, I felt I had been too gentle, too lenient. When I recovered I retorted, "a class action suit never crossed my mind."

In my mind I thought, *what a great idea.* Out loud I continued, "I am more than willing to go through the civil process if there's no other way to get a safe hearing." I mustered all my strength and asked Sister Mary Ellen directly, "what makes you think I am vengeful?"

"You have a tone about you," she snapped.

"A tone?"

"Yes."

I sat, dumbstruck—too paralyzed to go on. The strength I'd felt at the LINKUP conference seeped down to my feet and into the floor boards. Goodall's favourite manipulation had been 'pushy'. Now Sister Mary Ellen, the woman appointed to look out for me, labeled me 'vengeful.' I came within inches of simply walking out. Looking back, I think I should have. However, I restrained myself knowing that walking out would have given them justification for the label. Anything I did seemed to give them justification.

Sister Mary Ellen continued. "We will not use the legal system for this."

Apparently, my superiors had contacted Father Francis Morrisey—an internationally recognized canon lawyer in Ottawa. He informed them that it would cost a minimum of $100,000 to bring this to trial.

Sister Mary Ellen added, "However, if you want to go that route it is possible for you to get an *exclaustration* for a few years and then return to the congregation."

"What good is that since I have no money?" I asked.

"We are prepared to give you $40,000."

I wondered what I could possibly do with that amount if the estimated cost was more than double the amount offered. Moreover, how would I support myself plus go through a trial? I shook my head. That offer was totally inadequate. Furthermore, I did not have the stamina to do both—leave the order *and* pursue this case all at once. I needed help. Couldn't they see that?

Sister Rolande introduced a new topic. "We want you to consider taking a psychological assessment," she stated. They both emphasized that I was obsessed with this case and seemed to have little time for anything else.

I reminded them that I had held a full-time job and done additional work for Labrador Legal Services. I was in excellent physical health. Where did they get the impression that I had little time for anything but this case?

Neither of them responded. Nothing I said swayed them in the least. They were adamant. They were obviously afraid and intimidated by the men of the Church. I was drowning, and they wouldn't swim out to help me fearing they too would be sucked under.

I explained that Bell-Gadsby had been very positive about my mental health. I asked Sister Rolande to speak with her directly.

At one point, Sister Rolande, in tears, said; "I have little time for McManus but a lot of time for you, Yvonne."

Inside I screamed, *so why don't you help me!* Time for me? I refused to accept that. I felt I was becoming her caregiver—going easy on her and grateful for every crumb. I had done enough of that with Goodall.

She went on to say, "This case is very heavy on me. I'm doing it only because it is my job as provincial." Then came the most devastating comment of all. "Because I have to face issues all day in the office, I can't face more in the evenings. Yvonne, you'll be talking a lot about this. I want you to move out."

My heart contracted and my world fell apart. My only home in the whole world, and I was told to move out. Where was I supposed to go? I had no place to rest my head in Labrador, and now I had no place in Manitoba. Is this what a homeless person feels like? Thrown from place to place? Always begging for the necessities of life?

I sat absolutely still. All I could hear was my heart pounding in my ears. I looked at Sister Mary Ellen. Her face was blank.

Either they had agreed on this ahead of time or Sister Mary Ellen saw nothing strange in a superior ordering a sister to move out without giving her an alternative place to live. I was shocked and disgusted. I felt utterly betrayed. No one had stood up for me when my father molested me, and now no one blinked an eyelash when I was told to move out.

So why did she say she had lots of time for me? She didn't even want me under the same roof. I felt like that mouse again at the mercy of lions. I had no supporters—they all clawed at me for being a victim.

Sister Mary Ellen and Sister Rolande repeatedly suggested the Southdown Institute near Toronto as a good place for my psychological assessment. I feared any institute that was closely associated with any church. I suspected that in the final analysis they were more loyal to the Church than to the victims.

I asked what sources of information they had on me and my mental health since neither lived near me. No response. It seemed I was expected to respond to their questions but they gave me only evasions. After two and a half hours of grilling, they asked that I reflect on their offer for assessment during our summer days at Camp Morton. They then ordered me to meet with them immediately after. They pledged their concern and support. I staggered out of there feeling rotten, sick, humiliated. Did they hear me? Did they care?

Something broke within me that day. I had entered that meeting with my superiors enthusiastically, certain they would stand by me as a victim of clergy abuse. I had left, destroyed and homeless. For the first time since becoming a nun, I thought about leaving. Never had I felt so abandoned, so betrayed, so alone. I put on my survivor's mask, determined they would never see me cry again. They would never see me fall apart. A part of me has not yet recovered from that meeting.

During the three days at Camp Morton, I played, laughed, and renewed old acquaintances. I decided I would accept going to the Southdown Institute to prove myself to them.

On my birthday, 11 August, 1994, I met again with Sister Rolande and Sister Mary Ellen. I repeated my question about why Sister Mary Ellen found me vengeful. I was too insecure to tell her that being vengeful might just be healthier for victims than being forgiving. Goodall had put me through several pregnancy scares, an infectious disease, and years of depression. If asking for a proper investigation made me vengeful then perhaps Sister Mary Ellen didn't understand the meaning of the word. She didn't respond to my query. I learned that Sister Rolande had phoned Cheryl Bell-Gadsby only to find she was on holiday.

At this second meeting they stressed the positive. "We want you to be as ready as possible for the day you meet with the investigation team in the UK."

After the meeting, I drove to the St. Boniface residence with Sister Rolande. *En route* she said that since we had talked she felt better. Now she felt perhaps I didn't have to move out—at least not until the next dispute. I didn't respond. I wanted to ask her why she had the right to decide for both of us what a dispute was. What gave her the right to make all the rules for my life?

The next morning without informing Sister Rolande, I picked up my African packsack and hopped a bus to the McMillan convent. I decided I'd stay there instead of a hotel—afraid that a hotel would be misconstrued as a vengeful waste of money by Sister Mary Ellen. While at McMillan, I visited family and friends in the area and prepared for Southdown. I held myself together mainly by rereading my notes from my therapist, Cheryl.

One Flew over the Cuckoo's Nest

There I was chalking up more frequent flier points—this time flying to Toronto for a psychological assessment. One priest, also there for assessment, swore that his affair with his parishioner was consensual. I began to doubt myself again—perhaps I did freely consent to sex with Goodall at Durban. Did I say, I want to have sex with you? Did I imply it? Did I look at him seductively? Did I undress myself? Clearly, the answers to all those questions was *no*. But I still beat myself up wondering, did I do anything that lead him to believe it was consensual?

On Sunday morning I attended mass in the chapel—two stained glass windows peered down on me: both portrayed saintly men. The homily told of more men. I sat there, too miserable to get up and walk out.

The next morning, I met the spiritual director who asked me questions about my relationship with God. There wasn't much positive to report there. Later I completed several long questionnaires for my assessor. My first question to her was, "How does Southdown deal with clergy sex offenders?"

Her curt reply put me off. She said, "Oh, Yvonne, you are here for yourself, let Southdown worry about the treatment of sex offenders."

Why was I expected to trust an institute founded by priests for the treatment of priests? Only years later when the supply of priests had shriveled up, did they allow women inside the doors. Actually they had women there all along—as servants.

During my five day stay, I saw a nurse, a psychiatrist, a spiritual director, and an addictions counselor—each for about forty minutes. The psychologist gave me several more tests: Wechsler Adult Intelligence Scale-Revised (WAIS-R), Rorschach Test, and six others. All the tests seemed to be oriented to Western whites—white urban males.

Several of the women in treatment invited me to a meeting for women only. They had been refused permission to hold the meeting on grounds that this would be divisive. They went ahead anyway and I joined them. One participant complained that at the session on sexual addiction, the presenter had explained the four phases of the male cycle as attraction, involvement, guilt, and then recommitment. He then outlined the female cycle starting with seduction, involvement and, "I don't know the rest." For the remainder of the hour, he spoke only of the male cycle despite the fact that half the participants were female. Some women decided to bring this complaint to the director.

On the fifth day, Sister Rolande came in for the oral report with the psychologist and myself. The psychologist explained to both of us that I had personality disorders—histrionic, compulsive, dysphoric, and dependent, plus a few others. The labels gave me the shudders. Each sounded like a malignant tumor. I wondered how many of my great-grandmothers had been given similar labels in the low countries and suffered drowning or burning at the stake as a result. How many of those witches were simply protesting victimization by a husband or parish priest?

.ˑ. ˑ.ˑ .ˑ.

Once back in Winnipeg, Sister Rolande gave me permission to take the job in Happy Valley-Goose Bay, Labrador. We had never talked about the work in Labrador nor the living conditions. Why hadn't she granted this permission months earlier and saved me the anxiety and terrible feelings of homelessness? Again, I felt like a puppet. With a flick of her wrist Sister Rolande could dangle me or put me down wherever she wanted. Was she deliberately testing my mental equilibrium—keeping me off-balance, and then sending me for treatment so she could close the case against Goodall? I realized I was becoming bitter and suspicious of all authority.

In September, two days before my departure for Happy Valley-Goose Bay, I met with the three members of the Manitoba provincial council, Sister Rolande, Sister Marylyne Gibney, and Sister Leslie Sacouman. Sister Rolande said, "I have no time or energy for the case with McManus, but I have all the time needed for you, Yvonne." Exactly the same statement as in early August with the same tears too!

I insisted that canon lawyers as well as civil lawyers be consulted in the UK, Canada, and Africa. I begged that they check with a lawyer about the possibility of a defamation suit. Three different times I pleaded that they not put my case on hold. Sister Leslie finally said, "Yvonne, You've repeated this three times. We have heard you. We have been listening."

The night before I left for Labrador I wrote in my journal:

I am sad. The Holy Names will not take a strong stand against McManus and Goodall. I think it is time to tell

McManus that if he doesn't have a thorough investigation, I will inform the press.

At dawn the next morning, I flew out of the airport and looked down on the Red River. I could see two people in a canoe paddling upstream. I envied them—their unison. I felt as if my paddles had been snatched out of my hands, and I was left to drift as best I could. A sense of loss and betrayal flooded me. I had not experienced that before in my many previous departures from that airport.

My friend, Shirley Flowers, met me at the Happy Valley-Goose Bay airport. She gave me a place to stay while I searched for a place to live. I wanted to live near my work, knowing I probably wouldn't have a vehicle. My first purchase was a mountain bike which I used to get to the prison and my office everyday.

Shirley introduced me to Evelyn Keener, a gracious teacher who lived alone in a small, comfortable house on Corte Real Street in Happy Valley. Evelyn welcomed me in as a housemate and we soon became a happy household.

The place was perfect. The large westward-facing front window looked out over a forest of birch, tamarack, and black spruce. The sunsets from this window were breathtaking. In the back yard, I was delighted to find a miniature vegetable garden alongside aspen, mountain ash, alders, and Labrador tea bushes. Around the edges of the yard there grew dandelions and crackerberries. In true Labrador fashion, long poles of firewood were stacked vertically in a large teepee shape beside the garage. Not only did the wood dry better this way, but also it was easier to find in the deep snows of winter.

Inside the house I set up bricks and planks as shelving for my books. Evelyn helped me a great deal. Before long she became a major support for me. Finally settled, I had to keep busy. When I wasn't working at the prison or volunteering at the Mokami Status of Women, I embroidered, worked at a correspondence course from McMaster University, went berry-picking, and refined my report for the investigation.

Sunday I attended the morning mass at Our Lady Queen of Peace parish. The homily was a dry theological discourse by a priest who never looked anyone in the eye. I gazed around at the dead-pan faces everywhere. They sang hymns to "Father God." At the "I believe in God the Father almighty . . . ," my eyes fogged over and my throat burned. I biked back to my new home unable to see the road for the tears in my eyes. That was the last time I stepped into that church.

Linda Marcotte was the United Church minister and a feminist I'd met at the Take Back the Night Walk sponsored by Mokami Status of Women. I liked the service she led, but felt empty and lost without the rituals of the Catholic Church. After a few Sundays, I stopped attending church altogether and walked the forest and marshes behind my house instead.

✳ ✳ ✳

In late September, Jenny Fasal wrote that not a single canon lawyer would even read my story. McManus, however, had found two canon lawyers within days of my disclosure. I found this most revealing—victims receive no help, offenders receive plenty.

My work with Legal Services included counseling men individually at the correctional centre, as well as group work with batterers and sex offenders. Things went well, and I was able to recruit co-facilitators for these group sessions.

Fortunately, I found trails through the forest which led from my house and crisscrossed to the correctional centre. Every day before and after work I made a forty-five minute contact with nature. The exercise and the woods never failed to restore my spirits.

The dreaded Southdown report arrived in my mailbox all too soon. I tore it open. The first paragraph amazed me. According to my superiors I had been sent there because I was: *"preoccupied with seeking a more adequate response and appears to devote most of her attention and energy to this issue."*

I thought they had sent me to prepare me for my hearing in the UK? Not only had they pressured me, but they had also used false reasons to get me there. I was far from pleased. Furthermore, I held down a job, a household, and maintained good health, how did they conclude that I spent most of my time on this issue?

The report continued:

The community is attempting to help her rethink her position and consider some period of residential treatment in order to clarify her goals and fortify her for any eventual litigation or inquiry.

So, I was sent there to 'rethink' was I? And to clarify my goals. I had never once deviated from my goal of having an investigation of all the places Goodall worked and lived. Why did I need to clarify my goals yet again? How many times did I have to repeat them before they believed me. If I had said 'drop it all,' would they have pressed me over and over to clarify and rethink? I concluded the real purpose of the assessment was to silence me. Were they out to medicate me, brainwash me into proper female subservience so I'd free them of their responsibility to stand up to the priests?

Her position vis-à-vis testing was somewhat guarded and defensive, with a tendency towards denial and avoidance of self-disclosure.

This from the very psychologist who would not tell me how her institution dealt with sex offenders.

Her feminist perspective notwithstanding, appearances— both social and physical—are important to her . . .

Were feminists not to care about appearances? What was she driving at? She seemed to have a narrow concept of feminism— certainly not my brand.

In fact, there is a discontinuity between her apparent independence of thought and the underlying streak of dependency in her personality. It is her pressure of dependent needs that fuels her perfectionism, her compulsive efforts to do the right thing, and her willingness to accept excessive responsibility in many situations. Her need to be perceived by others as virtuous and composed, as well as to win their support and reassurance, is such that she has tended to defer or submit to them allowing them considerable control, which then only contributes to her sense of resentment and distrust.

Now *that* fit like a glove. My suspicion is that this fits most women in Western society. Women are expected to be dependent, to defer, to submit. Isn't that precisely why we are given first our father's name and then our husband's? Nuns fare no better; we go from father's care to bishop's care. The mother superior is just a cog in the bishop's machine. In all of this, deference and submission made us feminine and acceptable. When we speak up we are labeled shrill, un-feminine, aggressive—castrators.

> While currently not in a major depressive episode, she is nonetheless in greater distress and more depressed than she can recognize or acknowledge, a state that is at odds with her usual public presentation and with her inner sense of self. Whether she suffers from a true dysthymic disorder remains to be determined, but in the present circumstances one can observe glimpses of the sadness and anger that accompany her experience of rejection and betrayal.

They seemed to be waiting for me to fall apart so they could pounce on me and declare me properly ill. God the Father had a similar eye on me—waiting for me to make a mistake so he could punish me. It annoyed me to no end the way the psychologist defined me—telling me that I was more depressed than I could recognize. Hadn't Goodall spent years telling me the same thing? Her analysis implied I didn't know myself at all.

> Likewise her intense focus and preoccupation with the admitted sexual violations by her former retreat director, and with the church's attitude towards women, may be deflecting her attention from core issues that are less social than they are psychological in nature.

According to this theory, Goodall had actually admitted sexually violating me! All Goodall had said to McManus was that "his part" was wrong. That was hardly an admission of sexual violation. My training and experience with sex offenders had taught me that a statement of that nature usually meant grave mini-mization, if not outright denial of the offense. The offender usu-ally sought counseling at that point "to learn how to ward off seductive women and children." Obviously the Southdown asses-sors were not aware of such distortions and believed that "his part" meant admission of sexual violation. I refused to be duped by such language from Goodall and now from Southdown. The psychologist was making assumptions that put Goodall in a posi-tive light and me in a negative one. She had not grasped the issues I was dealing with and by that failure she was compounding my victimization. The director had countersigned the report.

According to the Southdown assessment, the core issue wasn't my victimization by Goodall, and revictimization by the Catholic Church authorities, but rather my obsession. They just didn't get it. Southdown didn't grasp the nature of the cover-up and yet proposed to be able to treat me. This was blatant revictimization by Church-affiliated mental health professionals.

∴ ∵ ∴

Soon after the report reached me I received a letter from Sister Rolande. She wrote:

> For me the report (Southdown) confirms our decision (Yvonne needs residential treatment) and it also shows that you have been badly hurt in the past. I think that the ques-tion is: What do you want for yourself? Do you want to deal with some of your psychological difficulties? Do you want to give attention to the core issues mentioned in the report?
>
> At this time, we the Congregation offers you this oppor-tunity. We ask you to consider some period of residential

treatment at Southdown. We will not pursue the case unless you accept willingly to go to Southdown in January—providing there is an opening . . .

How generous of them to offer residential treatment. They couldn't afford a lawyer, but they could afford treatment. According to them, my main psychological disorders were I didn't trust enough and I was too dependent on the opinions of others. Yet these same people would expect me to go willingly into residential treatment as a condition of pursuing justice in my case—an institutionalization that would clearly undermine my credibility and my ability to get the justice I deserved.

Enclosed in Sister Rolande's letter was a copy of her fax to McManus saying she was putting the process on hold for at least six months so she could do some consultation and research. She ended her letter to McManus with:

Let us support one another in prayer as we continue to try to develop a just, pastoral process within a canonical context.

So despite my pleas, she was putting my case on hold. Her last sentence repelled me. It told me that Sister Rolande was ready to crawl before McManus. She would support him in her prayers and asked him to do the same. The powerful boys had her under their thumb. I knew where that left me—rotting in Labrador.

∴ ❖ ∴

In November, I attended the second meeting of Voices for Non-Violence Advisory Committee in Winnipeg. I was eager to hear from the Baptist Minister again. She brought us up-to-date on

developments with her case of sexual harassment by a parishioner. The parish board had asked her to remove herself for a
time—implying that she was ill and needed healing. Wasn't that
familiar!

While in Winnipeg, Sister Rolande asked to see me along
with her council, Sister Marylyne and Sister Leslie. I insisted on
having an advocate with me. Sister Rolande refused the person I
wanted, so in the end I met with Sister Marylyne and Sister
Leslie alone. They asked me why I needed a support person with
me to meet with the three of them.

"Because the last time I met with the three of you I felt too
vulnerable. You said you'd heard my plea not to put my case on
hold, but you have done exactly that. What research and consulting are you doing? Why won't anyone tell me what is going on?"

I brought up my hurt at being labeled vengeful by Sister Mary
Ellen, and the betrayal at being told to move out of my home by
Sister Rolande. I asked point blank, "If Sister Rolande found it
too hard to see me around the house in the evenings why didn't
she move out?"

I informed them that I would never go to Southdown. I also
said that the closing sentence of Sister Rolande's last letter to
McManus, sickened me. I asked why Sister Rolande didn't get
legal advice on the possibility of my being charged with defamation? They shrugged their shoulders. I continued pelting them
with questions. "I want you to ask the UK exactly what restrictions have been placed on Goodall. Get a canon lawyer for me.
Get legal advice for everyone. I'd ask Sister Rolande again, but
every time I opened my mouth, she got nervous and defensive.
And you know what happened then? I limited myself, I slowed
down, I reduced my requests. In short, I took care of her! I
became her caregiver!" I blew out a big breath then looked
straight at Sister Leslie. I asked, "Why do I need treatment?"

"Because you generalize," she responded flustered. "You make these broad general statements." She did not back up her statement with an example. Was *she* generalizing perhaps?

∴ ∵ ∴

Back in Happy Valley-Goose Bay I prepared an eight page response to the Southdown assessment report. I pointed out that:

> ". . . he admits his part in the relationship with Sister Yvonne was wrong and harmful and apologizes for this," is not an apology but a manipulation so that authorities and psychologists pounce on my back instead of his.
>
> Women aren't allowed to be autonomous in our society and certainly not in the Catholic Church. So indeed I am in conflict constantly. When I expressed some autonomy and questioned Southdown's handling of sex offenders you squashed that soundly.

Meanwhile Cheryl Bell-Gadsby sent me a copy of the assessment she had sent to Sister Rolande. She said she found me articulate, clear and intelligent.

> She is openly confused about the 'conditional' support she has received from her community. On one hand there seems to be support but on the other hand there are also a lot of subtle negative messages that indicate perhaps Yvonne is overreacting to her abuse experience and that she is overly vengeful and motivated by a possible class action suit. There has also been pressure for her to submit to a full psychiatric assessment at Southdown in Ontario which would indicate that

her superiors and members of her community have doubts about her mental state.

Yvonne has displayed many effects and coping mechanism which are completely normal in the context of sexual abuse . . . It is the writer's opinion that Sister Yvonne is not the least bit 'crazy' but that she is merely responding normally to an abnormal traumatic experience. Unfortunately to the untrained eye a lot of these behaviours and emotions can seem 'dysfunctional.' It is also a frustrating fact that the medical and psychiatric professions tend to label and categorize survivors of sexual abuse as 'dysfunctional' rather than realizing that the many coping skills used by these clients are vital to their survival.

I have experienced Yvonne as very motivated to look objectively at her situation in order to reintegrate her experience in a healthy and productive manner. She is a very resilient woman who has continually worked at maintaining and developing her skills and profession as well as participating in other outside interests. I am concerned that Sister Yvonne's feminist perspective and courageous stand against her own abuse and sexual abuse in general, may be misconstrued as 'dysfunctional' as opposed to being a healthy and adaptive way of working through and dealing with her trauma. It is an unfortunate reality that all of us who do this work constantly come up against destructive and stereotypic attitudes toward women and that these attitudes collude with offenders to maintain the secrecy and isolation of the victim.

The writer is also concerned that the repeated questioning of Sister Yvonne's motives and emotional state around her disclosure due to the hierarchical structure of the church and misinformation regarding sexual abuse, will result in Yvonne's revictimization and this can trigger and intensify many of the previously mentioned symptoms and effects of the abuse. . . . that her exploration and vindication of her 'truth' be validated rather than challenged or judged. The collusion and defensiveness of the institution is maladaptive and dangerous.

I dropped the last page to the floor and laid back on the sofa. I looked out at the Labrador sky and wondered how these two reports could be so radically opposite—like I was Dr. Jekyl and Ms. Hyde. Southdown was caught up in the closed mentality of the Church—forgive the powerful offender, blame the weak victim. Then, quickly rehabilitate both to maintain the *status quo* of power and dominance. I concluded I was facing the worst.

A Lead-filled Life Vest

In November, 1994, Sister Leslie phoned. She said, "We have decided to go ahead with your case. Do you know what you want next?"

Did I know what I wanted next! Were they deaf? I was hoarse from repeating myself. I had never altered or faltered in my motives or my goals. I just gritted my teeth and waited for her to go on to more important business. She asked, "Would lawyer Mary Kate Harvie, be acceptable to you? She works for a well established firm here in Winnipeg?"

"What about a lawyer in the UK instead of here in Canada?" I asked.

"We are not considering a UK lawyer at this point."

Her tone confirmed what choice I'd have. It was Harvie or nobody. It felt like one more ultimatum. After eleven months of handling my case for me, they had finally decided to consult a civil lawyer but only in Winnipeg, Canada. I agreed that Harvie could read my material. My journal on that day was written in thick dark print:

> I feel isolated, unwanted, blamed and rejected. What can a lawyer in Winnipeg do for me?

∴ ❖ ∴

Meanwhile, on the local front, I had written Bishop Goudreault regarding my concern for the past and potential victims of one of his active priests. Goudreault wrote back stating that I seemed concerned only for the victims. He reminded me that others had rights also.

He added that my request for information regarding the status of the abuser priest in question was unacceptable and that he was handing my letters over to his lawyers. So my questions were worthy of spending money on lawyers. Great. I felt rather pleased thinking the lawyers would warn the bishop of the repercussions should a current victim come forward.

The last line of his letter said it all, *"You need to take more time for yourself."*

∴ ❖ ∴

Several months had passed since Sister Leslie had contracted Mary Kate Harvie as "our" lawyer and she had not yet contacted me. I became alarmed at this. Exactly whose lawyer was she since my superior would be paying her? It dawned on me that I would be very much secondary. I phoned Harvie to find out her position on all this.

"Who is your client? I asked.

"Sisters of the Holy Names. Well, Sister Rolande Joyal."

At least we had that straight, and I knew where I stood— on sand. "Have you read the correspondence with McManus?" I asked.

"Most of it. I understand your case perfectly."

"How can you?" I blurted, "You have never even spoken to me! What is your background? What experience do you have with sexual abuse?"

I learned she had 8 years experience in civil and criminal cases and had dealt with a few sexual abuse cases including one involving a priest. I became bolder and asked what position she had in the sexual abuse cases.

"Defense," she admitted.

She had been hired by sex offenders to defend them. Why hadn't victims hired her? My guess was that victims couldn't afford her or any other lawyer. But offenders could. Wasn't Goodall getting top-notch barristers in the UK? What was I getting? This lawyer, 3000 kilometers away, who hadn't even spoken to me up to this point, yet allegedly understood my case.

"Have you told Sister Rolande how defamation of character suits work? She keeps warning me not to talk because she fears I'll be liable for defamation."

"No, that hasn't come up."

After the phone call, I felt as drained and as empty as an Ethiopian rain barrel.

Not a week later Harvie wrote me a very formal letter informing me that I must not incur any costs or make any contracts with any lawyers or advocates without the express permission of my superiors. I figured they must have had a little chat after my call to Harvie.

So again I felt controlled; my superiors sat idly by, and when I pushed for information they threatened me. They knew that for 36 years I had kept my vows of obedience and poverty. They wanted to make sure I didn't deviate now.

⁘ ⁙ ⁘

Margaret Kennedy had found a sympathetic barrister in the UK. Margaret McCooey showed interest in my story. Immediately I asked her to check into the statute of limitations in the UK. She told me that her husband, Andrew, usually handled the court cases, and said he would be glad to read my material. I agreed to this like a fish gasping for the sea.

Andrew McCooey phoned a few weeks later. "I've read your story," he said. He felt my case could go to both criminal and civil courts.

"I don't have a good grasp of your case yet, but Yvonne, you have been horribly abused. I need to study it more. Would you say Frank Goodall took advantage of your naïveté—your training in the Church where women are submissive, and that you acquiesced to him? Goodall is obviously experienced at this!"

"Yes!" I sighed with relief. This lawyer validated me unlike Harvie who "understood perfectly," but refused to make a comment on the abuse itself. I also felt ashamed that I had acquiesced. I did not like to see myself as submissive and weak. When I hung up, I was affirmed by his analysis of the abuse but I also worried he might think me dirty.

On Feb. 23rd, 1995 I wrote in my journal:

Elie Wiesel once said, 'the silence of the bystander hurts the victim most.' I've sent my story to some twenty people. Only a few wrote back supporting me. What happened to my otherwise caring, compassionate friends when I brought up clergy sexual abuse? Don't they believe me? One wrote back that it takes two to tango. Murder also takes two!

Dad and I used to tango—actually, it was old time waltz but the principle is the same—two people dancing. Did that automatically mean both dancers were having a good time?

That was another assumption I had long thrown out but obviously others held fast that abuse never happened between two adults who danced. Naive isn't it? Only the powerful who have not experienced these multitudinous "small" abuses can make such assumptions. Well no. Perhaps the powerless like to cling to an illusion of equality so they don't need to face their own oppression. They can smile on, forgive forever and forget forthwith.

That week I wrote Sister Leslie informing her that I did not feel Harvie was competent to handle my case. I also expressed my hurt at the letter from Harvie reminding me that I must not incur costs without their permission. I had never broken that rule.

It took SNJM one full year before consulting a lawyer in Canada where the case is not to be heard. It took J. McManus about a week to find an experienced legal lawyer in the UK where the case will be heard. When I asked Sister Rolande on the phone last week if I am to go to a canonical hearing in UK without a canon lawyer to advise me, she said yes.

By return mail, I received a response signed by all three authorities in Winnipeg. The letter told me that Harvie was part of a well-established and respected agency and that they would retain her services. The letter ended with ". . . *As a provincial administration, we stand with you in your struggle to attain justice, to heal, and to ensure that further abuse is not perpetrated by Goodall.*"

They called it my struggle, but they dictated the means and likely even the end result. Certainly it felt to me that they were the worst part of my struggle. McManus had become a background figure by comparison. My agony was with the sniveling, sucking-up behaviour of my own. They claimed to support me, held all the power, and seemed determined to come out of this looking good in the eyes of the Church hierarchy. They'd take care of it all right—*we took care of that unhealthy troublemaker. Now, is there anything else we can do for you, boys?* While I was drowning, they were throwing me a lead-filled life vest.

About that time, Margaret Kennedy phoned from the UK to say she had a confusing letter from Mary Kate Harvie telling her she could not make any contract or incur any costs with me without the express permission of Sister Rolande Joyal. Margaret felt this was threatening language to use on her. She, Jenny Fasal, Bishop Budd and Father Ralph Brown, a canon lawyer, planned to meet that week to discuss my case. I authorized her to show them my Southdown assessment as well as Cheryl Bell-Gadsby's assessment.

Sister Rolande requested that I cancel that meeting on grounds that it would bring my case to the level of Bishop. I did no such thing.

There seemed to be more action with my advocates in the UK than with my superiors in Canada. I was thrilled with the news of the proposed meeting and since it was all free, I hadn't broken my vow of poverty. I wasn't so sure about obedience. Someone had once said that if your conscience leads you out of the Church then that is what you must do. I felt this just might apply to me. If no one in my community would stand for truth and justice, then I would do what I had to do. I asked Margaret Kennedy to go ahead with the planned meeting. I felt guilty but strong. Ralph Brown never showed up and later backed out entirely claiming that religious congregations have their own canon lawyers for such cases, fulfilling Tom Doyle's prophecy that no UK canon lawyer would help me.

Finally, at the end of February 1995, after eight months of silence, Sister Rolande sent a fax to McManus saying we had not been told the details of Goodall's suspension from retreat work. She noted that:

> Counseling of offenders is of questionable merit when the counselor has no access to the statements of the victims. We are very concerned that other individuals have been subjected to and may still be subjected to the same abuse to which Father Goodall has admitted he has subjected Sister Maes.

I was not at all convinced that Goodall had admitted subjecting me to abuse. Did Sister Rolande have information that I did not? I doubted it. My theory was that because Sister Rolande had no experience, she made invalid assumptions simply to make Goodall out as a responsible priest. On what she based these leaps of fact I had no idea. My impression was that Goodall was letting on to McManus that he (Goodall) was really the victim of my seduction. "His part" could well mean that he allowed himself to be seduced by me—and regretted that.

What Rolande wrote in this fax was far from complicated. Why had it taken eight long months to produce?

Within two weeks McManus wrote back:

> Thank you for your letter of 20th February, 1995 . . . our solicitor advised that: Given the delays, the personal involvement of Sister Rolande, the unspecified nature of their proposed consultation and research and the absence of reciprocity from Sister Yvonne, I am doubtful that any form of enquiry, Tribunal or investigation could now do justice to either party.

What about his own personal involvement, his research and consultation? How did these have any affect an enquiry? His letter was pure stonewalling of the finest order.

My four superiors requested a two day meeting with me in Montreal in June to look at a protocol—a community stance which they were preparing. So, I thought, they were preparing some process for me. Why were they doing things for me, without me? More alarm bells echoed in my head. I imagined they were setting out a policy that would silence me totally. They were deliberately keeping me in the dark.

They told me there would be a facilitator—of their choice. I insisted that Phyllis Clarke, my neighbour and good friend, participate fully at the meeting as my advocate. I wanted the sessions audio-taped. They accepted Phyllis, but refused the audio-taping. For weeks prior to this Montreal meeting, my stomach heaved and tossed with dread. I decided the time had come. I was determined to fight and fight hard.

Preparing for Battle

As we boarded the plane for Montreal, Phyllis Clarke handed me a hardcover notebook with a Norman Rockwell print on the front. Inside she wrote:

> *Into battle we go!*
> JUNE 14/95, PHYLLIS.

And what a battle it proved to be. We knew neither the location of the meeting, nor the contents of the protocol despite the fact that we had asked weeks in advance. This secrecy increased my fear that my superiors wanted to silence me. It was four superiors vs. one inferior supported by a lay woman. This brought to mind the Mohawks at Oka standing up against the Sureties de Québec—nose to nose.

Phyllis suggested that I make a list of things I considered my bottom line so we could discuss them before we met the superiors. I came up with nineteen items and ended with:

I may choose:
* to cry

- ❖ to refuse to respond, or
- ❖ to *not* make any decisions whatsoever.

As we flew over the Straits of Belle Isle I spotted an iceberg. It looked so small with only one-tenth sticking out of the water. My case was like a tip of that iceberg—a tip of the iceberg of sexual abuse in the Catholic Church.

> ICEBERG
> *Sturdy—shifting*
> *heavy—afloat*
> *growing in dark eons*
> *layer upon layer*
> *century by century.*
> *Invade my space*
> *push me down.*
> *I roll and rise*
> *beyond your lies.*
> *Gag me*
> *and my jagged edges*
> *slice your flesh.*
> *Confine me*
> *I melt free of your clutch*
> *Butt me*
> *and join the Titanic!*

While getting our connection in Halifax we managed to contact Sister Mary Ellen to ask where we should go once we reached Dorval Airport.

"Didn't you receive the priority post I sent eight days ago?"

"No!"

She directed us to a convent in Westmount, Montreal. She was waiting for us there and handed us a copy of the missing information. It was a two page letter saying she had met with the Manitoba SNJM provincial council in April: *"For all of us it seems essential to choose a path of action to bring this case to resolution in a timely fashion."*

For a year and a half they had procrastinated, and now suddenly they spoke about "timely". Whose time? And whose resolution, since I'd been banished from the process? Had it taken them this long to realize that I would not sink into oblivion, and so now they had come up with another strategy to silence me?

> . . . we have worked with Father McManus through Father Francis Morrisey to have a process like the one we envisioned in December 1993 but have not been able to bring to realization. We will give you the details of the plan when we meet with you. We assure you that it provides a person of your choice on the three person panel as well as the option for you to be accompanied by the person of your choice for the panel investigation.

So they had sent a world famous canon lawyer, the great Father Morrisey himself, to negotiate with McManus. McManus wouldn't deal straight with nuns, but the minute a man appeared he became cooperative. They had struck a deal for my good that I had no part in. I'd have my moment in the spotlight all right— just long enough for these chameleons to assure my demise. They could all get on with their lives again, the sooner the better: *"Our objective is to seek a solution in which all concerned will feel that they are choosing life."*

Who were all these concerned parties? Sounded peculiar. Were they really interested in me? My life hadn't counted for much this last year and a half so why this sudden talk about "choosing life?" One called me vengeful, and the other told me to move out. Was that how they chose life for me? The abuse itself had fallen by the wayside, and the discomfort of disclosure had taken over. Perhaps their concern was to prevent a scandal and to reinstate Goodall.

We do not agree to tape the session. However, at the end of the session we will come to an agreement on a written statement that will summarize where we are at the end of our time together.

Was this an ultimatum? Was I being told that I would have to come to some agreement within the two days? What if I didn't agree with their choices? It all felt rather crazy to me. I began to doubt myself again. Why was I so out of step with these four superiors. According to traditional theology of religious orders, the superiors have a position of power—inspired by the Holy Spirit who promised them wisdom that inferiors did not have. To me this sounded more and more like the powerful preserving their positions and using God's name to do so. Hadn't Europeans used the same theology to prove the divine right of kings in the Middle Ages? I couldn't believe how this entire thing was affecting me. I couldn't trust them anymore. They confused and betrayed me so badly that I was suspicious of every move they made.

That evening Phyllis and I studied the letter. I scribbled in the margins, "Why was I excluded from this process? *Too little, too late.*"

We met at 10 A.M. in a large room with seven school desks set in a circle. After introductions they told us that the meeting would end at eleven the next day.

"I understood this was going to be a two-day meeting," I commented with irritation in my voice. "Had I known it was to end at noon tomorrow, we could have arranged for Phyllis to return home. She has five children in her care at the moment."

Elaine Zimbel, a middle-aged Jewish therapist, facilitated the meeting. She asked that we share how it felt to be there. When it was my turn I broke down:

"For months and months I have been left out of these negotiations. The four of you even met together to discuss my case. I was not invited. I have been left to rot while you act on my behalf! Why?"

No response. Silence.

Phyllis shared how she witnessed my deterioration the previous summer after returning from Southdown and Manitoba. She said I was drained of self-confidence and it was obvious that I was struggling just to hold myself together.

When it was Sister Rolande's turn she stated, "It takes me a month to prepare each fax to McManus."

To this I rebutted, "There have been exactly two faxes this entire year. One was simply to say that you needed six months for consultation and research."

"I thought of resigning," she continued, ignoring my comment altogether. Did she want me to feel sorry for her, to back down so that her job would be easier? She certainly was acting as if she was now my victim. I blasted ahead, heedless of her tears, and asked if she had the right to tell me to move out that previous summer.

She said, "I would still ask you to move out but I would do it differently. I need a place to get away from my work."

At that Elaine Zimbel asked who lived in the house first.

"Sister Rolande was there first."

"Squatters rights," she announced and dismissed my question as if we were playing a silly board game.

The silence of the other superiors further shocked me; not one made a comment in my defense. They tacitly consented that making me homeless was appropriate. I realized that I would forever be an outsider to my Holy Names Sisters simply because I had served in remote areas instead of Winnipeg. I belonged nowhere.

Sister Rolande then said, "You moved several times: St. Mary's, St. Ignatius, and then St. Boniface in just a few years."

"Yes!" I responded, annoyed at the implication that I was difficult to live with. "Your predecessor asked me to move from St. Mary's to St. Ignatius while I was studying in Chicago, and when I returned she asked me to find another place to live because St. Ignatius Convent was closing. That is when I moved to St. Boniface."

Sister Rolande seemed surprised at my explanation, but never apologized for the rude accusation.

It was 1:30 P.M. before the "protocol" was handed to me. It was a done deal. No negotiation was permitted. The Redemptorists had already selected all three panelists, despite Sister Mary Ellen's promise that the Holy Names Sisters would select one. I would tell my story at a preliminary hearing in Canada, so the panel and Goodall could read my evidence. Goodall would respond. Likewise I would see Goodall's statement and respond to it. Then there would be a panel hearing by the end of 1995 at which Holy Names and Redemptorists would each be represented by a lawyer. I could have an advocate with me, preferably a canon lawyer, and Goodall would have the same right. I would tell my story first and then Goodall would tell his story. If both of us agreed we could have a "reconciliation."

Their use of the word reconciliation made me wince. They obviously had no notion of what was appropriate for a hearing on clergy sexual abuse, yet they were making the rules for the hearing. Face to face confrontation might be a possibility, but to bring up reconciliation was to pressure the victim into a stance of forgiveness. They seemed to believe the panel hearing would bring me to my senses and I'd kiss and make up.

Parts of the process were improvements on the earlier one, but the panelists were the same three: a Redemptorist, an employee of the Redemptorists and a third chosen by the Redemptorists. This panel was to make recommendations not decisions. They could recommend:

- if there had been abuse or not
- if anything would go on Goodall's record
- if actions needed to be taken regarding Goodall and Maes
- if there would be any payment of costs or damages.

Their recommendations would go to the two provincials who could, in fact, ignore them if they wanted to. Phyllis asked if there was any right of appeal if the hearing and recommendations proved unsatisfactory. Her question was completely ignored.

Sister Mary Ellen said they had spent a lot of time and effort on this protocol, and that this was the best they could do for me. If I chose not to accept this process as it stood, I seemed to have but two options—I could drop the whole thing, or I could leave the order. They did not offer me any money. They would not reveal who they would select as their lawyer, nor would they let me suggest names of lawyers I could trust. Sister Mary Ellen's next comment was:

"Yvonne, if you go ahead with this, I want the team representing the Holy Names to work together in harmony. There must be a spirit of cooperation among the three of you."

I was being given a sermon on submitting to whatever their lawyer thought best. Would they give that lawyer the same admonition? It felt like blind obedience. I had never been good at that and I had no intention of starting then.

Just when I thought there could be no more blows, the most outrageous punch was thrown at me in a sickly, sugary-coated voice. "I do not want you to feel pressured about this as you said you were regarding the assessment at Southdown."

Every hair on my body bristled. Let's see, I had to respond by noon of the next day and she didn't want me to feel pressured?. What a farce!

Later, Phyllis and I went to a nearby restaurant for dinner. I oscillated between rage and depression, while she calmly reflected back the day's traumas. I really wanted to hold out for two weeks before giving a response, but my knees were wobbling.

The next morning at 9 A.M. only one question was allowed; "Do you accept our process?"

"I need more time," I told them.

At this Elaine insisted on a "yes" or a "no" before 11 A.M. Since when did a facilitator have so much power? They must have primed her to force their agenda through. In any case they, not me, paid her, so she needed to dance to their tune or risk her job.

All the candy-coated sermons on "choosing life" and "no pressure" had obviously washed down the St. Lawrence Seaway. I knew that I did not have the emotional strength to simultaneously make a break with my order and handle my case. I felt too exhausted to cope with the amount of stress those changes would require. Furthermore, I was not at all sure the order would give me enough to get on my feet and handle my case—with the possibility of paying lawyers and travel to the UK. In a sense, I was opting for the devil I knew instead of the angel I didn't know. I also knew that going their route would at least give me first hand experience of an internal canonical hearing. That would be turning over new ground, and I could still make other decisions afterwards. By noon I had caved in to their ultimatum.

When everything was over according to their rigid agenda, Elaine insisted on hugs all round. It turned my stomach. These women just steamrollered me into the ground. Each hug jarred my eyeballs—two to tango—two to hug—two for assault. I felt I sold myself to assault for two pieces of silver with each embrace.

.·. ·:· .·.

Once back in Labrador, I needed to find someone to go with me to the preliminary hearing which would take place in Toronto. The protocol advised a canon lawyer. Was this part of the old boys network to keep them employed? When Joan of Arc was tried for witchcraft, sixty-five men were on the payroll. My case seemed to be going that route. Since no canon lawyer in the UK would touch my case, I asked Reverend Douglas Stamp from St. John's Newfoundland. He knew my story and seemed capable. I sent him my materials. He then agreed to be my advocate at the preliminary hearing. Later, when he told me that the preliminary hearing would take about one hour I became nervous. Was I expected to tell my tale of eight years of abuse in *one* hour?

Shortly after he agreed to take my case, Father Stamp asked me who in South Africa might have information on Goodall. I recalled Goodall referring to a Father Kevin Dowling as an

authority figure. Father Stamp told me that he'd write to Kevin
Dowling, Bishop of Rustenburg in South Africa, asking for any
information regarding Goodall. Why hadn't Sister Rolande done
this a year and a half ago? Father Stamp also warned me, "They
could still block us."

"Then I'll go to Cardinal Basil Hume and to the BBC," I
declared.

Father Stamp sent me a list of thirty-five questions for the
preliminary hearing. I felt a big issue was being left out so I
courageously added a thirty-sixth:

"What has been your experience in reporting this for a canonical hearing?"

I was told the interviewer would be the same Father Francis
Morrisey who had worked on the process with my superiors. He
had the sense to insist that I be given the option to reject him as
the interviewer. My superiors had not given me that option. This
gave me the impression that Father Morrisey had a better grasp
of abuse hearings than my superiors. Still, I wondered why they
chose a man, a priest, to interview me. Wasn't there an acceptable
woman somewhere for this?

JOURNAL, JULY 18TH, 1995, HAPPY VALLEY-GOOSE BAY
I caught myself humming while walking home from the correctional centre. I haven't done this in years and years—since
before I met Goodall. I am in good physical shape. I walk a
good half hour through the bush to the prison most days of
the week.

Wind, trees and sky had become my healing. I followed trails
and streams, seldom meeting anyone. It felt safe there, and no
matter how despondent I was with myself or my work, a few
minutes in the bush always seemed to console me.

In early August I flew to Winnipeg for a break. I planned to visit my sister Isabelle. When changing planes in Halifax, I spotted a lobster shop in the terminal. I had a bright idea. For once I was determined to treat my sister and her family, instead of her always treating me. I bought a huge box of live lobsters. I quashed my guilt at spending so much money—one hundred twenty dollars! At three different meals we donned bibs and cracked pincers. The lobsters were a hit!

These were summer days for the Holy Names Sisters of Manitoba. We discussed our vision for the future. Not a word had been said about my case. It felt as if I were carrying a black secret that the superiors did not want others to know about: as if I had AIDS. At the closing session Sister Rolande opened the floor to anyone to take the microphone and share. Several nuns spoke of new work or projects they were undertaking. I listened, then decided, *my turn*. I took the mike and told of my abuse. Not a pin dropped as I finished and walked to my chair. Afterwards several came to tell me they supported me. One asked me, "Why did you go back?"

I felt judged yet again and said, "Good question. Have you a few hours so I can explain?" I handed her my material and asked her to read it carefully. Later she wrote that I should forgive, and that God would take care of Goodall. Nuns had been trained well in submitting to priests and to trust in superiors. My training was wearing thinner than an egg shell. I felt disgusted by the childish trust preached at me. Do priests preach at each other in this fashion? Had Jesus sat down quietly and let God take care of the Pharisees?

∴ ❖ ∴

After a day of sailing the Toronto waterfront with a friend, I met my canon lawyer, Father Stamp, for the first time. He was a small, slender, dark-haired man with a deep voice and a big position as chancellor of the archdiocese of St. John's, Newfoundland. He was also pastor of St. Theresa's Parish at Mundy Pond. We ate at a local restaurant. It was a humid Toronto evening and I was nervous, knowing that his input would be crucial. After the meal, we walked along the lakefront. Father Stamp listened and shared well. I felt he believed me. He asked what I intended to do after the UK hearing.

"I'll watch to see whether they will investigate the places Goodall worked, and what kind of disciplining he gets. If I am not satisfied I'll take other actions."

Father Stamp then told me a story about another victim of a priest, a young boy, whose parents continued to make contact with the priest offender while he was in treatment. "The priest had been a close family friend, and they couldn't seem to let go of him and move on with their lives; the empty space needed filling," commented Father Stamp.

Was he telling me to let the panel make their recommendations and then trust McManus to deal with Goodall? Was he hinting that I best drop out of sight after the hearing: leave the offender and his supporters in peace—trust them to act justly?

The next morning we met at the Redemptorists' provincial house for coffee with Father Morrisey. I looked at them and thought, how can they be neutral? I am bringing a complaint against one of their brothers.

Father Morrisey was a tall, sturdy man. He wore a Roman collar—that irked me. Everyone seemed nervous, myself included. I smiled when I did not want to.

My story took three hours. The hardest part was telling about the blister, the pornographic pictures and the pregnancy scares.

The messiest part was trying to explain my dependence on Goodall's affirmation; no words seemed adequate to express that: "In my lifetime I had warded off my father and a date rape, but not Goodall, even though I was forty-six. I was so grateful not to be pregnant, that I determined to move on and get the relationship right."

"Was there ever a pregnancy?"

"No," I replied. Would they hold this as a plus for Goodall? Would they believe that since Goodall spared me an unwanted child that he was therefore a caring man and deserved credit not condemnation?

At the end Father Morrisey asked, "Would you consider yourself a Catholic?"

I answered him honestly. "A Christian maybe but not a Catholic. No. Not anymore." The words hung in my throat and then encircled me like a heavy funeral shroud. I had lost so much.

"The important thing in all this is that you need to get on with you life," repeated Father Stamp. He'd brought this up twice already. I knew I had to get on with my life. What did they think I was trying to do? How could I do that if I was stuck in this quagmire of abuse and cover-up? He seemed to be steering me away from any further action beyond a hearing in the UK. Why was he not encouraging me to go public or to the legal system? Why didn't he suggest that he make public statements regarding my case?

After the interview ended, I felt hollowed-out like an abandoned canoe, and exposed to the world for its pity and wrath. I waited, half expecting Father Morrisey or Father Stamp to show signs of disgust for me, for my rot. They didn't. Then I wondered if they were simply good at masking their feelings. I knew only time would tell how they really felt—how far would they support me? I was suspicious of everyone.

JOURNAL, AUGUST 14, 1995, TORONTO
Couldn't control Goodall's sexual behaviour.
Can't control how the church disciplines Goodall.
But I will make it miserable for them.

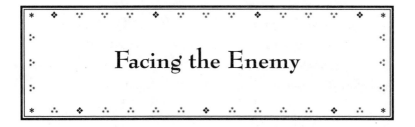

Facing the Enemy

I handed the immigration official at Heathrow my passport and thought *what a dull job it must be sitting in that high chair eight hours a day checking passports.* How many ways did he have of phrasing the same question?

"Why are you coming to England?" he asked in a monotone.

"For a hearing," I replied just as flatly.

"What kind of hearing?" he queried.

"A clergy sexual abuse hearing." I emphasized clergy. I thought this might give him something to tell his co-workers at break: *"I had this woman come through my queue today and you'll never guess why she was traveling to the UK?"*

He snapped the passport closed and handed it to me without making eye contact. I had been wearing civilian clothing since I left Africa. I wore brown corduroy slacks, a tan-coloured winter parka, and a bright red scarf. My hair had become dark brown. I kept it short and wavy. My weight remained steady at 140 pounds.

I swam through the sea of people and made my way to the luggage carousel. I picked up my bags, then waited for my sister Clarisse. She said she'd stand by me during the hearing. She was scheduled to arrive just one hour later. My distrustful mind wasn't going to count on her actually arriving. I would understand her not wanting to be there. Maybe this abuse was just my latest platform, as Goodall had put it. Perhaps I should just take the next flight back to Labrador and get on with my life.

When she did indeed appear, I let out the same uncontrolled high-pitched croak as I had eleven years earlier when she came to visit me in Maseru, Lesotho. I croaked in disbelief that anyone would care enough to be with me during this ordeal.

We chattered loud and fast on the top level of the double-decker bus from Heathrow to Euston Station—giddy with fatigue, but determined to make up for our eighteen months apart. The Northern Line took us to Camden Town where Sister Elaine Kelly and three other sisters welcomed us at Holy Rood Convent. Elaine, a friend from the Chicago days, knew the reason for my visit to London. After a short nap, Clarisse and I explored the canal walkways as darkness and dampness descended.

The next day, Sunday, we strolled along the Thames at Embankment to the Egyptian sphinx that faced Cleopatra's Needle. As I stood there, I recalled 1987. I told Clarisse, "Goodall brought me and three African sisters here in 1987. I was so confused then. I saw no light at the end of the tunnel. Maybe retracing my steps will rework the memories."

Clarisse smiled at me compassionately. "I bet it was confusing," she reflected. She looked up at the statues. "The sphinx has a woman's head. Isn't she supposed to pose riddles?"

"Yeah. And you know what mine was in '87? Why can't Yvonne straighten out her relationship with Goodall?"

"I suspect you have the answer now, don't you?" Clarisse leaned on the sphinx's shiny black paw.

"Yeah, I guess I do. Goodall had a hidden agenda and it didn't include chastity."

Next I paid a visit to Scotland Yard. I asked for their sexual assault squad. I wanted to rehearse walking into a police station to lay sexual assault charges just in case. It was Sunday so the man kindly gave me a phone number.

On Monday I had lunch with Margaret Kennedy and then tea and cakes with Margaret and Andrew McCooey at the Grosvenor Hotel, Victoria Station. My nervousness about meeting these two lawyers disappeared within minutes after their arrival. Both had an easy, gracious way about them. After tea, we moved quickly to the Jubilee Room at the House of Commons for Lord Longford's ninetieth birthday reception. Longford had spent much of his life visiting prisoners sentenced to life—prisoners who had no visitors. The hundred guests sipped champagne and milled about.

When I told Lord Longford why I was in the UK, he said, "May I kiss you, or would that be abusive?" I was so stunned that I acquiesced. The old lectures of *don't hurt a man's feelings, don't create a scene, you should be flattered* filled my head. He kissed me on the lips.

That was the second time an older man asked to kiss me after learning about my victimization by a priest. Did they want to comfort me—like a father? Lord Longford at least recognized the possibility that this could be another form of invasion. I felt uncomfortable the rest of the evening. I wondered if I'd do any better with invasive questions from the panel members or the lawyers?

The next day, Clarisse agreed to accompany me to Our Immaculate Lady of Victories Church at Clapham Common. Goodall had sent me a cassette tape from there in 1986. McManus had used this address also. They might both be there that very day. I wanted to see this residence and the adjoining church for myself, hoping this would reduce my fear of being in the same building as Goodall at the hearing. Mass was scheduled for noon. At 11:45, I sat in the back of the church. Fortunately my jacket had a hood. I peeped from under it only enough to see who stepped out to the altar and lectern. Was it Goodall? A slight man with a mop of curly white hair walked out. Goodall was taller and heavier but perhaps just as white by now: I hadn't seen him in seven years. After a few minutes I left the church. I felt proud and strong, knowing I could enter the living space of both McManus and Goodall without falling apart.

We stopped at a pub on the corner for a cup of soup.

"What brings you to Clapham, all the way from Canada and Camden Town today?" asked the proprietor, a young woman.

"I've come to report a monk from the church next door for sexually abusing me," I replied carefully articulating every word. She did not blink.

"Jolly good. I'm glad these things are coming out."

That afternoon, I sought out a photocopier and paid £20 to duplicate my materials for the hearing. Then I purchased the 1995 Catholic Directory of England and Wales. It lists all the priests, parishes, and organizations related to the Church. Sisters were not listed. There was little doubt in my mind that I would need this information in the future, and I intended to be prepared.

The next two days were delightful. We took in the musical *Crazy For You,* toured the National Portrait Gallery, and enjoyed a meal at Cafe Rouge in Soho. Friday morning the sun shone as I strode down Hampstead Heath to Jenny Fasal's flat. The lifting mists made the morning magical. We strolled Primrose Hill, a minor royal park overlooking London. That evening, six women met for supper; three had histories of sexual abuse by a professional.

I slept fitfully that night wondering how I'd face Goodall the next day. I didn't know what I was up against. Would he tell the panel that I had consented, or that I had seduced him? Long before dawn, I sat up and scribbled out some questions, one for each panelist and lawyer who would judge my case. It didn't help me sleep but it was therapeutic all the same.

By 7:30 A.M. December 9, Clarisse and I were on the Underground rumbling southward to Wimbledon. The panel members had arrived before us. McGreevy showed me around with nervous deference. I did my share of smiling. Father Stamp, Clarisse, and I were given a large comfortable room in one wing of the conference centre. This was the private hearing agreed upon by my superiors. Unfortunately they would not allow Clarisse to either participate or sit in. She felt angered at the exclusion. I felt like this was one more regulation imposed to intimidate victims from coming forward.

The hearing room was large with nine desks and chairs placed in a circle. I sat across from the panel, and Father Stamp sat on my left, Father Morrisey on his left. Hawthorne handed me two booklets of photocopied documents as I walked in. They contained letters and material that I had no time to browse, let alone study.

Crowley introduced everybody and asked me to tell my story. I started with the first meeting with Goodall on that infamous retreat in Durban so many years and miles away. As I moved along, I picked up strength and my voice became louder. I never cried or stumbled. The first three hours were simply telling my story; I passed out the eleven pages of quotes stapled together and then as each appendix came up I handed it along. I felt organized yet frustrated. My head swam with a sizzling barrage of voices, like ghosts hauntingly saying:

Yvonne, you have no scars—you seduced! You went back— you consented. Women are responsible—to blame! Boys will be boys—priests are just human. He protected you from pregnancy! Confidentiality first—scandal helps no one. Not all priests are bad—it takes two to tango. You are vengeful— half-demented! Get on with your life—he's learned his lesson. A priest is a priest forever—you generalize. Rethink your goals—you waited too long. Forget the past—move out. You are not the woman I first met—vitriolic, punitive.

In the fourth hour, each person could make comments or ask questions. Father Morriscy started, "Her statement is consistent with her preliminary inquiry. Very consistent."

Father Davey asked about my celibacy, "You said that you compromised celibacy with others on a few occasions."

"Yes. Until that retreat at Durban, this had never included sexual intercourse."

Mrs. Gallagher asked, "Did you see this as breaking celibacy?"

"Yes, clearly, and I took steps to change. I managed much better with others, but with Goodall I tried over and over to get sex out of the relationship, but it only got worse," I replied, feeling both disturbed and ashamed.

Then Hawthorne spoke up saying, "You are bringing in new material here. How do you expect Fr. Goodall to be able to respond?"

I must have looked as bewildered as I felt. Father Stamp stepped in quickly, "These are Goodall's letters to her and she has referred to them in her deposition. This is not new evidence!"

Hawthorne continued, "When did you write out these quotes?"

"Two or three weeks ago."

"How can you remember the events so well! Some happened ten years ago?"

"They were traumatic events. I remember them very well indeed." In fact, I had written the story out two and a half years prior, but had pulled out the quotes just a few weeks earlier.

"Why would you tell Fr. Goodall about incest early on in your retreat? You would have to build trust first?" questioned Hawthorne. Obviously he'd not been trained as a nun.

I frowned at the stupidity of the question. Father Stamp spoke up, "It is normal and even expected that retreatants tell their issues to the director very early on in the retreat."

"Even the first or second day?"

"Yes. Even the first or second day!"

"Why didn't you tell someone earlier than 1993?" he asked.

I was stunned by the question. I had made clear my reasons for that in the three hours of my story. I knit my eyebrows wondering how I could phrase a response to such an ignorant question. Did he ask Goodall why he hadn't report himself to his superiors and the police immediately? Or why he waited all these years before admitting anything at all? Why are victims held responsible for reporting?

"I thought it was my fault and that somehow I was responsible. And anyway, who would listen to me?"

In fact I had told my confessor—who saw no abuse in a retreat director having sex with a retreatant. He saw it as a breach of celibacy for both. Under the stress of the hearing, I had totally forgotten to raise this point. Neither Father Stamp nor Father Morrisey pointed it out either.

Father Stamp then intervened with, "The Provincial of the King William's Town Dominicans did report sexual abuse by Fr. Goodall in 1986 and was not heard. Sr. Yvonne would have received the same treatment. That is why she did not tell."

"You cannot answer for Sr. Yvonne," snapped Hawthorne.

"I can enlarge on her response," retorted Father Stamp.

"Only with consultation."

Hawthorne then launched into a story, "A man and woman at a bar are drinking and he is bigger and stronger. Then they have sex. This relationship goes on for three or four years. Can she then report him for rape at the first instance because he was stronger?"

I refused to be caught in his ridiculous example. I said, "I don't know about your example. What I do know is there was no alcohol involved. This was a retreat and not a bar. Goodall was the director and I was the client. He had certain responsibilities and I trusted him to fulfill them." The crude comparison annoyed me. He was miles off track—a retreat and a bar put into the same basket! Only one panel member *asked* a question. It was a simple question about my past life and not about the abuse or its impact. Were they out of their depth? Had they done any preparation for this hearing?

∴ ∵ ∴

Father Stamp brought Clarisse and me a tray of sandwiches and some hot soup. He ate quickly, then left saying he wanted to hear what the others were discussing in the dining room. Suddenly, it hit me like a brick in the forehead—once again I was excluded from my own process. Others were sitting together in the main dining room while Clarisse and I ate in isolation.

While Goodall testified, Clarisse and I walked the town of Wimbledon. Part of me badly wanted to face him, but another part was ashamed and afraid. It angered me to still want his affirmation. It was so confusing. I feared that if I did face him the panel and others would call it a "reconciliation" as they had in the procedure outline. This was about confrontation—that much I wasn't confused about.

Late in the afternoon, Father Stamp came to ask if I would agree to a reconciliation meeting with Goodall in front of the entire panel.

"This is not about reconciliation," I insisted. "Make it clear that I am prepared for a face to face confrontation, but I do not want this to be in any way seen as a reconciliation!" I felt feverish despite the cool room.

Father Stamp came back a few minutes later and said they were ready for me to meet Goodall. I asked if Clarisse could attend this, at least.

"No, but there is nothing saying she can't listen at the door," Father Stamp replied with a wink and an impish grin.

Clarisse, feeling she had been barred from the entire process solely for the comfort of the offender said, "I want to hear every word, Yvonne. I'll be at that keyhole!"

I squared my shoulders and walked to my chair. I looked Goodall in the eye as he entered. I didn't smile but I did nod at him. He wore a light blue suit. I felt a flash of pity for him thinking he must be dying from embarrassment—his face bright red. The flash of pity passed quickly. I determined not to spare his feelings at the expense of truth. I closed my eyes for a moment overwhelmed with sadness at my loss—all that nurturing and hope, his original promise of kindred spirits—they evaporated forever before my eyes.

Crowley looked at me ever so kindly and said, "Father Goodall has something to say to you."

So this *was* about reconciliation and not about confrontation! Would I even have a chance to speak? Was this a trick to silence me? If I walked out, would they accuse me of being vengeful, uncooperative, untruthful—just as Goodall had?

Father Stamp stepped in quickly. "Sister Yvonne needs to speak first!"

The chair nodded her agreement. They had no process in place—were they just winging it? I felt that I was in the hands of amateurs who had the right to decide my fate—like interns performing triple bypass surgery. I took a deep breath, looked straight at Goodall then launched in.

"I want you to know a few things," I began. "You made me special on retreat and led me to believe this was to be friendship. You then turned it into sex. I did not want the sex. I said I didn't want to be pregnant and you just went right ahead. My fears didn't count. Only your needs mattered. You undressed me. I did *not* undress you. When I left that retreat, I had a vaginal infection and a panic about pregnancy. You were annoyed that I wanted you to phone me. Then you were annoyed when I would not go to a hotel with you. But before that, you dismissed me because you thought I had broken your need for secrecy." I stopped long enough to take a breath. "Then you were annoyed because I didn't stop the van and cuddle you. You were angry because I had other male friends. When I told you I burned your self-portrait, you exploded. Why did you lie to me over and over? You didn't hear me. You just told me what to do. You talked and joked so much I couldn't get a word in."

Goodall sat pink and silent. He didn't respond, so I continued, "Do your superiors know you had a gun? I bet they never knew. That you practiced not to ejaculate? How many other women have you abused?"

He looked at me pleadingly and turned up his palms in supplication.

There was a pause and Sister Crowley interjected, "Frank would you like to say something?"

Goodall crossed his chest with both arms and said ever so gently, "I'm sorry for hurting you. I hope your life gets back on track."

I shot back, "Sorry for what? A few weeks ago you wrote the panel that you were in counseling because of *my* punitive behaviour! In your last letter to me you told me I was sick and half-demented. Now you say you're sorry!"

"I felt guilty about the failure in celibacy," he responded.

"You never told me that. Just the opposite. You were angry at me for questioning your sexual behaviour. You showed no shame or guilt to me. So what are you in counseling for?" I demanded, looking directly at him.

No response.

"Does your therapist know what you've done?" I demanded.

"She does now. She has all the reports."

"What reports?" I didn't trust that either Goodall or McManus had given her my entire story. No one responded. "Does she have the one telling about the anal rape?" I put emphasis on *anal* and *rape,* and swept my eyes over everyone in the room. I felt dreadful saying this in front of six men and two women. But I knew this would be my one and only chance to speak. I had waited many years for this. I was not going to curb myself for their comfort. Dead silence.

I waited. Then, feeling the need to appear somewhat gentle I broke the silence. In retrospect, I regret doing that—I had taken care of others again and let Goodall off the hook.

"So you never told your therapist the story. Remember when I said 'Sex was not on my agenda'? You answered that you had 'an open agenda?' I felt so stupid when you said that. I felt the sex was all my fault." My whole body shook.

"Yvonne," Goodall finally spoke up, his blue eye peering from his pink face. "How can you feel stupid, you have two degrees."

That caught me off guard. I couldn't see the connection. I felt stupid again. Was he defining me as stupid for having felt stupid? Had anyone noticed how he deflected my question?

"So celibacy doesn't matter to you, does it?" I asked.

"It does now."

"And how come you know so much about sex?" I continued.

"I told you about the nurse."

"And the other women, the other victims?"

At this Goodall threw up his hands in innocence and rolled his eyes.

Crowley intervened, "Yvonne do you accept this?"

I sat stunned. What exactly was I expected to accept? Did she think this was an apology?

This was not acceptable at all, so I continued. I repeated, "Why did you lie to me? I haven't been able to make retreats—I haven't been to mass in two years."

I went on for some minutes until it all felt too futile to continue. I was not getting through to anyone. They wanted this to be an apology and a reconciliation. They had a fixed agenda. I refused to cooperate.

Crowley thanked us all for our time and courage in coming to this hearing. I stood up and walked out immediately without a word or a nod. I fled to find Clarisse and wailed uncontrollably in her sturdy arms. The sounds that escaped from my throat were loud and foreign to me. Then I stiffened up, pushed her to arms length and looking her in the eye. "I was great! You can be proud of me. To hell with what they think of me!"

Father Stamp affirmed that I had indeed done well, I had spoken clearly and forcefully. "If they did not hear you that is their problem. You did a fine job. And now you can get on with the rest of your life."

There it was again. I had become suspicious of people who tried to hurry me.

As we walked to the Underground station in the dark, Clarisse described what she'd heard. "I stayed glued to that keyhole except when someone came along the hallway. Then I pretended I had to tie my shoes. I'd hear your voice, then some quiet and then you'd start again with *rat-a-tat, rat-a-tat.*" She flapped her hands in the air giving wings and power to my *rat-a-tat*. Several times we stopped on the sidewalk in fits of laughter. I had to wipe my eyes watching her describe her key-hole story.

She then added soberly, "Yvonne, they all looked scared! It was clear they never dealt with this before. They don't know what they're doing. It's sad. I think they still protect the priests. I doubt you'll get anywhere with this hearing. You were a very, very credible witness but their loyalty will be with the men and not with you—you nuns have little power in the Church. No, they'll make some gesture of discipline, and then Goodall will be on the loose again and no one will know." She paused watching my face. "Furthermore, I get a funny feeling Father Stamp wants you to forget this just like your superiors do. Why else is he suggesting you get on with the rest of your life?"

"I agree. Truth is, I have lots of options left and I intend to use every single one." I felt weary but determined. "They all want me to get on with my life? I will. I figure I have a good twenty years left in me, and I plan to use them exposing clergy abuse. It probably won't end, but at least it'll be out in the open. Someone has to stand up. Imagine, a little farm girl from Manitoba challenging the Church!"

The thought gave me chills. I was reminded of a photograph taken by Paul Weinburg. It was of a black servant woman in South Africa standing between two armoured trucks waving her fists at the soldiers and their guns. I felt like that woman waving my fists at the sisters on one side and at the priests on the other. They'd be just a little less comfortable with me around disturbing their power and entitlement.

What would Father Stamp and my superiors do about that, I wondered? What could McManus do? They had already run me over a few times, but I had sprung-up again much like my name-sake, Madiepetsane.

JOURNAL DECEMBER, 9TH 1996
Since my teen years I have felt that someday I would face severe oppression and suffering, including imprisonment. When I reached Africa I had assumed that it would come in the form of political dissension perhaps against apartheid. Never did I dream it could be dissension against my own church and religious order. I am facing a form of imprisonment—political cover-up within the church to protect the powerful. The abuse wasn't the problem—my disclosing it was.

The Witches of Belgium

How does one celebrate surviving an internal Church hearing? Margaret Kennedy seemed to know. She inviting us to a Christmas meal attended by eight other survivors of sexual abuse. We met at a café in Trafalgar Square. All ears perked-up when they learned what I'd been up to that day. Before long, Clarisse was entertaining us with her blow-by-blow keyhole account.

That night, I slept fitfully, moving between euphoria and disgust. My delivery lacked nothing, yet I wondered if the panelists were even breathing under their deadpan faces? How could they break through Church loyalty and act responsibly? It would mean admitting to grave scandal, and confronting priests for perpetrating abuse. If they did so, would McManus still hold them in high esteem? Would they lose their jobs as I had?

I was awakened in the silent hours of the London dawn by a strong and recurring dream. I wrote about it in my journal:

DECEMBER 10, 1995, LONDON

I dreamed that I was telling my story to a room full of people—mostly men. One of only two women present interrupted me, "Yvonne, how did you survive? This was such insidious abuse!" She looked at each person in the room and added, "Did you hear that? Yvonne was in a war zone. Not only the enemy but her own battalion tried to kill her."

I shook Clarisse from her sleep to tell her my dream. "That's what the panelists should have been telling me!" I said. "The lawyers too. Instead they asked degrading questions or sat with deadpan faces. No matter what they say now I will not allow them to define me. If they minimize or white-wash this, I'll go public. I am not begging for justice. I'm taking it."

Clarisse, half-awake, muttered, "Right on, Yvonne! You sound every bit as strong as that suffragette, Nellie McClung who faced the Canadian politicians. She had it right: politicians weren't giving women the vote—women were taking it!"

Now that was a compliment I rather liked. Imagine me next to Nellie McClung!

From that day on, I started calling myself neither victim nor survivor, but *thriver.* To mark my new status I bought a green and gold scarf: green for life and gold for the sun. I wore it every day for weeks. Now I wear it only on special occasions when I need to remind myself that I am a thriver.

Father Stamp called to tell me that he and Father Morrisey had met with the panel and the other lawyers. Father Morrisey had informed them that this was his sixtieth case and stressed the need to take it seriously. Father Stamp told me the panel had found me clear and credible. All three panelists admitted to having no experience and very limited knowledge of clergy sexual abuse of adults; only one had read a book on the subject. My hopes of obtaining even minimal justice seemed as remote as Mars.

This information horrified me. My fears about their incompetence were being vindicated. They hadn't just looked blank: they *were* blank. They had been appointed over a year in advance, yet had made no effort to become informed. These uninformed persons presumed the right to judge. I was disgusted. My disillusionment was turning to hate. How dare these panelists and lawyers play with my life.

Father Stamp explained the *second accident* theory to me. It went something like this: a car was damaged in one accident but still functioned well despite several cracks. When a second accident happened the gas tank blew up. It was the second accident and not the first that caused the car to become dysfunctional.

Apparently Father Stamp had used this theory to convince the panel that I deserved compensation for the second accident—Goodall's abuse. I wasn't sure about the theory—would it give the panel room to blame my father and exonerate Goodall?

Over the telephone I asked Father Stamp, "Is there any hope? They acted more like peace-makers than judges. They looked thoroughly stunned—out of their element like lobsters piloting airplanes."

"All in all I am not hopeful," he admitted, sounding tired. "They appear to be twenty years behind North America on sexual abuse issues."

"Well, even if they are in the Middle Ages they ought to know when they're being conned! Did they even notice how Goodall gave that one line "so-called" apology as if he'd stepped on my toes at the bus stop?"

I feared Goodall had hoodwinked them all with his charm. Most sex offenders are charming people. They hone their people skills to a fine craft. I worried the panel had swallowed his version of the story.

Father Stamp told me that Goodall had behaved like a grade four pupil. He had walked in and told the panel to do with him whatever they wanted. He offered to become chaplain to old nuns.

This really set my blood boiling. Great, more easy targets for him to seduce! And this is supposed to be penance? If I had anything to do with it I would not let him near any women—old or young. He could dig God's gardens instead of preach God's word. And the garden better not be near a convent or he'd be pawing the ground outside the windows.

Father Stamp cleared his throat then stunned me even more by saying, "Actually, Goodall was drunk."

I had noticed he was pink, but figured it was from having to face me. It had never, ever occurred to me that he might be drunk! I remembered his telling me that he had had a few binges in his younger days, and simply vowed he would never drink again.

After the call I returned to my room. I wept, too tired to wail.

Needing to do something positive, I decided to gather together my best books on the topic. I posted them to McGreevy with a little note suggesting the panel read these diligently prior to writing any report. It was a feather in the wind I feared, but it felt more assertive than crying in my bedroom.

Then I called Bishop Christopher Budd. He listened well and commiserated with me. Still he did not offer to intercede in any way. Could he not speak up and say something to McManus and the panel? Was he too afraid of rocking the boat? He was at the helm, so why the timidity?

Next I phoned Jenny Fasal. She and Margaret Kennedy drafted a letter to send to the panel insisting that my case be taken seriously. They offered their professional help. These lay women were acting courageously. To this day I regret having taken Father Stamp instead of one of them as my advocate to the panel. Either of them would have stopped the hearing on the following grounds:

- ❖ Goodall was drunk
- ❖ I was obliged to face Goodall for reconciliation not confrontation
- ❖ The apology was extremely inadequate
- ❖ The panel was negligently unprepared.

That afternoon, Clarisse and I bade goodbye to our wonderful London hosts and left for Itegem, Belgium for a visit with relatives. Two events stand out from that visit. The first was an extraordinary piece of luck—like finding a needle in a haystack, even though I wasn't looking.

After hearing my story, my cousin, pulled out a picture of herself with a priest who had been her retreat director. The priest had his arm wound tightly around her waist just as Goodall had wrapped his arm around me. Both pictures had been taken at the closing of a retreat. Was there a connection? Was I becoming overly suspicious?

My cousin said, "His name was McManus but I don't know where he is now. That was in '83 or '84." She said she could find out from a friend where he was now. She left the room leaving the photo with me and Clarisse. When she returned, she confirmed that the priest in question was indeed James McManus, the UK provincial superior, *the* Jim McManus handling my case!

I glared at the picture. There was something about it that upset me. I thought maybe I was just being paranoid and judgmental. I made no comment.

Later when Clarisse and I were alone, I asked, "Did you have a good look at that picture? Did you notice anything peculiar?"

"Besides the position of McManus's arm?"

I nodded.

Clarisse huffed, "Pardon my brashness, but I sure did. I find it inexcusable that Father McManus had an erection!"

"You noticed that too, huh?"

She raised her eyebrows. "Kind of hard to miss! I wonder what in the world that man was thinking to produce such a trophy in his pants. And I find it too coincidental that he was clutching her the same way Goodall clutched you. What do they do? Compare women at the end of the retreats? Maybe it's a Redemptorists' trade mark: get a trophy to show the boys. Like jocks on a hockey team bragging about all the women they've had."

I groaned, what a horrible thought. This was shattering more myths about the safety of retreats. I was no longer the innocent nun thinking the best of everyone regardless of the evidence before my eyes. My trust was gone. I was in the fast lane now, enjoying the freedom of the iconoclast.

The other highlight of the Belgium visit was not a surprise, but the result of a diligent search. I spent a few days at the Louvain Central Library researching my witch ancestors; I was determined to find at least one—and I did! Her name was Pense Maes. In addition, I discovered that one of the most famous magistrates who prosecuted fifteen witches between 1599 and 1601 was a Jacobus Maes. This last bit of information left me raw. I hadn't anticipated ancestors on both sides of the witch hunts!

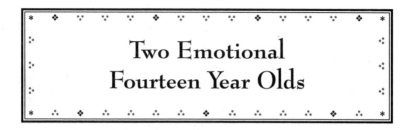

Two Emotional
Fourteen Year Olds

The dreaded panel report reached me on January 29th. It came with a tiny note from Sister Rolande saying she was eager to hear my comments. She hadn't even phoned to tell me the report was on the way, so I doubted her sincerity.

The report was five pages long without the appendix. My heart thumped as I read. The further I read the louder it thumped. They wrote that the issues raised were complex and challenging. Did they think sexual abuse was ever simple and straight forward?

They said there were *"a number of unsubstantiated claims and counter-claims by both parties."*

They spoke of concern *"that a complaint about Father Frank Goodall from the Dominican Sisters in South Africa had not been adequately pursued or reported to the Ordinary Provincial Council of the Redemptorist London Province by the Superior of the South African Vice-Province at that time."*

They did not recommend anything be done about that previous allegation. It was simply left in the hands of McManus and now seemed to be a totally dead issue.

The Panel upheld the charge:

One count of pastoral sexual abuse: fondling and sexual intercourse which occurred in July 1985 at the Dominican Retreat Centre, Brighton Beach, Durban, Republic of South Africa, during a directed retreat.

Now that was good to see in print. The Church could never again say that Goodall was never convicted. This one sentence could take me a long way. But why only one charge? What happened to all the rest—the eight years?

Father Frank Goodall did not dispute the event. He gave an unconditional face to face apology in front of the Panel and the legal representatives of both parties.

How outrageous. They seemed to be bragging that they had achieved a fine miracle in one quick sitting. Who were they trying to convince that this so-called one-line "apology" was unconditional? The one thing that seemed unconditional to me was their wish to sweep this all under the carpet of the Holy Roman Catholic Church—to bury the abuse in some tightly sealed Vatican sarcophagus.

The Panel considers that Father Frank Goodall totally betrayed his role as a priest and retreat director in July 1985 at the Dominican Retreat Centre. His actions were wholly wrong and inappropriate.

I gave a little sigh of relief. At least they realized that raping a nun on retreat was not kosher. However they spoke only of his actions on the retreat and nothing else. Was the rest all my fault? Was the unconditional apology only for that one abuse? Who was to answer for the following eight years?

There were a number of references to elements of abuse in her childhood. Although there was no statement of actual sexual abuse (her sister Clarissa does appear to have been a victim).

So what in the world did they define as "actual sexual abuse?" Was having your breasts groped and constantly being preyed upon not sexual abuse? And my sister, who wasn't even allowed to sit beside me during this hearing, is Clarisse not Clarissa. You'd think they would at least take the time to get her name right—especially since Father Morrisey went to the trouble of spelling it correctly in the preliminary report.

There was some contact with a couple of boy-friends whilst at College but any sexual advances left her feeling guilty and degraded. Her statement illustrates her discomfort at being female, a jealousy of her male siblings and clear evidence that she had become very angry towards men.

I had described an attempted date rape at the preliminary hearing yet not once did my childhood or teenage years come up at the UK hearing. Somehow they took the report Father Morrisey had given them and interpreted it, turning me into a manhater. I was stunned at this interpretation of my life. Just what difference did it make how I felt about men anyway? The issue we were supposed to be addressing was how Goodall had abused me not whether or not I liked men.

About Goodall they wrote *"He admits to some sexual contacts which he feels affirmed his "normal sexual orientation" . . . finding in the process that "women liked him and wanted to be friends."*

They did not seem concerned that these sexual contacts could have been abusive. A blind eye appeared to have been the order of the day.

Further on they describe how both of us were products of the times and *"useful workhorses to their respective congregations"* and *"that there were elements here of two emotional fourteen year olds frozen in time and nobody had noticed."*

Why was my emotional age or work capacity any concern of this panel? This was not a marriage nullity but a sexual abuse hearing. They seemed to invent a level playing field so that Goodall could be excused and I could be given at least half the blame for my own abuse.

Finally came the recommendations. This, if anything, would carry some weight with McManus. There were five in total.

They first recommended that Frank Goodall not work with women, *"pending a full, professional assessment by Father Fitzgerald of Our Lady of Victory, Stroud."* Further plans regarding Goodall's ministry would be *"based on the completion of this assessment and any treatment recommended."* The panel then recommended that a copy of their report be put in Goodall's file.

The third dealt with the costs of bringing the case forward. The Redemptorists were to pay the Holy Names once itemized invoices were presented to them—this would be in the range of $10,000 to $12,000. I knew my travel alone had cost that much. If I added the travel of my superiors, it would be much higher.

The next recommendation bowled me over. They said that both congregations had to take responsibility for their respective members before and after the fateful Durban retreat of July 1985. *"Each Congregation bears responsibility for on-going care and healing process required by both parties."*

Now wasn't that just fair and square. Everybody was at least partly guilty for producing these two emotional fourteen year olds. Therefore, everyone was somehow guilty for the rape of one fourteen year old and the rapist had no responsibility to make restitution to his victim. The victim and her irresponsible congregation had to do their own healing and pay for it themselves. There didn't seem to be any logic in this whatsoever.

The final recommendation was the climax. They quoted a canon law code that didn't exist and noted that they had been, *"approached by third parties not directly concerned with this hearing. This appears to involve breaches of agreed confidentiality."*

I had to read it over and over again. It was a thinly disguised gag order with a threat of defamation charges if I didn't comply. I had never heard of a gag order without compensation. I was astounded that they had given themselves such unlimited power.

Why didn't they name these mysterious third parties? How dare they attempt to muzzle me! I threw the report on the floor and vowed, Never! I will never be silenced. They will never succeed in that. Anything but secrecy. Goodall muzzled me for over eight years, my superiors for another two and a half, and now the kangaroo court. *"Never. Never!"*

Eventually I picked up the neatly bound report and continued where I had left off. The next paragraph was in bold print and described the tragedy of this case. I did not find my name in the tragedy. I was nowhere to be seen. According to this panel the disaster was the conflict between these two wonderful congregations:

Tragically, the outcome of this case has brought two well-known and highly respected Religious Congregations into a conflict which is far removed from their commitment and mission in the service of the Gospel. The constructive manner in which these delicate issues and tensions have been addressed is a credit to the mutual patience, charity and generosity of the Superiors and Canon-lawyers involved.

That was their conclusion. Sadly, the superiors had wasted precious time on me—time that obviously should have been spent spreading the Gospel. Furthermore, to add insult to injury, the panel congratulated the superiors on their fine work handling this "delicate issue."

So sexual abuse, Goodall's lies, and McManus's mismanagement were minor compared to the tension between the two congregations. The fact that my life had been in tatters for over a decade was not the tragedy. Goodall's blatant breach of both professional and Gospel values was not the tragedy. All that was inconsequential in comparison to the stress this had created between the two congregations. I felt I was a non-entity. Or at best a workhorse with no individual worth or rights. The congregation was the entity and held the rights. I was faceless and voiceless once again.

That evening I phoned Clarisse and read her the most bizarre sections. She sighed and had a few choice words for the entire process. Finally she said, "Yvonne, it looks like you've been sold down the river."

JOURNAL, FEBRUARY 5TH

I learned what 'chilled to the bone' means today. This afternoon when I left the correctional centre the guard told me that the wind-chill factor was over 3000—exposed skin freezes in a few seconds. By the time I reached home the cold had gone through my clothes, my skin, my layer of fat, my muscles and was fast penetrating my bone marrow. Only my walking felt real. I knew I had to find shelter soon or die. I'm out in the cold with the Holy Names too, so I have to find shelter elsewhere else or die.

Aftermath

A few nights later I awakened with a single thought scratching at my brain. It was a startling discovery—I belonged to a cult. Just how different was this from say the Jonestown Cult where members poisoned themselves as ordered by the leader? Members were sacrificed for the glory of the man or men on the top. This was the Catholic version of Jonestown. My thoughts felt neat and tidy like freshly clipped finger nails.

The secrecy demanded by Goodall from the Durban retreat onward had driven me into depression. Now the panel demanded the same secrecy of me—and about the same man. No, I would not let that happen twice.

Who believed Galileo when he claimed the earth moved around the sun? How many excommunications had it taken before the Church started to listen? This era is no different.

Forgiveness is a big issue for most Christians. I've noticed that it is the weak who are asked to forgive the strong over and over again. Jesus talked about a brother forgiving a brother not a son forgiving his father. Forgiveness is between equals. If the Church counsels forgiveness, then the Church has but one choice: strip the priest abuser of ordination—then and only then is there a possibility that the victim can be equal to the offender. After restitution is made, the victim could choose to forgive—any other scenario is further coercion of the victim so the offender can feel good. Goodall had not even made a sober admission, let alone any restitution!

Shortly after I read the panel report I talked with Father Stamp. He thought it a good report though not perfect. The fact that they had upheld one charge of clergy sexual abuse seemed to impress him considerably more than it did me.

He didn't see the gag order. This was my canon lawyer and he couldn't see it! What good had his doctorate done him? As we spoke, my voice became louder and sharper. I felt my blood pressure rise until I had a headache. He shrugged off my concerns—flies in the ointment. I had hoped he would refute this report with me.

Exasperated by what I felt was his collusion with the panel, I asked point blank, "Would you want Goodall saying mass at your parish in St. John's on Sundays?"

"Yes!" he answered with no hesitation whatsoever. So this had been well thought out. Father Stamp had already considered having sex-offender priests active in his parish. Maybe this had already happened.

"Why?" I questioned horrified. "You'd willingly have a priest who can't apologize to the woman he'd abused preaching in your church!"

"We can't just lock him up for the rest of his life."

"He's not locked up!" I yelled into the phone. "And incarceration is not what I'm asking for—it never was. If he were a university professor found guilty of sexually abusing one of his students, he'd lose his job. Why does the Church insist on protecting men like him? Because I'm a woman, I'm barred from the priesthood, yet I manage to earn a living. So can

Goodall!" I took a deep breath and continued articulating each syllable, "Priesthood is a privilege, not a right. Goodall could be a gardener!"

It was obvious that Father Stamp no longer represented me or my interests. He would do nothing to declare this report inadequate or invalid. Would my superiors gaze through the same rose-coloured glasses? I knew the answer was yes—and their glasses would have a heavier tint than Father Stamp's.

In the days that followed I sent copies of the panel report to Budd, Kennedy, McCooey, Fasal, and Higgins—exactly as the panel recommended I *not* do. I scribbled the following on each copy.

> I suggest this panel report be returned as INADEQUATE and INVALID. I am appalled that nothing is said about my courage or hurt. Rather, they focused on the "tragedy" of the religious orders. The unethical conduct of McManus in his handling of my case is whitewashed. They have the nerve to congratulate themselves on a job well done.

When Sister Rolande phoned me the following week, I voiced my reactions loudly. She made no comment whatsoever, but changed the subject to the sick and elderly sisters in the infirmary.

I drafted my response to the panel report. I drafted on and on. Then I attached appendices and still I was not satisfied. It was too long and scattered. I pruned, snipped, and sliced until it was just ten pages plus seven appendices. I sent Father Stamp a copy. Perhaps he would recognize my logic better in writing than on the phone. Instead of being impressed with my arguments he was disappointed. He informed me that all was in the hands of Father McManus. I cringed. I had no reason to trust those hands. I was positive he would never hold Goodall accountable or even investigate the allegation from South Africa. Stamp repeated that he considered it to be a good report except for the failure to provide for compensation. He closed the letter with:

I believe your primary task now should be your own health and plans for the future. I do not believe there is anything to be gained by pursuing the matter of Father Goodall.

My journal that night reads:

What a great report—for Goodall and his cohorts—for all male church leaders! It certainly tells us women where our place is: under the soles of their shoes.

I wrote Father Stamp again. I forced myself to thank him for "the concern and support" he had provided me earlier on. But then I added that his advice felt condescending. I haven't heard from him since.

I have heard *about* Father Stamp however. Ironically, his name has been on the CBC national news several times, first in August of 1996 and again in February of 1997. The last report stated that Father Doug Stamp, who says he was once abused by a priest himself, was charged and has pled guilty to sexual abuse of minors in Peterborough, Ontario, from 1979 to 1983.

.∴. *∵* .∴.

My superiors, all four of them, requested to meet me in Montreal to *"discuss the report and put closure to this case."* Needless to say, I did not take kindly to the word 'closure.' They wouldn't send me their draft response, so I didn't send them mine. Phyllis Clarke agreed to go with me once again as my advocate.

Sister Mary Ellen confirmed the dates and informed me that once again Elaine Zimbel would facilitate. I phoned Elaine and told her how I felt—that last time she had taken the agenda of the superiors.

Incredulously she asked, "Did you feel you got an ultimatum at the last meeting?"

"Yes," I responded. "Absolutely."

"Did Phyllis think you got an ultimatum?"

"Yes."

"Well I didn't think so!" she spat.

Since when was giving someone less than a day to say "yes" or "no" to a non-negotiable, packaged protocol anything less than an ultimatum! How could these otherwise intelligent women become so blind? Was sexual abuse an issue they couldn't see? Or was it something they just couldn't bare?

Sadly, I sensed I was close to the end of the road with my congregation. I had many good memories and a few good friends after a lifetime of service. It seemed pitifully ironic—as the woman in me grew stronger and sought justice, my superiors ostracized that woman. I cried quite often and felt very alone.

In Montreal, the four superiors politely asked about the hearing in the UK. Father Morrisey had told them that Goodall was "inebriated." No one seemed upset by this. They took an extended lunch hour to read my response to the panel report and the actions I wanted including:

- the panel report be declared invalid
- criminal charges be laid against Goodall
- McManus be reported to Church officials for "mismanagement"
- that retreat centres, parishes and dioceses in South Africa,

the UK and Ireland, and Zimbabwe be informed of
Goodall's abuse
❖ my story be told at conferences and in the media
❖ to write a book
❖ *no gag order!*

When we returned from lunch, I asked if they had seen the
1986 allegation against Goodall from South Africa. They hadn't
seen it. Why hadn't Father Morrisey shared this vital information
with them? When I got no reaction regarding the 1986 allegation
and my response to the panel, I broke into tears of frustration.
That got a response!

"Yvonne, we are on your side. We really care and we are
doing our best. You do not seem to appreciate our efforts. Your
anger is misplaced!"

When Phyllis asked if there was an appeal process in place,
they did not respond to her question. I wasn't the only one being
ignored.

They prepared the points of their response to the panel report.
It began with an expression of satisfaction that the one charge of
pastoral sexual abuse was upheld. They regretted the panel's failure to mention me as a victim and the damages I had incurred.
They commented on ". . . *Goodall's inebriated state the day of the
hearing and therefore question the possibility of an unconditional
apology on his part,"* but made no demand that the hearing be
declared invalid.

They did say, *"We disagree with your definition of sexual abuse
which you seem to equate with intercourse."* and that ". . . *the
expression 'unconditional apology' is a judgment impossible for the
panel to assess.*

They objected to being held at the same level of responsibility
with the Redemptorists, and accepted that the Redemptorists pay

the costs of bringing the case to light. We agreed on the hefty figure of $500,000 for compensation. This figure was dropped after I left and no figure appeared in the final version.

In the closing session, Sister Rolande announced that she was giving me "permission" to write a book. I did not want her permission. I did not need her permission. I had taken that right and resented her assuming she had anything to do with that decision. I was the little submissive nun no more. I could see how much they loathed and perhaps envied my tenacity. Then Sister Rolande added the caveat: "Be respectful!"

"What do you mean?" I asked rather astounded. "When in my thirty-six years in the convent have I been less than respectful?

She raised her eyebrows but bit her tongue. "Well, be respectful of the sisters." She clearly meant "say nothing that could put any sister in a bad light." Especially herself!

As minutes dragged into hours I knew—as did they no doubt—that there would be no resolution to this impasse. I saw things one way, and they another. I was impressed with their solidarity—their unified stance as religious superiors. Although I was on the outside looking in, I was proud not to be in their shoes—I felt sickened.

Once again Elaine Zimbel insisted on hugs all around as closure to the session. I resented the pressure to cooperate, but didn't want to be seen as less than respectful. If I had walked out, I would have been given a label stronger than Sister Mary Ellen's 'vengeful,' so I stayed.

When I hugged Sister Rolande, I broke into sobs. My body shook so violently that it vibrated and shook her too. I sensed she admired me in my quest for justice, yet she seemed unable to comprehend any of it. She seemed to live in a world of contemplative meditation—a religious bubble where prayer was the solution to the world's evils. I felt she was more terrified of my victimization and revictimization than I was.

I was clinging to a rope that was fraying fast. This rope—this lifeline for thirty-six years had very few strands still intact. Was I to continue holding on, knowing there was no safety net to catch me? In my gut I knew the time had come for me to reach out and help myself. I had lost faith in my religious congregation as a place to live out truth and justice.

Having nothing left but my pride and self-respect, I marched from the room. A claustrophobic feeling burned around me, like a thousand hands clutching my throat. I fought suffocation. I couldn't wait to get out of that building. It had become a smoke-filled prison with invisible bars on tightly sealed windows. If I stayed, I would choke; my heart would stop beating even if my body lived—like a zombie.

I packed quickly. With determination I strode down the corridor. As I passed the room where Mother Marie Rose Durocher died in the 1800s, a few tears blurred my eyes. She had demonstrated courage. She stood up to priest offenders in her day. I felt she understood me, her spirit encouraged me to stand firm and walk tall in my convictions. As nuns, we seemed to have lost that ability and had become part of the *status quo*.

Phyllis called a taxi and was waiting for me at the front door. With my sturdy African packsack slung across my back, I paused on the circular stairs in the gracious front entry. Although sad, I could hold my head high. Slowly I looked around for what I sensed would be the last time. I whispered my good-byes to the spirits that had assisted me in my vocation as a nun.

∴ ❖ ∴

After walking out of the Montreal convent I went to work finalizing my own response to the UK panel report. I sent a copy to Father Francis Morrisey. In addition, I confronted him on making statements like ". . . the Redemptorists cannot just sit back and let Sister Yvonne threaten them." He refused to respond to any of my questions, stating that this "would serve no pastoral purpose."

By May 1996, I had begun the first draft of my memoir. Although recounting the initial abuse was painful and depressing, it was also therapeutic. Writing about the process of disclosure helped me realize the many ways I had been ostracized by my own superiors as well as by the Redemptorist superiors.

Sister Rolande Joyal wrote me to say that there would be no further consultation on the case against Father Frank Goodall. She stated that the only point still being negotiated was the "cost of bringing the case forward" because Father McManus refused to pay the account. Lawyers were dealing with this. To date, it appears the amount is still outstanding.

I wrote to Sister Claver Maier in South Africa asking whether anything had been done regarding the 1986 allegation she had made against Father Goodall. Another Sister, Aloysia Zellman, responded saying she was the new Prioress General and that she had heard rumours about Goodall. Zellman added that she did not know his whereabouts and suggested that I contact the Redemptorist provincial. She made no reference whatsoever to the 1986 allegations against Goodall made by her predecessor.

I sent a request to Cardinal Hume asking that he investigate my case and the 1986 allegation from South Africa. Hume passed my request to his assistant who passed it on to another where it ended with a pat on my head.

In the summer of 1996, I spent five days kayaking the length of Grand Lake in Labrador and then holed up in my basement with my computer, working on my memoir. One day when I emerged from my basement for exercise I found a letter from Sister Rolande informing me that my manuscript would be examined by two censors appointed by the Holy Names superiors. When Phyllis learned this latest development, she laughed, "When those censors are through with your manuscript all that'll be left is page numbers."

My sister, Clarisse wrote the panel an excoriating letter asking why they had allowed a drunken priest to give testimony at a hearing on sexual abuse. Father McGreevy responded that the panel had fulfilled its mandate.

Sister Marjorie Moffatt visited me and apologized for not supporting me adequately during our time together in Labrador. My Belgian cousin wrote to Father McManus upbraiding him for the way he had handled the charge against Father Goodall. He responded that he had done his utmost to see justice done.

Meanwhile, I wrote to Father McManus asking about the status of Goodall and the status of the 1986 South Africa allegation. Father McManus sent a response to Sister Rolande Joyal, who phoned me, but would not reveal any information regarding Goodall. I suspected that Goodall was back in full ministry and no one dared tell me. Margaret Kennedy confirmed that Goodall was giving missions and retreats to sisters.

I sat down that evening and wrote the Pope and my superiors, requesting a dispensation from my vows on grounds that the Church protects priest sex offenders, and had failed in its fiduciary duty to me. A few months later Sister Rolande asked me on the telephone to say "yes" or "no" to the question, "Do you wish to leave the congregation?" Upon saying "yes" I was relieved of my vows. A few days later the Pope's official letter of dispensation arrived at the Happy Valley-Goose Bay post office in Labrador.

After more than thirty-seven years of service I left the congregation with no pension, a very small inheritance left by my parents, and no property except a second-hand computer and a used car. Canon law states that I can demand no recompense for my years of service, but that my order needs to deal with a departed member with charity and equity. Later I did receive a "gift" of $65,000 from the Holy Names Sisters.

In July of 1997, I stuffed my sturdy African pack sack into the trunk of my maroon 1989 Volkswagen Golf and drove across Canada—from Happy Valley-Goose Bay, Labrador to Vancouver, British Columbia.

Epilogue

It has been two years since I left the convent and the Church. Remarkable changes have taken place. I feel a vibrant sense of choice that was absent during my convent years: I can speak up now without looking over my shoulder, I don't have to worry to about who is censoring me. I buy brighter clothing. I tell people about *The Cannibal's Wife* and feel believed and even accepted. As a result of all this truth-telling, I am able to hold my head higher. Even my chin sticks out from time to time.

Central to my emergence from abuse is breaking silence: over and over. I am convinced that had I fallen silent I would have become suicidal. Furthermore, because I am telling my truth to the world through this book, closure is finally starting to happen. I am slowly starting to heal.

I think when this *memoir* is in the bookstores I will feel vindicated. Someone once said, "If a person realizes they have a right, then they also have the duty to take that right." I have taken my right to tell my truth and the telling has set me free. Once my truth is out, I suspect I will experience a final fitting closure to my long ordeal.

Fortunately, I do not live anywhere near the abusive party. This distance gives me safety and allows me to speak and write. I would like to study the influence of physical distance on the ability of survivors to speak and write about their victimization. Is it ever possible for a victim to feel their abuser is 'out of sight, out of mind?'

My current goal is to advocate for survivors and write articles and offer seminars that will stimulate discussion on issues related to professional sexual abuse. I see the publication of *The Cannibal's Wife* as a vehicle for my work: it will put my name and my experience out into the realm of public opinion. Some may think I am a fool, some may think I'm naïve, but if my story helps one victim, then I will feel success.

It is my hope that *The Cannibal's Wife* will be used in reading circles and in therapeutic settings. I sincerely hope it will illustrate the dynamics of abuse of adult women by clergy, in particular, and professionals in general. Clergy sexual abuse has parallels with abuse by medical practitioners and mental health workers. Nonetheless, the manipulation of faith that occurs in clergy sexual abuse is so profound that it merits discussion on its own. I welcome any individual or group to contact me for further information. You can also ask your bookseller about the *Reading Group Guide* that is available for this book from the publisher.

Except for two family occasions, I have not entered a church of any denomination for more than five years. On the two occasions that I did, I felt nostalgia for the rituals, especially the singing and camaraderie church services can offer. But each time I came away disappointed that the God language continues to be exclusively male and the stories are still largely told from the male perspective.

Despite my disillusionment with the Church, I see nuns as part of a long line of strong women who in many ways continue to make the world a better place. Joining the nunnery remains a valid alternative to marriage and in some societies it's the only alternative a woman has. For these reasons, I believe convent life continues to have value. The dilemma is that at the same time as nuns find value in the Church, they also prop up a system that keeps them and all women in inferior roles.

Imagine if one fine Sunday not a single woman showed up for mass. Or they neglected to urge their children and husbands to attend. Imagine if one Sunday not a single woman prepared the altar, the bulletin, taught catechism. Churches would be empty without women. And so would the collection plates. How many Sundays would it take to bring Rome to its knees?

Priests are being recruited from Africa and Asia to minister in North America. It's hard to imaging why, when there are thousands of perfectly qualified women already running parishes, albeit under titles like assistant or administrator. I can't help but find that insulting. The next pope might be able to drop the celibacy rule for parish priests, but would he dare open the question of ordination of women? I doubt it. The Roman Curia are so threatened by women that it would never allow a pope to ordain a woman. Wasn't Pope John Paul I (Albino Luciani) in office just a few weeks when he issued a pastoral letter in which he used a female image for God? Didn't he die rather suddenly a few days later?

Abuse has definitely changed me. I still cringe at letters and phone calls, bracing myself for yet another denigration, pat on the head, or restriction. I remind myself that no one can control me unless I allow it. Victimization is not overcome quickly. I believe my story contributes to the discussion of the psychology of victimization.

Ten years ago I had a dream about a little girl. I had her squeezed in my hands so she would not escape and desert me.

* Epilogue *

She did escape my clutches, but to my surprise, she did not run away. Instead she turned to face me, opened her arms wide, and invited me to dance with her. I have come to the realization that I am both that little girl and the adult who clutches her.

Ever so slowly I am learning to clutch less and dance more.

MARCH 1999
VANCOUVER, CANADA

A NOTE ON THE TYPE

The text was set in 11.5 point Granjon with a leading of 15 points space. Granjon was designed in 1928 for Linotype by George Jones. It is named after the sixteenth-century French printer, publisher, and lettercutter Robert Granjon, who is noted in particular for his beautiful italic types. A common pairing is the romans of Claude Garamond (a contemporary of Granjon's, whose roman types were of exceptional quality) and the italics of Robert Granjon.

∼

The display font, Bernhard Modern, was originally cut in metal in 1937. Bernhard Modern seems to presage the demise of letterpress printing and the eventual rise of digital typography. Witness this comment on the typeface by its designer, Lucian Bernhard: "My aim was to get all the spice and contrast into the contour . . . without counting on the ink spread." Lucian Bernhard was one of this century's eminent graphic designers, and Bernhard Modern is his enduring masterpiece of type design.

Composed by Charles B. Hames
New York, New York

Printed and bound by
Haddon Craftsmen